SUSHI COOKBOOK FOR BEGINNERS

A Simple Book for Making Sushi with Over 200 Recipes to Make at Home

By: Bonnie N. Fagan

TABLE OF CONTENT

INTRODUCTION

Sushi's Brief Historical Background

Omakase sushi is a kind of sushi where the chef prepares the food in front of you.

However, sushi has been around for far longer than most people realize, but not in its current form. The development of sushi across time is a fascinating narrative of the evolution of a basic dish. Long before it became famous around the globe, sushi was originally referenced in China in the second century A.D. Sushi's roots may be traced back to an old technique of food preservation known as nihonbashi. Fish was put in rice and left to ferment, enabling a person to keep the fish palatable for a longer amount of time than would otherwise be possible. In this household, rice was thrown away, and fish was consumed as and when it was required or desired.

The technique spread across China, and by the seventh century, it had made its way to Japan, where fish has long been a staple of the cuisine there. On the other hand, the Japanese took the concept a step further and began to eat the rice with the salmon. At one time, the supper was prepared similarly to how it is now. On the other hand, Matsumoto Yoshiichi of Edo (now Tokyo) began seasoning rice with rice wine vinegar in the early 17th century while preparing his sushi for sale in Edo. This allowed the meal to be enjoyed immediately rather than having to wait the months that it would typically take to cook the sushi.'

Sushi Has Undergone a Revolution

When a gentleman who lived in the early nineteenth century came up with a new way to make and serve sushi, it resulted in a massive advance in how the dish was prepared and presented. He no longer wrapped the fish in rice but instead placed a piece of fresh fish on top of an oblong-shaped part of seasoned rice to make a sandwich out of the two ingredients. Known now as "nigiri sushi" (finger sushi) or "edomae sushi" (after Edo, the name of Tokyo at the time), this style of eating sushi has become the most common technique of ingesting sushi in Japan, accounting for more than half of all sushi consumed in the country. Long ago, sushi was sold from vending machines on the street, and it was meant to be enjoyed as an after-school snack or as a quick meal to be had while on the go. Not only was this the world's first true "fast food" sushi to be served from a stand, but it was also one of the most extraordinarily popular of its kind, gaining immense popularity in a shockingly short period of time after its introduction. As a result of the Great Kanto earthquake of 1923, which forced many people to lose their homes & businesses and relocate away from Tokyo, this technique of delivering sushi quickly became popular throughout Japan.

so uniquely cultural may take the world by storm and influence the direction of food in other cultures, it is considered a significant event. According to all indications, demand for sushi is on the rise, and that the market is constantly evolving. Traditional sushi restaurants and fusion restaurants coexist in the same neighborhood, and both are popular for reasons that are very different from one another. Sushi's lengthy and famous history is far from over, and it is continually evolving.

In the aftermath of World War II, the sushi booths were shuttered and transferred indoors, where they could be stored in more sanitary conditions. More formal seating was provided (the early prototypes were just indoor versions of the sushi booths), and sushi grew from a "fast meal" notion to a complete dining experience. Sushi became increasingly popular throughout the world. With the promotion of seafood in the United States, this novel technique of presenting fish was quickly adopted by western cultures, who were always on the lookout for something new, particularly something as sophisticated and distinctive as sushi.

Sushi in the Twenty-First Century

Sushi, the creative eating experience formerly exclusive for the Japanese, has now advanced to a greater level of complexity beyond traditional Japanese customs and is now available worldwide. California rolls and the countless complicated 'fusion' compositions presented at luxury sushi businesses exemplify how Western concepts have inspired the creation of new forms of sushi, such as the California roll. However, even though sushi has been around for a very long time (at least 1,800 years), the current form is prevalent worldwide, and for a good reason as well. In the rare and fantastic event that something

1. CRISPY CRAB ROLLS

Total: 45 min
Active: 45 min

INGREDIENTS

- Approximately 8 ounces of jumbo lump crab meat
- Freshly ground white pepper
- 1 pinch nutmeg
- 1 pinch cayenne pepper
- 1/4 cup of mayonnaise
- 1 large egg yolk, reserve egg white
- Zest of 1 lemon\
- 5 scallions
- Dipping Sauce
- 1/2 cup of Thai sweet chile sauce
- Juice of 1 lime
- 1 tbsp black sesame seeds
- kosher salt
- Crab Rolls
- 1-quart vegetable oil, for frying
- 1/4 cup of cornstarch
- 2 tbspWater
- 2 large egg whites
- 1 cup of all-purpose flour
- 9 slices white Wonder Bread, crusts removed

DIRECTIONS

1. Crab filling: In a medium-sized mixing bowl, combine the crab meat, white pepper, nutmeg, cayenne pepper, mayonnaise, egg yolk (reserving the egg white) and lemon zest until thoroughly combined. To make the scallions green, thinly slice them on an angle (reserving the white portion for later) and add them to the bowl. Gently blend the ingredients, making sure to retain the crab flesh bits as intact as possible while doing so.

2. To make the dipping sauce, combine the chile sauce, pineapple juice, tahini, and a teaspoon of salt in a small mixing bowl.

3. Heat the oil in a big, deep skillet until it reaches 375 degrees F. To prepare a slurry, whisk together cornstarch, water, and 3 egg whites (reserving 2 egg yolks) in a large mixing basin until smooth.Flour and salt should be combined in a separate big mixing dish. Every slice of bread should be flattened using a rolling pin. Place the bread on a flat surface with the short sides facing you. Distribute a heaping tablespoon of crab mixture over the center of each slice, leaving a 12-inch border on all edges. Spread a little amount of the saved egg yolk around the underside of the flattened bread using your index and middle fingers.Press the rolls together to seal the bread around the crab. Rest the rolls, seam side down, for 5 minutes.

4. Whisk the egg white mixture a second time to include any cornstarch that has settled to the bottom of the bowl. Every crab roll should be dipped into the mixture and then dredged in the flour. Carefully put the rolls to the oil and fry them in batches without crowding them until golden brown, about 8 minutes each batch, rotating once or twice while cooking. Using a slotted spoon, carefully transfer the crab rolls to a dish lined with paper towels. Garnish the chili sauce with the white portion of a scallion, which has been finely chopped. Using a sharp knife, cut the crab buns in half and serve with chile sauce.

2. GUNKAN SUSHI WITH NORWEGIAN PRAWNS

40-60 min

INGREDIENTS

- 100gprawns, peeled
- 2tbspsugar
- 1tspsalt
- 6tbsprice vinegar
- 8dlsushi rice
- 1tspchili pepper, red
- 3tspginger, pickled (gari)
- 1tbspshallot
- 1tbsptarragon
- 4leavesnori seaweed sheets
- lime juice
- salt
- Serve with
- soy sauce
- wasabi
- ginger, pickled

DIRECTIONS

1. While stirring, cook rice vinegar and sugar over low heat until the sugar melts. The rice marinade is done when the sugar and salt are entirely dissolved.
2. Allow the marinade to come to room temperature before using.
3. You may either follow the recipe for sushi rice, which specifies how to cook the rice, or the directions on the package.
4. Gently stir in part of the marinade into the rice in a large bowl. Add a bit at a time to keep the rice from becoming too wet.
5. Set the rice out in the open air to cool down.
6. Shrimps should be diced up into tiny bits.
7. Mix the prawns with finely chopped chile, ginger, shallot, and tarragon.
8. Add lime juice and salt to taste.

9. Cut the nori into eight 3 cm broad strips.
10. You may use water and rice vinegar to keep the rice from sticking to your hands.
11. Make a 2-centimeter-tall oval ball of sushi rice with about 1 tbsp of the rice in your hand.
12. Nori is a great way to add a little extra flavor to your rice. The ends may be glued together using water.
13. Prawn mixture on top of the pieces.

3. SPRING ROLLS WITH GINGER-LIME DIPPING SAUCE

PREP TIME: 40 minutes
TOTAL: 40 minutes

INGREDIENTS

- marinade and dipping sauce:
- 6 tbsp tamari (90 ml)
- 3 tbsp vegetable oil (such as sunflower) (45 ml)
- zest of 1 medium lime
- juice of 2 medium limes
- 3 medium cloves garlic, pressed or minced
- 1 ½ tsp finely grated fresh ginger
- ½ tsp finely grated fresh turmeric (or ¼ tsp ground)
- 1 tsp chile-garlic sauce (or Sriracha)
- 2 tbsp rice vinegar (30 ml)
- 2 tbsp maple syrup (30 ml)
- spring rolls:
- Oil for the grill
- 12 ounces extra-firm tofu, cut into strips
- 1-pound asparagus, ends snapped

- ¼ medium jicama, peeled and sliced into matchsticks
- 1 small watermelon raBowl, peeled
- 2 large carrots, scrubbed
- 3 scallions, cleaned and thinly sliced diagonally
- 1 small bunch cleaned and dried
- mint leaves
- pea sprouts, a huge bunch
- 2 medium avocados, seeds and peeled, ripe yet firm
- 20 rice paper wrappers

INSTRUCTIONS

1. the marinated and dipping sauce: prepare
2. Combine tamari, oil, lime zest and juice, garlic, carrot, turmeric, and chile-garlic sauce in a bowl or measuring pitcher. Whisk vigorously to ensure that the oil does not separate from the rest of the mixture. Add rice vinegar and maple syrup to the marinade to make a dipping sauce. In the following stage, marinate the tofu with the remaining (a scant 12 cup).
3. preparing the spring rolls
4. Put the tofu strips in a shallow baking dish, pat them dry with paper towels, and then pour the remaining marinade (about 12 cups) over them, tossing to coat. Leave for at least 15 minutes or up to two hours before serving (or cover and chill for up to 2 days).
5. Before cooking on the grill, you should preheat it (or use a stovetop grill). Tofu and asparagus should be grilled in batches until they are cooked through and browned. Remove and allow to cool before putting it back in. The tofu and asparagus can also be fried at the same time in a large pan covered with a thin coating of cooking oil.

6. Set up separate bowls of jicama, watermelon raBowl, carrots, scallions and mint with the pea sprouts and avocados. Warm water should be poured into a broad, shallow dish. Remove a rice paper wrapper from the water and set it on a chopping board for 10 to 20 seconds. Trim asparagus and jicama to fit the wrapper, then add it to the lower part of the plate along with the carrots, radicchio, onions, mint, pea sprouts, and avocado. In order to enclose your filling, fold the bottom of the wrapper upwards. Continue rolling up after folding in the edges.To get the paper or plastic as securely as possible over the filling without damaging it, you may have to give it a few attempts.To keep the final rolls wet, keep them covered while you work.
7. Serve the rolls with the dipping sauce once they've been sliced in half. They'll last up to a day in an airtight container.

4. TUNA AVOCADO AND CUCUMBER SUSHI

Prep Time: 20 minutes
Cook Time: 38 minutes
Total Time: 90 minutes

INGREDIENTS

- 1 1/2 (300g) cup of Sushi Rice
- 2 tbsp rice wine vinegar
- 1 1/2 tsp caster sugar
- 1/4 tsp salt
- 185g canned tuna
- 3–4 tsp mayonnaise
- juice of 1/2 lemon
- pepper as need
- 1/2 avocado sliced lengthways

- 150g cucumbers de-seeded and cut into sticks
- 3 Nori sheets

INSTRUCTIONS

1. Rinse the rice in a colander for about a minute under cold running water. Drain thoroughly.
2. Mix 1 3/4 (435ml) of cool water with the drained rice and toss it around once to make sure the water is well distributed.
3. Bring the water to a low and steady simmer over medium heat, and it will begin to bubble and froth. This project will take a long time to finish. Do not disturb the rice while it is in this state.
4. Simmer for 18 minutes, covered and on a low heat. Keep the lid on.
5. Remove the rice from the fire and let it sit for an additional 15 minutes after it has been cooking for 18 minutes. While the rice is still cooking, do not remove the cover.
6. Prepare the seasoning while the rice is standing. Make a small bowl and add rice wine vinegar, sugar, and salt. Stir until the sugar and salt have dissolved. Serve immediately. Remove from consideration.
7. When the rice is done cooking, use a wooden spoon to spread it out on the bottom of a large bowl. Pour half of the spice over the rice and gently fold it in with a wooden spoon. Then, using the leftover seasoning, do the same thing all over again. Allow 30 minutes for the rice to cool in an open window. If you want to speed up the chilling process, turn on a fan while the rice is cooking.
8. In order to make sushi, you will need to let the rice chill down first. The smooth/shiny side of a nori sheet should be down on a bamboo rolling mat while rolling.
9. Using moist hands, press and spread 1/3 of the rice uniformly over the nori sheet and to its edges, excluding a 2cm strip on the side closest to you. This is necessary to guarantee that the sushi roll may be properly sealed.
10. This is how you should arrange the strips of Tuna, Avocado, and Cucumber: on the side nearest to you, arrange them in strips width-wise.
11. Then, using the bamboo mat, roll the sushi lengthwise from the side closest to you to the side farthest away from you, firmly. Make sure the nori is tucked in and beneath the sushi roll when you are rolling it.
12. Remove the bamboo mat when you've completed rolling the sushi and moisten the remaining nori strip with water to seal the sushi roll, then continue rolling the sushi.
13. Cut the sushi roll in half using a sharp, wet knife to form two hand rolls or eight bite-sized pieces for lunchboxes.

NOTES

The blog page includes detailed instructions and a rolling lesson.

5. CAULIFLOWER SUSHI STACKS

PREP TIME:0 HOURS 15 MINS
COOK TIME:0 HOURS 10 MINS
TOTAL TIME:0 HOURS 25 MINS

INGREDIENTS

- FOR THE 'STICKY RICED CAULIFLOWER'
- 1 pkg. Green Giant® Riced Veggies Cauliflower
- 4 tbsp. flax powder (ground flax seeds) rice vinegar
- 1 tsp. rice vinegar
- 1/4 c. crumbled nori (cut nori sheet or snacks into very little pieces)
- FOR THE SPICY SHRIMP SAUCE
- 3 tbsp. mayo
- 1 tsp. rice vinegar
- 2 tsp. sriracha
- 1/2 tsp. miso paste
- 1/2 tsp. togarashi (Japanese chili powder)
- Granulated sugar or agave
- 1 1/2 c. chopped cooked shrimp
- FOR THE SUSHI STACKS
- 1 avocado, sliced thinly or chopped
- 1/3 c. 1/3 cup of cucumber, finely chopped
- Spice Islands Sesame Seeds

DIRECTIONS

1. STICKY RICED CAULIFLOWER CAN BE MADE
2. In a nonstick pan set on medium heat, gently break up one package of riced cauliflower. Stir and mash the riced cauliflower with a wooden spoon until it's smooth. Add rice vinegar and crushed flax seeds. Continue mashing and stirring until the mixture is sticky and cooked through, about 6 minutes.. Pour into a serving bowl, then whisk with the nori pieces. Mold should be lined with plastic wrap, and the mixture should be pressed firmly and uniformly into any mold.
3. To make the spicy mayo sauce, combine all of the ingredients in a mixing bowl and fold in the shrimp.marinade your meat while you're prepping other things.
4. Assembling
5. Riced cauliflower may be molded into a loaf pan, a dry measuring cup, or any other container. The cooled riced cauliflower may now be cut into cubes on a cutting board. With the shrimp mixture on top, sprinkle sesame seeds and togarashi on top of the avocado slices and the cucumbers. Serve with a little spatula after carefully slicing the meat into pieces.

6. CALIFORNIA ROLLS WITH CREAM CHEESE

INGREDIENTS

- 270 ml White rice
- 2 tbsp ☆Rice vinegar
- 3 tsp ☆Sugar
- 1/2 tsp ☆Salt
- 1/2 Avocado
- 1/2 Cucumber
- 4 stick Imitation crab sticks
- 30 grams Cream cheese
- 2 large sheets Nori seaweed
- 1 Mayonnaise
- 1 White sesame seeds
- 1 dash Lemon juice

STEPS

1. After you've washed and dried the rice as usual, reduce the amount of water you need to boil it. When the sugar and salt have dissolved than take the pot from the heat and let it to cool fully.

2. Step 1: Mix the vinegar and water together. Step 2: Add the vinegar mixture to the hot rice. Step 3: Cut the rice. Rice is ready to be served once it has cooked and turned shiny.

3. Slice the avocado about 5 mm thick and spray it with lemon juice to keep it from turning brown. Quarter a cucumber by cutting it in half lengthwise.

4. The imitation crab should be removed from its packaging, and the cream cheese should be sliced into sticks.

5. Start with half of the rice noodles from step 2 and spread it out evenly over the nori seaweed on the mat (if you have one). Spread it out evenly and sprinkle sesame seeds on top of it.

6. Flip the nori over and cover with a piece of plastic wrap that is twice the size of the nori seaweed. Seaweed side up, place a layer of cream cheese in the middle and dab some mayonnaise on top.

7. On top of the cream cheese, place the avocado and imitation crab, then drizzle with a little extra mayonnaise.

8. Roll the ingredients in plastic wrap before securing them in a container. Shape the roll, making ensuring the plastic wrap's end is at the bottom. Repeat the process for the last roll.

9. Remove the plastic wrap, cut into serving-size pieces, and serve immediately. Use wasabi and soy sauce to your liking if desired.

7. PEANUT AVOCADO SUSHI

Prep Time 15 minutes
Cook Time 20 minutes
Total Time 35 minutes

INGREDIENTS

- ⅔ cup of sushi rice
- ¾ cup of + 2 tbsp. water
- ¾ tsp. salt
- 1 tbsp. rice vinegar
- FOR THE FILLING
- ½ cup of roasted and salted peanuts
- 1 tbsp. natural peanut butter
- 1 tbsp. agave
- ½ avocado sliced into thin strips
- FOR ROLLING AND SERVING
- 2 nori sheets
- 2 tbsp. sesame seeds
- wasabi
- soy sauce
- pickled ginger

INSTRUCTIONS

1. WASH AND COOK THE RICE
2. A few minutes of flowing water will do the trick.
3. Add the rice and other ingredients to a small saucepan and bring to a boil. For about 21 minutes or until the liquid is absorbed, place the cover on the pan and cook on low heat. Allow it cool for another 10 minutes, covered, before serving.
4. INSTALL THE FILLINGS.
5. Process the peanuts, peanut butter, and agave in a food processor until finely ground.
6. Pulse till the peanuts are roughly diced and all of the other components are fully incorporated in a food processor.
7. It's sushi time!

8. Put a plastic-wrapped bamboo mat on top of a nori sheet. Keep a basin of water handy and moisten your fingers.

9. Using a spatula, spread half of the rice evenly on top of the nori sheets. Sprinkle half of your sesame seeds on the dough.

10. Turn the nori over gently so that the rice surface is on the plastic wrap and the nori is facing up.

11. Assemble a strip of peanuts about an inch distant from you on your nori sheet. The mixture should be pressed together as you do this to make it more solid.

12. Slice half of an avocado and place it next to your peanuts.

13. Squeeze and tuck the nori end closest to you over the peanut/avocado strip until it is tightly wrapped around the ingredients. Make sure to keep rolling until you reach your destination.

14. Place your roll seam-side down on a cutting board and cut it into desired lengths. Use a broad, sharp knife to slice the meat into eight pieces.

15. It's time to repeat this process with the remaining supplies.

16. Serve with soy sauce, pickled ginger, and wasabi.

8. CUCUMBER AND AVOCADO QUICK NORI ROLL

Prep Time: 15 minutes
Total Time: 15 minutes

INGREDIENTS

- 4 sheets nori seaweed
- 450 grams cucumbers
- toasted sesame seeds
- ground chili powder
- 1 ripe avocado
- 100 grams tofu
- long-stem sprouts
- soy sauce, for serving
- Optional additions
- simple tahini sauce
- raw cashew cheese or other spread
- pink raBowles, thinly sliced with a mandolin slicer
- large handful of small salad leaves, such as baby spinach or baby kale
- fresh herbs, especially shiso or cilantro
- 1/2 ripe mango, sliced into strips
- 1/2 small jicama, peeled and cut into strips

INSTRUCTIONS

1. Make sure you have everything prepped and divided into four equal amounts before you begin cooking.

2. The glossy side of nori should face down and the longest edge toward you on a clean and dry chopping board.

3. As you work your way around the nori, make sure to leave about an inch of exposed nori on the right side of each row of cucumber slices.

4. If using ground chili powder, sprinkle sesame seeds on top.

5. Apply tahini or cashew cheese to the cucumber now if you're using them.

6. Sliced raBowles or salad leaves can be arranged in a single layer on top of the cucumber at this stage.

7. Assemble the thicker ingredients (avocado and tofu), starting approximately 2 inches (5 cm) from the left border of the wrapper and arranging them vertically.

8. The Nori Roll

9. A quarter of a turn counter-clockwise rotates the cutting board such that the exposed nori strip extends the furthest away from you. Start by rolling the nori sheet from the edge closest to you, folding it over the contents, and then tightly rolling it away from you (see note).
10. Dip your fingers in the bowl of water and softly dab the nori so that it adheres to the end of the nori strip.
11. Three additional rolls may be made by repeating this process with the rest of the components.
12. The Nori Roll
13. Chef's knife: Slice in half or thick slices. Serving Suggestions: Soy sauce dipping sauce.
14. The Nori Roll

NOTES

This recipe doesn't really care what kind of cucumber you use. Smaller cucumbers that feel hefty for their size and are firm throughout are more significant than older cucumbers that begin to wilt at the tips. To ensure that the cucumber won't be bitter when sliced, taste it first. If it is, peeling it could make it more appealing.

A sushi-rolling mat isn't essential in this instance, in my opinion. If you stretch your fingers broad across the roll, you'll soon get the hang of it.

9. NIGIRI SUSHI

INGREDIENTS

- 320g sushi rice
- 80ml sushi vinegar
- nori seaweed
- nigiri sushi mould
- wasabi paste
- soy sauce
- pickled sushi ginger
- ideas for nigiri sushi toppings
- fresh raw fish such as salmon, tuna
- smoked salmon
- cooked prawns
- cooked octopus
- grilled eel
- crab sticks
- tamagoyaki Japanese style omelette
- avocado
- shiitake mushrooms

HOW TO PREPARE

1. Once the sushi rice has been prepared, we may begin the process of making nigiri sushi. Use our digital rice recipe if you'd want to learn how to make sushi rice that's perfectly sticky. For those who enjoy Japanese cuisine, a rice cooker may make the process of making sushi rice a lot easier.
2. Using our microwaveable rice will save you a lot of time in the kitchen. To make sushi rice vinegar, just combine 250 grams of cooked rice with 1 tablespoon of sushi rice vinegar.
3. Rice is cooking, so you can start preparing the fish or other toppings. Tamagoyaki, a Japanese-style omelette popular as a sushi garnish, is also on our recipe list. When it comes to sushi, nothing beats smoked salmon, parma ham, deep-fried tofu, shiitake mushrooms, pickles, or avocado. To obtain the full flavor of the rice, don't worry about getting the slice exactly the right size; just make it big enough to cover the majority of the pod.

4. The rice pods are now ready to be made. Sushi experts use a mixture of water and sushi vinegar to keep their hands clean and prevent rice from adhering to them. Using a nigiri sushi mold is a simple technique to ensure that your rice pods are perfectly round every time. It's best to spread the rice around evenly, then push the lid firmly in place before flipping it over and pressing it out.

5. The underside of the topping is a good place to sprinkle some wasabi if you want it spicy. Finally, press the topping onto a pod of sushi rice firmly while keeping your hands moistened with water and vinegar. To protect the tamagoyaki's nori seaweed from coming off the rice pod, some items, like the tamagoyaki, have a very thin strip of nori seaweed.

6. Traditionally, sushi is served with a little amount of wasabi paste, as well as a container of soy sauce. Dip the sushi in the soy sauce before you eat it to add a little bit of wasabi flavor. The subtle flavors of the various toppings are better appreciated when the palette is cleansed with pickled sushi ginger, which is taken in between mouthful.

10.   QUINOA AVOCADO SUSHI ROLLS

INGREDIENTS

- 1 cup of quinoa
- 3 sheets of nori (sushi paper)
- 1 1/3 cup of water
- 1/2 cup of rice vinegar
- 2 Tbsp. sugar
- 1 tsp. salt
- 1 ripe, Fresh California Avocado, seeded, peeled and sliced
- 1/2 cup of oil, drained
- 3 strips of crispy cooked bacon
- Spicy Mayo, (see make-ahead recipe below)
- Spicy Mayo
- 2 Tbsp. Japanese mayonnaise, as needed
- 2 tsp. sriracha hot sauce
- Dash of sesame oil, as needed

INSTRUCTIONS

1. Remove any residue by rinsing the quinoa in cold water. Add quinoa and water to a saucepan and bring to a boil.When the water reaches a boil, immediately increase the heat to high and whisk often. On low heat, cover and simmer for 12-15 minutes.

2. Meanwhile, in a small saucepan, add vinegar, sugar, and salt and bring to a gentle boil. Once the sugar and salts have been dissolved, remove the pan from the heat and allow the mixture to cool completely. When When the quinoa is done cooking, scoop it into a bowl using a wooden spoon. Gently mix the vinegar mixture into the quinoa. Let the quinoa get down to room temperature before eating.

3. To begin, put down a bamboo rolling mat on the ground, followed by a piece of plastic wrap and then a piece of nori.

4. Spread the cooked quinoa evenly over the nori with the back of a wooden spoon (approximately 1/4-inch thick). At the end closest to you, leave approximately 1/4-inch of the nori exposed.

5. A few slices of sun-dried tomato and two to three pieces of avocado should be placed on

the quinoa (the side nearest to you) before topping with the crispy bacon.

6. When you've lifted the end of the mat, carefully roll it over the ingredients and press lightly. Make a complete roll by rolling it forward. Removing the roll from the plastic wrap and reed rolling mat with care is necessary. Make 1-inch circles with a sharp knife.

7. Repeat with the remaining ingredients.

8. Serve immediately with a sprinkling of Spicy Mayo.

9. Instructions for making spicy mayonnaise

10. In a small bowl, combine Japanese mayonnaise, sriracha, and oil. Before drizzling over sushi or serving on the side as a dip, mix thoroughly.

11. SMOKED SALMON AND AVOCADO SUSHI

60 minutes

INGREDIENTS

- SALMON URAMAKI
- 250g of sushi rice
- 2 tbsp of rice vinegar
- 1 tsp caster sugar
- 4 sheets of nori seaweed, square
- 1/4 cucumber
- 1 handful of coriander leaves
- A half avocado, ripe and tiny, that has been finely cut into cubes.
- 4 tbsp of mascarpone
- 200g of smoked salmon

METHOD

1. In a large bowl, add the rice. Using your hands, swirl the rice in the water until it becomes hazy. You'll probably need to perform 4–5 water changes until the water is nearly clean.

2. Drain and refill the pan with 285ml of water after the mixture is nearly clear. Add a pinch of salt, cover, and come to a boil. To begin, bring the bring to the boil, then decrease the heat and simmer for 10 minutes. 10 minutes after taking it off the stove, add it to the dish

3. During the time the rice is cooking, combine the rice vinegar and caster sugar. Turn out the cooked rice into a big basin and fluff it up. Before adding the sushi vinegar, allow the mixture to cool for a few minutes.

4. Your bamboo mat is a good place to start. Lay a nori sheet on top of a piece of cling film and press it firmly into place. Rice should be pressed over two-thirds of the nori with wet fingertips, leaving a 2cm strip exposed. The rice side should be facing up

5. on the nori sheet now.

6. Spread a little amount of ricotta at the base of the nori

7. that is not covered with rice.

8. With the assistance of the bamboo mat, a moistened nori sheet is wrapped over the filling and further rolled to form a Bowle.

9. Spread a little mascarpone on the sushi roll before serving it (to ensure the smoked salmon will attach). Flatten the salmon with your hands as you lay it on top of the sticky rice.

10. Cut the meat into roughly 2cm circles using a very sharp knife. Nigella seeds and a little soy and wasabi are all that's needed to accompany this dish.

12. EASY SUSHI BAKE RECIPE

Prep Time 20 mins
Cooking Time 10 mins
Ready In 30 mins

INGREDIENTS

- 200 grams salmon, about 1 fillet
- 14 pieces crab sticks
- 1/3 cup of + 2 tbspJapanese mayo
- 1/2 cup of cream cheese, softened
- 1 tbsp sriracha chili sauce, + more as need
- foretake seasoning, (for topping)
- 4 cup of Japanese rice, (or jasmine rice), cooked
- 1 1/2 tbsp sushi vinegar, (or regular vinegar)
- 1 1/2 tbsp sesame oil
- 1/2 tsp salt
- pepper, as need
- nori wrapper, (Optional)

HOW TO COOK

1. Rice is ready to eat. 4 cups of cooked Japanese or jasmine rice. Remove from consideration.
2. Bake salmon for 15 minutes at 250 degrees F or 180 degrees C after seasoning it with salt and pepper.
3. Set aside the crabsticks that have been shredded.
4. Shred the salmon into flakes as soon as it's done baking.
5. CONTINUE READING BELOW THE ADVERTISEMENT
6. Pour 1/3 cup of Japanese mayo and cream cheese into a bowl and mix in the salmon and crab sticks. In addition to the Japanese mayonnaise, add as much pepper as necessary after mixing. Remove from consideration.
7. Mix cooked rice with rice vinegar (you may also use ordinary vinegar or sushi vinegar) and sesame oil to make the sushi foundation.
8. A casserole baking bowl or oven-proof glass container is ideal for this task.
9. Toss the rice with some foretake spice (Japanese seasoning).
10. CONTINUE READING BELOW THE ADVERTISEMENT
11. Spread the salmon and crab stick mixture on top of the rice.
12. sriracha chili sauce and additional furikake spice on top of the mayo.
13. Bake for about 10 minutes.
14. Serve it with nori wrappers once it has cooled down a bit.

13. BACON-WRAPPED KETO "SUSHI"

Total Time 20min

INGREDIENTS

- 6 slices Wright® Brand Smoked Bacon
- 1/2 cup of Cream Cheese, softened
- 2 Persian Cucumbers, thinly sliced
- 2 Medium Carrots, thinly sliced
- 1 Avocado, sliced

INSTRUCTIONS

1. Add some olive oil to a skillet and cook the Wright® Brand Slab Bacon in it at a low to medium heat (6 slices). A total of 3-4 minutes should be allotted for each side. Bacon must not be overcooked in order to be able to be folded.

2. Mix half a cup of Cream Cheese with salt and pepper in a dish while the bacon is frying. Before it's smooth, mash and blend.

3. Lay the bacon out on a sheet or other flat surface once it has cooled. Cream cheese and Persian Cucumbers (2), Carrots (2), and an Avocado (1) are spread on one side of the bacon.

4. Roll the bacon tightly, and the cream cheese will aid in the process. Wait until the bacon is done cooking before serving it

14.   EASY SUSHI BAKE

Prep Time 20 mins
Cooking Time 10 mins
Ready In 30 mins

INGREDIENTS

- 200 grams salmon, about 1 fillet
- 14 pieces crab sticks
- 1/3 cup of + 2 tbspJapanese mayo
- 1/2 cup of cream cheese, softened
- 1 tbsp sriracha chili sauce, + more as need
- foretake seasoning, (for topping)
- 4 cups of Japanese rice, (or jasmine rice), cooked
- 1 1/2 tbsp sushi vinegar, (or regular vinegar)
- 1 1/2 tbsp sesame oil
- 1/2 tsp salt
- pepper, as need
- nori wrapper, (Optional)

HOW TO COOK

1. Rice is ready to eat. 4 cups of cooked Japanese or jasmine rice. Remove from consideration.

2. Bake salmon for 15 minutes at 250 degrees F or 180 degrees C after seasoning it with salt and pepper.

3. Set aside the crabsticks that have been shredded.

4. Shred the salmon into flakes as soon as it's done baking.

5. Pour 1/3 cup of Japanese mayo and cream cheese into a bowl and mix in the salmon and crab sticks. In addition to the Japanese mayonnaise, add as much pepper as necessary after mixing. Remove from consideration.

6. Mix cooked rice with rice vinegar (you may also use ordinary vinegar or sushi vinegar) and sesame oil to make the sushi foundation.

7. A casserole baking bowl or oven-proof glass container is ideal for this task.

8. Toss the rice with some foretake spice (Japanese seasoning).

9. CONTINUE READING BELOW THE ADVERTISEMENT

10. Spread the salmon and crab stick mixture on top of the rice.

11. You may also add extra foretake spice on top of the Japanese mayo.

12. Bake for about 10 minutes.

13. Serve it with nori wrappers once it has cooled down a bit.

15. APPLE CINNAMON BANANA BREAD

PREP TIME 15 mins
COOK TIME 1 hr
TOTAL TIME 1 hr 15 mins

INGREDIENTS

- 2 cups of all-purpose flour
- 1 Tbsp all-purpose flour
- 3/4 cup of sugar
- 3/4 tsp baking soda
- 1 tsp ground cinnamon
- 1/2 tsp salt
- 1 1/2 cup of mashed ripe, darkly speckled bananas
- 1/4 cup of buttermilk
- 2 large eggs
- 6 Tbsp unsalted butter, melted and cooled
- 2 tsp vanilla extract1 1/4 cup of small diced (peeled) Granny Smith apples
- 2 Spading sugar (optional)

INSTRUCTIONS

1 Preheating the oven to 351 degrees Fahrenheit is required. Spray a 9-inch loaf pan with cooking spray after lining it with parchment paper.

2 In a large mixing basin, combine 2 cups flour, sugar, baking soda, and cinnamon. Allow yourself to let go of the bowl.

3 Whisk the mashed bananas, buttermilk, eggs, melted butter, and vanilla extract into a separate medium bowl.

4 Just before combining, mix in the wet components with the dry.

5 Add 1 Tbsp flour to a small bowl and stir the chopped apples until they're completely covered. Bake the bread for an hour after you've poured the batter into the pan.

sprinkling a good amount of sugar on top (optional).

6 After 55 minutes of baking, a toothpick inserted into the middle of the loaf should come out clean. Transfer the bread to a cooling rack

7 once it has cooled in the pan for 10 minutes.

16. BANANA SUSHI

INGREDIENTS

- Banana
- Dark chocolate
- Pistachios

INSTRUCTIONS

1. Melt the chocolate and coat the bananas.

2. Make it simpler to grasp the bananas while they're being covered in chocolate by inserting a toothpick into either end of each one.

3. Before adding the chopped pistachios, put the bananas in the freezer for a few minutes to set the chocolate.

4. Cut the banana into bite-sized pieces of sushi once the chocolate has hardened.

5. So that's all, I swear reading the recipe will take longer than preparing it!

6. To demonstrate how simple it is, I've included a video lesson.

17. SUSHI WITHOUT A MAT

PREP TIME 30 minutes
COOK TIME 20 minutes
TOTAL TIME 50 minutes

INGREDIENTS

- 1 cup of uncooked white rice (sushi rice if you can get it // or use short-grain)
- 2 cups of water
- 3 Tbsp rice wine vinegar
- 2 Tbsp sugar
- 1/2 tsp salt
- EVERYTHING ELSE
- 1 cup of chopped veggies (carrot, cucumber, red pepper, avocado)
- 4 sheets nori (dried seaweed)
- Soy sauce/tamari, pickled ginger, wasabi (optional // for serving)

INSTRUCTIONS

1. Prepare your rice first. Before your water clears, rinse rice in a fine-mesh strainer. In a medium saucepan, heat the water to a boil, and then add the pasta. Cover and simmer for 15 minutes or until water is absorbed.
2. Mix the sugar and salt in the vinegar in a small saucepan.Refrigerate uncooked rice in a container or dish.
3. Remove from heat and whisk in vinegar mixture using a rubber spatula or fork to avoid overcooking. It will look moist, but as you stir to release heat, it will dry up. Upon completion, it should be tacky and dry to the touch.
4. Prep your vegetables by slicing them into tiny slices as you wait. Bulky rice won't allow sushi to roll smoothly.
5. Grab a thick towel and fold it into a rectangle, then arrange it on a flat surface. Now it's time to roll. A sheet of nori is then placed on top of the plastic wrap. A thin layer of rice is patted onto the nori, ensuring sure it isn't too thick else your roll would just rice and no filling if there isn't enough.
6. Fill down the bottom third of the rice with a serving of your favorite vegetables or other filling (see photo).
7. With your fingers, roll the nori and rice over the vegetables, and then roll the plastic wrap and towel over the roll to compress and shape it (see photo). Begin the process of unrolling before it's completely wrapped up.
8. Set aside after being sliced with a sharp knife.
9. Follow this detailed guide to learn how to roll an inside-out cigar. Applying a layer of avocado on the exterior as shown in the images.
10. As soon as possible, garnish with pickled ginger and wasabi.

18. ALMOND BUTTER BANANA SUSHI

Prep Time: 10 minutes
Cook Time: 0 minutes

INGREDIENTS

- 1 medium banana
- 2 tbsp almond butter
- 1/2 tbsp hemp seeds
- 1/4 cup of mini chocolate chips, semisweet

INSTRUCTIONS

1. Peel your banana first.
2. Finish by snipping both ends.
3. Sprinkle hemp seeds and chocolate chips over 1 to 2 tablespoons of almond butter.
4. Prepare your meal by slicing it up and serving it up!
5. For a dipping "soy" sauce, combine 1 tsp melted coconut oil, 1 tsp maple syrup, and 1 tsp cocoa powder.

19. QUICK AND EASY CHIRASHI SUSHI

PREP TIME: 20 mins
RICE COOKING: 1 hr
TOTAL TIME: 1 hr 20 mins

INGREDIENTS

- For Chirashi Sushi
- 2 rice cooker cup of uncooked Japanese short-grain rice (2 rice-cooker-cup of (180 ml x 2 = 360 ml) yields roughly 4 servings (3 ½ US cup of); see how to cook short-grain rice with a rice cooker, a pot over the stove, an instant pot, or a donabe)
- 400 ml water
- 1 packet chirashi sushi mix (I used "Sushi Taro brand")
- For Toppings
- kinshi tamago (shredded egg crepe)
- ikura (salmon roe)
- snow peas (blanched)
- shredded nori seaweed (kizami nori)

INSTRUCTIONS

1. Make a shopping list of all the ingredients.Using a rice cooker, an Instant Saucepan, or a pot on the stove, cook 2 rice cooker cups of rice. While the rice is cooking, make Kinshi Tamago.
2. Using a Hangiri or Sushi Oke, place the cooked rice in a big salad bowl or baking sheet. Hangiri is an excellent size for a family of four because it measures 10" (26 cm). Add one package of Chirashi Sushi Mix to the rice while it is still warm.
3. Combine all of the ingredients. Use a rice paddle to "slice" the grains apart instead of "mixing."
4. Serving suggestion: Serve in a dish, garnished with ikura (salmon roe) and snow peas. Sashimi, for example, can be added as a garnish. Add shredded nori to the mix.

TO KEEP ACCESSIBLE

To keep rice from becoming mushy or watery in the fridge, wrap it with plastic or a thick dish towel.

20. BARBEQUE HOT DOG SUSHI ROLL

Prep Time 0 Hours 15 Minutes
Cook Time 0 Hours 30 Minutes
Total Time 1 Hours 15 Minutes

INGREDIENTS

- 1 cup of water
- 1 cup of short-grain sushi rice
- 1 tbsp rice vinegar
- 1 all-beef hot dog
- 1 sheet nori (dry seaweed)
- 1 tbsp diced red onion
- ¼ cup of barbeque sauce, divided
- ¼ cup of shredded Cheddar cheese, divided
- 2 tbspFrench-fried onions

DIRECTIONS

1. Bring 1 cup of water and the rice to a boil in a small saucepan.Allow for at least 15 minutes for rice to become soft on a low heat setting with a lid on. With the water absorbed, remove from heat and let rest for 10 minutes, covered. Mix rice with vinegar. Refrigerate for about 30 minutes before using 1/3 cup for each sushi roll.

2. Bring water to a boil in a small saucepan. Add a hot dog and reduce the heat. 5 minutes of simmering before heating through is plenty.

3. The plastic wrap should be placed on a level surface. Set up a nearby cup of hot water. Nori should be placed 2 inches from the edge nearest to you. Using damp fingertips, apply a thin layer of chilled rice over the nori sheets. A hot dog should be placed one inch from the base of the rice and nori. Set out a hot dog with onions arranged in a row alongside it. On a plate, place the hot dog and two tablespoons of barbecue sauce. Top with 2 tbsp of Cheddar cheese.

4. Lift the nori by carefully grabbing the edge of the plastic wrap nearest to you. Pulling on the plastic wrap, tightly roll the sushi into a thick cylinder, enclosing the contents with a fold over. Removing the plastic wrap To seal the nori, wet your fingertips and delicately pat the edge.

5. Split the sushi roll in six equal pieces using a sharp knife. Serve the slices in a bowl. Add 2 tsp barbecue sauce and 2 tsp Cheddar cheese on the top of the pizza crust before serving. French-fried onions can be sprinkled on top.

21. KIWI AVOCADO SMOOTHIE

PREP TIME 5 minutes
TOTAL TIME 5 minutes

INGREDIENTS

- 1 avocado, peeled and seeded
- 2 kiwi fruits, peeled and halved
- 2 cups of green grapes
- 1 granny smith apple, peeled and cored
- ½ cup of crushed ice
- ½ cup of water
- ¼ cup of fresh mint

INSTRUCTIONS

1. Mix everything together in a blender before smooth.
2. To serve, divide the mixture into four glasses.

NOTES

Bananas can also be added to the smoothie to add sweetness. It's also great with protein powders!

22. UNAGI DONBURI (EEL BOWL)

Prep Time 5 Minutes
Cook Time 5 Minutes

INGREDIENTS

- 2 cups of Cooked Sushi Rice You can substitute with white rice
- 12 oz Unagi Whole or cut into pieces
- 1/2 whole Cucumber Cut into slices
- 1/2 whole Avocado Cut into slices
- 4 oz Seaweed Salad
- Black Sesame Seeds Optional
- Unagi Sauce As need

INSTRUCTIONS

1. Use the package directions to prepare unagi.
2. Divide the ingredients into two separate dishes.
3. That's all I can say. Nothing else to do. Isn't it crazy?

NOTES

The recipe and directions for sushi rice may be found on this page.

The Unagi Sauce from Kikkoman is one of my favorites. It's a little thicker and a little sweeter than the regular version.

23.   BEEF SUSHI ROLLS
PREP TIME 15 min
COOK TIME 20 min
TOTAL TIME 35 min

INSTRUCTIONS

- Sushi rice
- ½ cup of (125 mL)15-minute dry short grain brown rice
- 1 cup of (250 mL) water
- 2 tbsp (30 mL) rice wine vinegar
- 1 tbsp (15 mL) sugar
- ¼ tsp (1 mL) salt
- Beef
- 2 tbsp (30 mL) soy sauce
- 2 tsp (10 mL) sesame oil
- 1 tsp (5 mL) honey
- ¼ tsp (1 mL) every salt and garlic powder
- 1 tsp (5 mL) sesame seeds
- 1 lb (500 g) thin-cut beef steaks, around 4 steaks
- Sushi roll

- ½ cup of (125 mL) every julienned carrots, julienned cucumbers, enoki mushrooms and chives
- 1 tsp (5 mL) vegetable oil

INSTRUCTIONS

1. Cover the rice and water in a pot.Once it's at a boil, reduce the temperature. The cover should be on for 15 minutes. For another 10 minutes, turn off the heat and keep the cover on. Ensure that the rice is done. Toss the rice with rice wine vinegar, sugar and salt in a large bowl and mix thoroughly. Mix and let the rice cool.
2. Salt, garlic powder, and sesame seeds go into a small dish with the soy sauce, sesame oil, and honey.
3. A meat mallet or heavy fry pan can be used to tenderize each steak. 3-mm thick, 6-inch x 3-inch steaks are ideal. Soy sauce mixture is brushed over both sides of the steaks, with half reserved for dipping.Every beef slice should have a layer of the rice mixture covering it. Make an even layer of rice on top of which you may evenly distribute carrot, cucumber, mushrooms, and chives. Starting with the short side of the steak, wrap up each piece like a jelly roll. Using 2 to 3 lengths of butcher twine, secure each knot.
4. Medium-high heat is ideal for heating oil in a big oven-safe nonstick pan. Add the rolls and cook for about 4 minutes, until they are golden brown.
5. Preheat the oven to 400°F (200°C). A digital instant-read thermometer should register around 140°F (60°C) within the rolls after about 10 minutes of cooking. Before serving, take the bread from the oven and cut it into 1-inch slices.

COOKING ADVICE

Cover and chill the rolls before cooking for up to three days in order to make them ahead of time. If you prefer, you may prepare them ahead of time and slice them right before packing them for lunch.

24. MAGIC MAKI ROLLS WITH CAULIFLOWER RICE

INSTRUCTIONS

- 2 large Cauliflower heads
- 200 g cream cheese
- 4 Tbsp rice vinegar
- 2 Tbsp sugar
- sheets of Nori Seaweed
- 200-250 g fresh, raw sushi fish
- 1 small cucumber
- 1 large avocado
- 1/2 ripe mango
- 2 tbsp Chili mayo

TO SERVE

1. Paste with soya and wasabi
2. Seaweed salad with pickled ginger
3. Wakame
4. Steamed edamame beans in their pods with salt and lime juice sprinkled on top.

DIRECTIONS

1. Use a grater or a food processor to shred the cauliflower. For 5 minutes, cook cauliflower rice in a saucepan. Pour the riced cauliflower into a strainer, add cold water, and let the extra liquid to drain. To make dry cauliflower rice, place all of the cauliflower rice in a Bowltowel and squeeze out as much water as possible.

Cauliflower rice, cream cheese, rice vinegar, and sugar should be combined in a bowl.

2. Cut long and thin pieces of fish, veggies, and mango. Place a piece of nori on top of the bamboo mat, rough side up. Remove only the top 15 inch (0,5-1,5 cm) of the nori sheet before adding the remaining 4–5 tablespoons of cauliflower rice (see picture). Place your filling in a thin, straight line down the bottom of the nori sheet (see picture). For each roll, I use all the ingredients.

3. Once the filling has been tucked in, fold it up and gently press it into place with the bamboo mat and your hands. Continue rolling the maki with the bamboo mat and 'closing' it by dabbing some water on the free tip of nori weed and rolling it all the way up. Repeat with the remaining maki rolls.You must keep rolling the roll firmly in order to maintain its integrity.

4. Before supper, put your sushi rolls in the refrigerator. To serve, cut them into 2,5 cm (1 inch) pieces and serve with your favorite sushi fixings!

25. VEGAN SUSHI WITH AVOCADO, BELL PEPPER AND CUCUMBER

Prep time 20 minutes
Cooking time 30 minutes
Total time 40 minutes

INGREDIENTS

- For the Rice
- 2 cups of short-grain rice
- 4 cups of water
- For the Sushi

- 1 avocado (sliced)
- ½ cucumber (sliced)
- sheets nori dried seaweed sheet
- 1 medium red bell pepper (sliced)
- For the Dip
- tbsps soy sauce
- 4 tsp wasabi

DIRECTIONS

1 For around 30 minutes, cook the rice in the water.

2 Seaweed and rice should be placed on a bamboo mat, along with the veggies.

3 Using a bamboo mat makes it simple to roll out a beautiful sushi dish.

4 To eat, cut the sushi roll into pieces and serve it with wasabi and soy sauce.

26. WASABI SALMON BOWL RECIPE

Prep Time 10 mins
Cook Time 25 mins
Total Time 35 mins

INGREDIENTS

- 2 salmon filets 6-8oz every
- 1 sheet nori thinly sliced
- 1 avocado chopped or sliced
- 6-10 pieces pickled ginger
- 2 Tbspcashews chopped
- For the Sushi Rice
- 1 1/2 cup of sushi rice uncooked
- 2 cup of water
- 1/2 cup of Mizkan rice vinegar
- 1/2 cup of sugar
- 1 Tbsp salt
- For the Wasabi Mayo
- 4 Tbsp mayonnaise

- 1 tsp Mizkan rice vinegar
- 1 tsp wasabi
- 1 Tbsp sugar
- Juice of 1/2 lemon

INSTRUCTIONS

1. To Prepare the Rice for Sushi
2. Package instructions should be followed.
3. MixMizkan rice vinegar, sugar, and salt in a small pot.
4. When the sugar and salt are all dissolved, bring the mixture to a boil over medium heat.
5. Set aside the vinegar and sushi rice in a large mixing basin to chill.
6. Prior to uniformly soaking the sushi rice in vinegar, stir the vinegar mixture with a fork. While sticky, but not dripping, rice is the ideal texture.
7. To Prepare the Salmon, follow these instructions:
8. Salt, pepper, and sesame seeds can be used to season the fish (optional).
9. Sauté the meat in a medium-sized pan. Using 1-2 Tbsp of coconut oil, coat the pan. Skin side down, place the salmon in the pan.
10. Make sure the skin side of the salmon is facing up when it's halfway done cooking. If you look in the centre of the fish, you'll see an unique line.
11. Remove heat from the pan, cover the salmon, and let it steam for 10 minutes (for medium doneness).
12. Recipe for Wasabi Mayo
13. In a small bowl, combine the wasabi mayo ingredients and whisk until smooth.
14. With 1/3 cup sushi rice, half an avocado, nori strips, and cashews layered on top of each other in your salmon bowls, you'll be

ready to drizzle with wasabi mayo and serve.

NOTES

As a suggestion only, the nutritional value will vary depending on the materials used and the amount of food cooked.

NUTRITION

A serving of this meal provides 795 calories, 65 grams of carbohydrates, 42 grams of protein, 6 grams of saturated fat, 99 milligrams of cholesterol, 190 milligrams of sodium, 1433 milligrams of potassium, 9 grams of fiber, and 5 grams of sugar.

27. SPICY SALMON, AVOCADO AND RICED CAULIFLOWER SUSHI

Prep Time: 15 minutes
Cook Time: 5 minutes
Total Time: 20 minutes

INGREDIENTS

- 3 cup of grated cauliflower rice
- 2 Tbsp rice vinegar
- 2 tsp tapioca starch
- pinch of salt
- 1/2 lb sushi-grade salmon (or tuna or smoked salmon)
- 1/2 Tbsp Franks Red Hot (if not worried about Whole30/Paleo, use siracha instead)
- 1 large avocado, sliced
- 1 cup of cilantro
- 1/2 cucumber
- 3–4 sheets of nori
-

- Coco amino and some red pepper flakes
- Spicy Mayo (optional):
- 3/4 cup of Compliant mayo
- 1–2 TbspFranks Red Hot or Siracha (not Whole30) – (mix per your desired spicy level)

INSTRUCTIONS

1. Cauliflower can be grated (I would HIGHLY recommend grating it so that it is the right texture)
2. Toss the cauliflower into a pan and crank the heat up to medium-high, then remove it from the heat.
3. Using a wooden spoon, stir the cauliflower continually for about 3 minutes.
4. Salt and rice vinegar should be added.
5. About 2 minutes later, continue to mix to ensure that the vinegar coats the cauliflower well.
6. Stir in the tapioca starch until smooth.
7. Take the rice from the heat and transfer it to a separate bowl to cool down a bit.
8. Wrap a paper towel in plastic wrap and place it on a large dish.
9. To absorb extra water, lay another paper towel on top of the rice and push down.
10. Return the cauliflower rice to the serving dish.
11. Cut the salmon into cubes and set them in a serving basin.
12. Franks Red Hot or Siracha can be added and stirred in to coat; set aside to cool.
13. Place the bamboo sushi roller on the cutting board before assembling the sushi roll.
14. Place one nori sheet on top.
15. You can use a metal spoon to spread cauliflower rice evenly across the nori sheet by pressing down with the back of it.

16. Work your way up the nori sheet, away from your body, starting at the bottom and covering the top 1 inch of nori with rice.
17. Lay some cucumber, cilantro, salmon, and avocado across the nori sheet, around one inch from the bottom, parallel to the nori sheet
18. To fold over your salmon, etc., draw up the bottom of the nori sheet closest to you, tucking the nori sheet under, and then continue dragging the bamboo roller away from your body while you press down hard on the roll as you do.
19. You should continue to pull away from me until the end of the roll.
20. Slicing the beef into one-inch pieces with a very sharp knife, clean your knife after each cut.
21. Serve with coco aminos right away.
22. Add more cilantro, black sesame seeds, and spicy mayo to the dish.

28.   SMOKED SALMON AND CREAM CHEESE ROLLS

30m prep
15m cook

INGREDIENTS

- 430g (2 cup of) SunRice Japanese Style Sushi Rice, rinsed, drained
- 750ml (3 cup of) cold water
- 125ml (1/2 cup of) sushi seasoning
- 8 nori sheets
- 240g smoked salmon slices, torn
- 80g-piece cream cheese, cut into 1cm-thick batons
- 1 1/2 Lebanese cucumbers, cut into 5mm-thick batons
- 100g snow pea sprouts
- Soy sauce, to serve
- Pickled ginger, to serve
- Wasabi, to serve

STEPS

1. Pre-rinse rice before it becomes transparent. Cook the rice and water in a large pot on high heat until the rice is tender. Low is the new high. Cover. Cook for 12 minutes or until all the water has been absorbed.
2. Cover and steam for 10 minutes. Fold in the seasonings with a rice paddle or wooden spoon. Stir occasionally for 15 minutes to cool down the mixture.
3. On a bamboo mat, spread out one nori sheet. Apply rice to the nori with damp fingertips, leaving a 2cm boundary at the farthest edge away from you.
4. Sliced salmon, cream cheese, cucumber and snow pea sprouts should be arranged around 5cm from the edge nearest to you on the rice.
5. While rolling to enclose, grab the mat's edge and keep the filling in place. Shape and seal the mat by gently pressing it. Seven additional rolls can be made by repeating this process.
6. Slice each roll into six equal pieces with a damp, sharp knife. Pickled ginger and wasabi can be added to the dish for additional flavor.

29. SALMON NIGIRI

Hands-On: 15 mins
Total: 30 mins

INGREDIENTS

- ¼ cup of unseasoned rice vinegar
- 1 tbsp granulated sugar
- 1 tsp kosher salt
- 1 cup of uncooked short-grain rice
- ¾ pounds sushi-grade salmon, thinly sliced
- Wasabi paste
- Soy sauce

DIRECTIONS

1. In a small big pot, combine vinegar, sugar, and salt and stir until dissolved.
2. Cook the rice according to the package recommendations after thoroughly rinsing it under running water. In a large glass baking dish, spread the rice and sprinkle with the vinegar mixture. Gently fold the rice into the vinegar mixture to combine.
3. Form the rice mixture into 16 (3-inch by 1-inch) pieces; top with salmon slices and wasabi to taste. ' Soy sauce is a good accompaniment.

NUTRITIONAL INFORMATION

A single serving provides 317 calories, 5.7 grams of fat, 0.9 grams of saturated fat, 20.1 grams of protein, 43.7 grams of carbohydrate, 1.4 grams of fiber, and 3.4 grams of sugar.

30. SPICY SALMON SUSHI ROLLS

Total Time: 60 minutes

INGREDIENTS

- Bamboo Rolling Mat
- 4 or more sheets of Nori
- SUSHI RICE SEASONING
- 1 cup of rice vinegar
- 1 2 inch square kombu
- 3 tbsp sugar
- 1 tbsp kosher salt
- SUSHI RICE
- 2 cup of short-grain rice
- 2 ¼ cup of water
- SPICY MAYO
- 1 cup of kewpie mayo
- 2 tbsp sriracha
- 2 tsp gochujang
- 1 green onion thinly sliced
- Salt as need
- Couple drops sesame oil
- SPICY SALMON FILLING
- 3 tbsp Spicy mayo mix
- 8oz Kvarøy Arctic Salmon
- 2 tsp furikake seasoning
- 1 tbsp soy sauce
- 1 tbsp sriracha
- 1-2 cucumber sticks per roll
- GARNISH
- Sliced green onions
- Sesame seeds
- Furikake
- Spicy mayo

INSTRUCTIONS

1. In a saucepan, combine the rice with the water to make the rice.
2. For 20 minutes, bring to a full boil, then decrease the heat to the lowest setting and cover.
3. At least 20 minutes
4. before serving, take the food from the oven and allow it to cool.To make the rice

seasoning, put all of the ingredients in a small pot and bring to a simmer. Take from heat and allow to cool to room temperature. Remove and discard the kombu.

5. Make sure the rice and spice are both at room temperature before mixing them together. Using a fork ensures that the rice doesn't become too mushy. You only need a sprinkling of the spice and a fork to fluff the rice.

6. In a pot, combine all of the ingredients for the spicy mayo and whisk until smooth.

7. If not used straight away, store in the refrigerator.

8. Squeeze some into a sushi chef's squeeze bottle and you'll look like the real deal!

9. The filling for the salmon is a spicy sauce.

10. Make sure to remove and dispose of the skin from the fillet.

11. Make cubes out of the salmon by slicing it into long strips first. You may create them as big or little as you like, but I prefer around a quarter of an inch.

12. In a mixing dish, combine the salmon with the rest of the spicy salmon filling ingredients and mix thoroughly. frigerate if you're not going to use it straight away.

13. To put together

14. On your bamboo mat, place a nori sheet with the dull side up. Rice should be distributed across the surface, ensuring sure your fingers are wet at all times.

15. Then, on the side nearest to you, run a thin strip of filling from left to right. Use the bamboo mat to assist keep the roll in place while you add a few strips of cucumber and a sprinkling of sesame seeds or foretake spice.

16. Here's a video that could be of use: Sushi Rolling Instructions

17. Slice it into rounds once it's rolled out and placed on a cutting board. Even if the ends are a touch sloppy, the flavor is still there.

18. Pour a generous amount of spicy mayo on top of your sushi, garnish with tobiko, sesame seeds, and foretake and ENJOY!

31. SALMON SUSHI BOWLS

Prep Time: 10 minutes
Cook Time: 40 minutes

INGREDIENTS

- 1 ½ pounds wild-caught salmon from Kroger Easy for You! Seafood with lemon slices, cilantro and butter sealed in the pouch.
- 1 avocado sliced
- 1 cucumber peeled and sliced
- 3 green onion sliced
- 4 sheets nori cut into strips
- sesame seeds for garnish optional
- sushi rice see recipe below
- sriracha aioli see recipe below
- soy-ginger dressing see recipe below
- 2 cup of short-grain white sushi rice such as Cal-Rose
- 3 cup of water
- 2 tbsp rice vinegar
- 1 tbsp sugar
- Work From Home
- Sponsored by Work From Home
- Work A US Job from Home in Bangladesh
- 1/2 tbsp salt
- For The Soy Ginger Dressing:
- 1/2 cup of soy sauce

- 1/4 cup of rice vinegar
- 2 tsp sugar
- 1 tsp sesame oil
- 1-2 tbsp fresh grated ginger root
- 3 garlic cloves minced
- For the Sriracha Aioli:
- 1/2 cup of high quality mayonnaise
- 1-2 tbsp sriracha to desired spiciness

INSTRUCTIONS

1. If you don't have a packet, roast salmon on a baking sheet at 425°F for about 20-30 minutes, or until it's cooked through.
2. Rice for sushi should be made. Before the water flows clear, rinse the rice. Add to a medium saucepan of water, stirring often until the water reaches a boil. Cover and lower the temperature. Cook for about 21 minutes, or until the water has evaporated. Make sure the rice has had time to cool somewhat before serving.
3. Rice vinegar, sugar and salt are all you need in a little bowl to get the job done. Stir for about 30 seconds in the microwave before the sugar and salt dissolve. Mix in the vinegar mixture before serving the rice.
4. Aioli made with mayonnaise and hot sauce can be made ahead of time and stored in the refrigerator.
5. To make the soy-ginger dressing, combine the soy sauce, rice vinegar, sugar, sesame oil, ginger, and garlic in a bowl and whisk until well-combined. Before the sugar is completely dissolved, begin whisking the mixture. Set away for later.
6. Add sushi rice to the bowl before assembling the salmon sushi bowls. Toss in a few pieces of nori, a few slices of avocado, cucumber, and green onion. Pour sriracha aioli and soy ginger dressing over top.

NOTES

Keep an eye out for tiny bones in wild salmon. If it's feasible, I attempt to remove them before serving.

As a convenience to you, we've included nutritional information for your use. If you have certain dietary requirements, please do your research before making this dish.

32.   SALMON SUSHI ROLLS
1h 50m prep
20m cook

INGREDIENTS

- 1 cup of sushi rice, rinsed
- 1 tbsp seasoned rice vinegar
- 4 nori sheets (dried, roasted seaweed)
- 1/2 avocado, sliced lengthways
- 105g can red salmon, drained, flaked
- 1/2 Lebanese cucumber
- 1 small carrot, grated
- soy sauce, to serve

STEPS

1. Place rice and 1 1/2 cup of cold water in a pot over high heat. Bring the water in a boil, cover, and reduce to a low heat. When the rice is tender and the liquid has been absorbed, reduce the heat to low and continue to cook for another 16 minutes. Take the pan off the heat. Take a five-minute rest from moving.
2. In a bowl, combine rice and vinegar. Mix everything together. Ensure that the rice has cooled sufficiently before stirring often to avoid it getting mushy and sticky.

3. The shiny side of a nori sheet should be down on a sushi mat. Spread one-quarter of the rice mixture over the nori sheet, leaving a 3cm-wide border around the edges, with moist hands. Place a quarter of the avocado on the side that is facing you and press it down firmly. Top with a quarter of each of the salmon, cucumber, and carrots. Make a tight roll using the sushi mat to encompass the filling. Repeat with the rest of the nori, rice mixture, fish, and veggies.

4. Cut each roll into four equal pieces. To keep it safe, wrap it in a plastic bag or another container.

33. RINSE AND WASH SUSHI RICE

Total Cook Time 25 mins
Prep Time 15 mins
Cook Time 10 mins

INGREDIENTS

- For The Sushi Rice
- 1/2 cup of Japanese Sticky Rice
- 1/2 cup of Vinegar 1/5 cup of Sugar
- 1 tsp Salt For The Sushi Rolling
- 1/2 cup of Smoked Salmon
- 1/2 cup of Gari 1 tsp Wasabi
- 1 nos Sushi Nori
- 2 tsp Soya Sauce 1 tsp Cream Cheese
- 1 tsp Spring Onion (Fine Chopped)
- 1 tsp Sesame Seeds (Black)
- 1 tsp Sesame Seeds (White)
- 1 nos English Cucumber

INGREDIENTS

1. Rinse and wash sushi rice under running water to remove any excess starch. It is necessary to perform this procedure five times.

2. Prepare the sushi rice by first bringing it to a boil in a 1:114 water mixture.

3. Make sushi vinegar by combining vinegar, sugar, and salt in a small saucepan.

4. Before using the rice, combine it with the sushi vinegar and keep it moistened with a towel.

5. In order to make sushi, you'll need:

6. Sushi rice should be evenly distributed on the nori sheet, which should be placed on a sushi mat.

7. Sushi rice should be sprinkled with a combination of white and black sesame seeds.

8. Make sure that the sushi rice is face-up on the sushi mat by flipping the nori sheet.

9. Sliced spears and the fried gari tempura should be placed on top of

10. the cream cheese.

11. cut the sushi into eight equal pieces by gently rolling it into a square form.

12. Gari, wasabi, and soy sauce should accompany it.

34. SCALLOP SUSHI

PREP TIME: 10 mins
TOTAL TIME: 10 mins

INGREDIENTS

- 2 sushi-grade scallops
- ⅓ cup of sushi rice (cooked and seasoned)
- wasabi (optional)
- Tezu (vinegared hand-dipping water):
- ¼ cup of water
- 2 tsp rice vinegar
- Toppings (optional):

- 2 tsp yuzu-flavored tobiko (flying fish roe)
- 2 tsp spicy mayo
- 2 chives

INSTRUCTIONS

1. Gather all of the ingredients before starting the cooking process.
2. Scallops should be de-muscled.
3. Using a pair of scissors, cut the scallops into quarters.
4. Pick up a tbsp-sized ball of sushi rice and dip your hands in tezu (vinegar dipping hand). Shape the rice into a rectangle with rounded corners and slips by gently pressing it in your right palm to produce the shape. As you're molding the rice into a firm foundation for the scallops, apply pressure on it.
5. Add a little amount of wasabi (if desired) and a scallop to each formed piece of rice. Decorate each scallop with tobiko and spicy mayonnaise. It's best to eat raw scallops on the same day they're harvested!

NUTRITION

36 kcals per serving This meal has 6 grams of carbohydrates, 2 grams of protein, and 1 gram of fat. It also contains 4 mg of cholesterol. Calcium is 2 milligrams, iron is one milligram, and sodium is 60 milligrams. Fiber and sugar are each one milligram.

35. SEARED SCALLOPS SUSHI

Prep: 15 min
Cook: 5 min

INGREDIENTS

- 5 sea scallops
- Vegetable oil
- 1 cup of sushi rice, recipe follows
- Wasabi
- Daikon sprouts, for garnish
- Sushi Rice:
- 5 cup of short-grain sushi rice
- 6 cup of water
- 1/2 cup of rice vinegar
- 2 tbsp sugar
- 1 tsp salt

DIRECTIONS

1. In a saute pan, bring the oil to a boil. Make sure the pan is gently coated with oil. Add the sea scallops and cook for 30 seconds to a minute on each side until golden brown. Avoid overcooking your food! Serve right away with lemon wedges and olive oil on the side.
2. Pick up a golf-ball-sized rice ball. Using your right hand, gently squeeze the rice to form a rectangular block with rounded corners and sides. As you're molding the rice into a firm foundation for the scallops, apply pressure on it. Each piece of rice should be topped with a little amount of wasabi and a half of a scallop. Serve each slice garnished with a few daikon sprouts.
3. Remove any dirt from the rice by rinsing in cold water and vigorously stirring. Drain all of the rice. Cover a medium pot with a tight-fitting lid and add the rice and 6 cups of water. Over a medium flame, bring the

water to a boil. Cook for 18 minutes without lifting the cover once the water has boiled for three minutes. Remove the top from the rice and turn off the heat (the water should no longer be visible). To uniformly distribute the rice, use a spatula or a rice paddle to spread it out on a baking sheet. Before the rice reaches room temperature, add the vinegar, sugar, and salt and stir with a spatula or rice paddle. When the rice isn't ready to be used, cover it with a moist paper towel or napkin.

36.   SPICY SEATTLE TUNA ROLLS

Active Time 40 minutes
Total Time 40 minutes

INGREDIENTS

- 4 green Thai chiles, stemmed, coarsely chopped
- 1 tsp grated peeled fresh ginger
- 1 tbsp toasted sesame seeds
- 1 garlic clove, coarsely chopped
- 1/2 tsp kosher salt + more for seasoning
- 1/4 cup of sunflower
- 2 tsp toasted sesame oil
- 1 tsp distilled white vinegar
- 1 pound sashimi-grade yellowfin tuna fillets, cut into 1/8" cubes
- 4 toasted dried nori sheets, halved lengthwise
- 1 1/2 cup of (about) cooked short-grain rice, cooled

STEPS

1. Mini-processor: Pulse ginger, sesame seeds and garlic in a food processor until a paste forms. Pour into a medium basin. Toss in both the vinegar and the oil. Salt to taste the dressing. Toss in the tuna with a light hand to evenly cover both sides.

2. With the short side facing you, place nori sheets onto a work area. The bottom third of each sheet should be uniformly coated with 2 rounded tablespoons of price. Cook rice and divide the tuna mixture among the buns. Fillings can be added to the top. Use a few grains of cooked rice as "glue" to seal the cones or logs.

3. Making Spicy Tomato Tuna Casserole - Each Step in the Process (And Why)

37.   SALMON SUSHI BOWL RECIPE

prep time: 15 MINUTES
total time: 15 MINUTES

INGREDIENTS

- Sushi Bowls
- 2 Cup of Prepared Brown Rice or Cauliflower Rice
- 1 Cucumber, (sliced or chopped)
- 1 Cup of Matchstick Carrots
- 1 Avocado, (sliced or chopped)
- 4 ounces Smoked Salmon Lox
- 1 Small Lemon, (thinly sliced)
- 4 Roasted Seaweed Sheets, (crumbled)
- 1 Cup of Shredded Cabbage
- Black & Tan Sesame Seeds
- 1 Cup of Shelled Soy Beans - Edamame, (optional)
- Sushi Ginger, (optional)
- Wasabi Paste, (optional)

- Dressing
- 2 tsp Toasted Sesame Oil
- 1 tsp Rice Vinegar
- 1 Tbsp Coconut Aminos, (or soy sauce)
- 1/4 tsp Grated Ginger, (or dried ground ginger)
- 1 tsp Mayonnaise
- 1/2 tsp Chili, (optional)

INSTRUCTIONS

1. Sushi bowls should be assembled.
2. To make this dressing, combine all the ingredients in a small bowl and pour over the sushi bowls.

38. KIMBAP (KOREAN SEAWEED RICE ROLLS) RECIPE

Active: 60 mins
Total: 60 mins

INGREDIENTS

- Save Recipe
- 1 large (12-ounce; 340g) cucumber
- Sea or kosher salt
- 3 large eggs
- Vegetable oil, for greasing the pan
- 6 long strips ham for kimbap (every about 1/4 inch or less thick)
- 1 medium carrot, julienned
- 3 sheets flat odeng fishcake, cut lengthwise into 1/4-inch strips
- 2 tsp (10ml) grain syrup or oligosaccharide syrup (sold as "oligodang" at the Korean markets)
- 1 tsp (5ml) soy sauce
- 1 whole danmuji

- 6 long pieces Korean braised burdock root for kimbap
- 3 long strips of artificial crab meat (surimi in Japanese), cut in half lengthwise for a total of 6
- 3 cup of cooked short-grain (sushi) rice, hot (see note)
- 1 1/2 tbsp(22ml) sesame oil, + more for brushing
- 1 1/2 tbspcrushed roasted sesame seeds
- 6 square sheets gim (sold as nori in Japanese) for gimbap or sushi

DIRECTIONS

1. Split the cucumber in half and take the ends. Scrape the seeds out of each half using a spoon. Make six strips by cutting each half into three long strips. Toss the cucumber slices with salt and pepper on a platter and serve. Set away for later.
2. Beat the egg & salt together in a small bowl. Make sure the pan is preheated but not scorching hot by lightly sprinkling some vegetable oil on top of it. Stir in half of the egg, swirling to coat the entire bottom of the pan, and cook for 3 minutes, or until the egg is just set on top. Using a rubber spatula, remove the egg from the pan and set it aside to cool. If necessary, lightly oil the pan again and cook the remaining egg in it. Remove the food from the pan and wipe it down.
3. Thinly slice an egg in half lengthwise. Set away for later.
4. Squeeze gently to remove extra moisture from cucumber after rinsing under cold running water. Set the skillet over medium-high heat until it shimmers, wiping it gently with extra vegetable oil before doing so. In

about a minute, add the cucumber and simmer for another minute or two until it's softened. Take a break and allow the food to cool down before serving.

5. Cook for 1 to 2 minutes, swirling and turning occasionally, until ham is cooked through. Take a break and allow the food to cool down before serving.

6. Carrot should be crisp-tender after 1 to 2 minutes of swirling and tossing in a skillet with a heavy teaspoon of salt; if the pan needs extra oil, do so at any time. Take a break and allow the food to cool down before serving.

7. Reduce the heat to medium. Fishcake strips, oligosaccharide syrup, and soy sauce should be added to an oiled pan and cooked until the fishcake strips are softened, about 1 to 2 minutes. Take a break and allow the food to cool down before serving.

8. Rice should be mixed with sesame oil, crushed sesame seeds, and 1 tsp salt in a big dish before being served. Using a scale, divide the rice into six equal pieces.

9. Prepare a work surface with a kimbap/sushi rolling mat. Place a nori sheet on top of it. Place a quantity of rice on the seaweed sheet and spread it evenly with both hands, leaving approximately one or two inches of the sheet exposed at the top edge. Using plastic gloves, do this. Top the cake with a few rice grains (they will help it stick together later).

10. Assemble your fillings by placing them down the middle of the rice: There is a cucumber stick, some egg strips, some ham strips, one-sixth of a carrot, some fishcake strips, one danmuji strip, one burdock strip, and one crab stick strip.

11. Use both hands to keep the filling in place as you roll it with your thumbs, then lift the bamboo mat away from you and wrap the seaweed sheet and rice around the contents. Use the seaweed sheet's uncovered flap to secure the roll. Make a little squeeze on the top and side of your seaweed roll to compress it and seal it; if necessary, you may damp the seaweed seam to help it stick.

12. Repeat with the remaining seaweed sheets, rice, and other ingredients.

13. Gently smear a sharp knife blade with sesame oil before cutting the rolls. It is simpler to cut through two rolls at a time rather than one at a time, so place two rolls next to each other and slice them both into half-inch thick pieces.

NOTES

Compared to ordinary rice, you'll want to use a bit less water. It's not unusual for me to adjust my typical rice-water ratio from 1.2 parts water to 1 part by volume to 1.1 parts water to 1 part rice if the rice is more humid (often true of fresh rice). You should use a 1:1 ratio if you're using a pressure cooker or a pressure rice cooker.

I propose substituting the rice seasoning above with a vinegar marinade made with 1 part water, 1 part rice vinegar, 1 part sugar, and 1/2 part salt during the summer months.

39. INARI SUSHI

prep time: 20 MINUTES
total time: 20 MINUTES

INGREDIENTS

- 4 cup of sushi rice – visit my post on how to make sushi rice
- 1 can inarizushi no moto
- 1 tbsp black or white sesame seeds

INSTRUCTIONS

1. Gently fold the sushi rice after you've added the sesame seeds, if desired (not too much otherwise the rice will get mushy).
2. Make rice balls by grabbing a little amount of rice with your hands and rolling it into a ball.
3. Wash your hands with the inarizushi no moto liquid after pouring it into a dish.
4. Place a rice ball into an inarizushi pocket that has been opened. Repeat this method until all of the pockets have been emptied.

NOTES

Despite the fact that inari sushi is best consumed immediately, it can be preserved in an airtight container in the frigerator for up to two days. Avoid warming them up and enjoy them at room temperature instead.

40. SHIITAKE MUSHROOM AND AVOCADO SUSHI

Prep Time 10 mins
Cook Time 25 mins
Rolling Time 30 mins
Total Time 1 hr 5 mins

INGREDIENTS

- 1/2 cup of dried shiitake mushrooms
- 2 tbsp soy sauce
- 1 tbsp sesame oil
- 2 large eggs beaten
- 4 big sheets seaweed
- 1 1/3 cup of freshly cooked hot rice
- 1 avocado sliced
- 1 Persian cucumber halved lengthwise
- 4 green onions
- 1/4 cup of pickled ginger

INSTRUCTIONS

1. Mushrooms may be cooked in a medium skillet. Swirl them around in the water to make sure they're completely submerged. Boil for 10-15 minutes, or until most of the stems are pliable, whichever comes first. Trim the mushrooms' stems, then cut them in half.
2. In a separate skillet, heat a little quantity of oil over medium-high heat.Sauté the mushrooms for 5 to 10 minutes, or until they're brown and aromatic, then remove from the heat. Mix in the soy sauce, and simmer for a few more minutes, until the mushrooms have darkened. Add the sesame oil after removing the pan from the heat.
3. Another skillet should be preheated with a small amount of oil on low heat. Then, add the egg, sprinkle it with salt, and cook until the top is done.Remove from the pan and put aside to cool completely before slicing into four similar-sized pieces.
4. You should have enough plastic wrap to completely cover the sushi rolling mat before you begin rolling the sushi. Fill a small basin with water and keep it close by for emergencies.

5. The glossy side of a sheet of seaweed should face down on the plastic wrap. Break up and distribute about a third cup of rice with your fingers, leaving the top and bottom borders free of rice.Whether it looks a little spotty or not, there is nothing to worry about

6. Mushrooms can be placed in two rows, running from left to right, in the centre of the rice. Gently press them into the rice to aid in their adhesion. Cover the mushrooms with a thin layer of egg white. Make sure you place a couple avocado slices on top of the egg, but keep them closer to the bottom half of the sushi canvas. Right above the avocado, place two cucumber slices and one green onion. Slices of pickled ginger can be draped on top of the avocado.

7. Use the bamboo mat to firmly wrap up the sushi from the bottom to the top. While rolling, you can use one hand to keep the cucumber/green onion in place with the other, if necessary. Using the plastic wrap to guide the rest of the roll after you're a few inches from the top edge is a good idea. To ensure that the sushi is properly sealed, give it a few squeezes before unwrapping it from the plastic wrap and sushi mat.

8. Slice the sushi using a serrated knife. The sushi will hold together better if it is cut into thicker pieces. Serve it at room temperature. Rice will harden if it is kept in the refrigerator.

41.   AHI SHOYU POKE
Prep: 20 mins
Total: 20 mins

INGREDIENTS

- 1 pound fresh ahi steaks, cut into small cubes
- ¼ cup of soy sauce
- ¼ cup of chopped Maui onion
- ¼ cup of chopped green onion
- 1 chile pepper, seeded and diced (optional)
- 2 tsp sesame oil
- 2 tsp toasted sesame seeds (Optional)
- 2 tsp finely chopped toasted macadamia nuts
- 1 tsp grated fresh ginger
- sea salt as need

DIRECTIONS

1. Soy sauce, green onion, chilli peppers, sesame oil, and sesame seeds are added to a big dish of mixahi cubes, along with macadamia nuts and ginger.
2. If you don't want to use the Maui onion, you may use a yellow onion instead.

42.   TUNA TARTARE IN SESAME GINGER SAUCE
prep time: 15 MINS
cook time: 0 MINUTES
total time: 15 MINS

INGREDIENTS

- 300 grams of sushi-grade Tuna, cut into small cubes
- 4 green onions, finely chopped
- 2 tbsp toasted sesame seeds
- 1 avocado, chopped into small pieces

- 1/2 cup of diced cucumber
- A handful of cilantro, chopped
- 1 tbsp lime juice
- pinch of salt & pepper
- Sauce
- 2 cloves of garlic, minced
- 1 tbsp. grated ginger
- 2 spring onions, chopped
- 2 tbsp soy sauce, gluten-free if needed
- 1 tbsp sesame oil
- 1 tbsp rice vinegar
- 1 tbsp honey

INSTRUCTIONS

1. The sauce may be made by mixing all of the ingredients together in a basin. Set away for later.
2. Make sure the sauce is well mixed before adding the chopped tuna, green onions and sesame seeds.
3. Finely chop avocado, cucumber and cilantro in a separate bowl and combine with lime juice, salt and pepper.
4. Plate your tartare in a mould (like this) or a round ramekin (like this)

NOTES

A side of rice crackers will complete the meal!

To serve your tartare, place it in a ramekin and then carefully turn it over onto a serving dish.

sriracha, cilantro, and sesame seeds may be added to your tartare to enhance the flavor and aroma.

43. RAINBOW SPICY TOFU SUSHI BURRITOS {VEGAN}

PREP TIME: 40 minutes
COOK TIME: 15 minutes
RESTING TIME: 1 hour

INGREDIENTS

- pickled carrots:
- ½ tsp sugar
- ¼ tsp fine sea salt
- splash hot water
- ¼ cup of (60 ml) rice vinegar
- 2 medium carrots, scrubbed, cut into long matchsticks
- rice:
- 1 ½ cup of white, short-grain sushi rice
- 2 cup of water, + water for rinsing the rice
- 1 ½ tbsp sugar
- 1 ½ tsp fine sea salt
- 3 tbsp rice vinegar
- tofu:
- 12 ounces firm or extra-firm tofu, grated on the large holes of a box grater
- ¼ cup of good mayonnaise
- 1 ½ tbsp sriracha
- 1 tsp finely grated ginger root
- other goodies:
- 4-5 nori sheets
- 2 small Persian cucumbers, seeded
- 2 cup of pea sprouts
- handful sesame seeds
- 4 scallions
- 1 cup of coarsely grated watermelon raBowl or daikon raBowl
- 1 large firm-ripe avocado, peeled, pitted
- wasabi and tamari

INSTRUCTIONS

1. In a medium bowl, pour boiling water and stir in the sugar and salt until the sugar and salt are completely dissolved. Stir in the rice vinegar and the carrot matchsticks, and serve. Set aside for about an hour while you finish the rest of the ingredients, stirring regularly.

2. prepare the rice:

3. To release the starches in the rice, place it in a bowl, cover it with lukewarm water, and swirl it about. Using care, drain the water, then repeat the process 2-3 times more thoroughly. Drain thoroughly. Add the rice, sugar, and salt to a small pot and bring to a boil. Bring the saucepan to a simmer over a medium temperature. Cooking time should be reduced by 10-15 minutes to allow the rice to absorb all of the water. Allow to cool for ten minutes after removing from heat. If the rice is too firm, add a few tbsp additional water and repeat the steaming/standing process until the rice is cooked but not mushy. Toss the rice with a spoon to incorporate the vinegar, then fluff the rice with a fork. (To avoid the rice from turning mushy, handle it as little as possible and carefully.) Spread the rice out in a large bowl and let it there for 31-1 hour to speed up the chilling process.

4. how to make tofu:

5. Gently combine the sriracha and ginger with the grated tofu in a large bowl. Make sure you like the seasoning by giving it a taste test. (You may make this a few days in advance and store it in an airtight container in the fridge if you choose.)

6. Prepare and have on hand the remaining components.

7. Lay a nori sheet, shiny side down, on top of a bamboo sushi rolling mat (or a piece of Bee's Wrap). While you spread a layer of rice on top of the nori, leaving about an inch of space on all three sides, a basin of cooled water will help keep your fingers from sticking to the nori. To prevent your fingers from sticking together as you work, dip them in water. Making a layer of rice that's thin but not mushy is what you're going for.

8. Every one of the following should be topped with one-fourth or one-fifth a nori sheet:

9. As you grip the mat or Bee's Wrap and the bottom of the roll with your thumb and forefinger, begin a smooth, decisive action with the roll, folding the bottom of the rollover the fillings and securing them in place with your other fingers. Make a strong push on the roll to ensure that it is firmly coiled, then switch to holding it with your palms instead of your fingers to prevent it from unraveling. After removing the mat from the middle of the roll, wet the naked nori with a touch of water, and roll the burrito tight with the seam down, give it a last squeeze. The tortilla should be removed off the mat so that you may proceed with the rest of the ingredients before they're all gone.

10. Burritos can be served with tamari and wasabi to drizzle or dab on top of the burritos. Even though the burritos may be stored in the refrigerator for up to three days if they are airtight, they are at their finest when eaten within 24 hours of being assembled.

NOTES

I can generally get by with one of them, but if I'm very peckish, I'll eat up to one and a half.

Sushi rolling takes some skill, so don't be discouraged if your first few rolls are loose and under-filled or over-filled and coming apart; they will still be tasty.

Using one of the four servings, nutritional values are calculated

44. SIMPLE SUSHI ROLLS W/ SPICY CRAB

45 mins

INGREDIENTS

- 4 servings
- 1 cup of chopped crab meat
- 1 cup of jasmine rice - cooked or steamed
- 1 tbsp rice wine vinegar
- 1/4 cup of mayo
- 1 tbsp sriracha
- 4 sheets of Nori Seaweed

STEPS

1. Steam the rice for 30 minutes to cook it. Jasmine has a delicate sweetness to it that I find appealing.
2. Set the rice aside to cool before adding the rice wine vinegar.
3. Then, while the rice is cooling, dice the crab meat and mix it with mayonnaise and a little bit of Sriracha sauce.
4. A plastic-coated bamboo mats
5. Lay down a glossy side of a Nori sheet.

6. Cover the Nori sheet with rice using moist palms or a wooden spoon. (It should already be sticky)
7. of the recipe for spicy crab sushi rolls.
8. After pressing down, flip the rice sheet over and spread a thin coating of spicy crab across the surface of the grain.
9. of the recipe for spicy crab sushi rolls.
10. Roll the nori and rice sheets tightly to make a long roll covering the crab mixture with both hands on the bamboo sheet.
11. the simple recipe for spicy crab sushi rolls
12. Enjoy your sushi roll by cutting it into bite-sized pieces. A sushi roll can be stuffed with a variety of different items. avocado. Cream, shrimp, and cucumber Cheese and other dairy products I've simply put up the easiest one.

45. SPICY TOFU ROLL

INGREDIENTS

- 3 cup of cooked seasoned white medium grain rice or more if using more rice in your rolls
- 1 oz. half package Tamanoi Sushinoko powder
- ¼ cup of Japanese mayonnaise
- ½ tbsp Sriracha sauce + more if desired
- 6 sheets dried roasted seaweed gim
- 2 large carrots peeled and julienned
- 1 red bell pepper sliced thin lengthwise
- 1 zucchini julienned
- half package tofu pan-fried and sliced thin into strips
- sushi ginger
- wasabi
- low sodium soy sauce

- Special equipment:
- A bamboo rolling mat
- Disposable gloves
- A small bowl of water
- A wood cutting board
- A sharp knife

INSTRUCTIONS

1. Place cooked white rice in a large mixing bowl and set aside for 10 to 15 minutes to cool. Mix in the Tamanoi Sushinoko (Sushi Rice Mix Powder) once it has cooled. Although the packaging suggests using additional vinegar powder, I like to use about half of the recommended quantity. Taste and, if necessary, adjust the quantity.

2. Blend the Japanese aioli and sriracha sauce in a small bowl. If desired, season with extra sriracha sauce.

3. Place a single sheet of dried gim on your bamboo mat (make sure the bamboo sticks are horizontal). Spread roughly a half cup of cooked, seasoned rice evenly over 2/3 of the gim using your fingers. At the top, you can leave one inch exposed (with no rice at all). This will aid in the final sealing of the roll, or you may use it to cover the entire seaweed sheet (gim) if desired.

4. Place all of the raw vegetables on top, then top with the pan-fried tofu, leaving approximately an inch of rice exposed at the bottom. Serve with a dollop of spicy mayo on top. Roll the bamboo mat from the bottom up and over the ingredients (as if you were rolling a sleeping bag), pushing down softly but firmly to keep the contents in place. Pull the mat up and straighten it as you roll to keep it from becoming stuck in the roll. Continue even if you haven't reached the gim's edge.

5. Dab a little amount of water along the top seam of the dried seaweed with your fingertips and roll to seal it shut. With the bamboo mat, roll and gently squeeze one last time, then set aside and proceed with the remaining seaweed sheets.

6. When you've done all of the rolls, plunge a sharp knife into the water and raise it up so the water flows down the blade. This will assist you in achieving a great, clean cut. Each roll should be cut into 8-10 pieces. Enjoy your sushi with ginger, wasabi, and soy sauce!

46.   TURKEY SUSHI ROLL

INGREDIENTS

- 300g cooked rice
- 80ml sushi vinegar
- 1 sheet nori seaweed
- cooked turkey (or chicken)
- 2 tbsp teriyaki sauce (optional)
- soy sauce (optional)
- wasabi (optional)
- sesame seeds (optional)

HOW TO PREPARE

1. We must first prepare our sushi rice before beginning to make our makizushi. Sushi rice is made by mixing sticky short-grain rice with a specific sushi rice vinegar. More information on how to produce great sticky rice and sushi rice may be found in our recipe.

2. Cover two-thirds of one side of the nori seaweed with sushi rice to a height of about one centimeter. Turn it over onto a piece of

cling film with the rice side down and the nori seaweed strip on top.

3. On top of the nori seaweed, place your cooked turkey (or chicken). Before pouring the teriyaki sauce evenly over the turkey, you can add some veggies if desired.

4. Now comes the fun part. Begin rolling up the components, keeping the roll as tight as possible. After you've rolled it up the first time, use cling film and a rolling mat to make sure it's as securely curled as possible. Make sure the cling film doesn't become stuck inside the roll. Without coming apart, the sticky rice should keep everything together.

5. Finally, cut your roll into 7-8 pieces and, if desired, sprinkle sesame seeds over the rice for added flavor. Blend some fish sauce and a pinch of wasabi paste in a small dish and use as a sushi dip.

47.   VEGAN SUSHI

Prep Time: 30 mins
Cook Time: 1 hr

INGREDIENTS

- For the beets
- 2 pink Chioggia beets
- Extra-virgin olive oil, for drizzling
- 1 tbsp rice vinegar
- 1 tbsp tamari
- ½ tbsp sesame oil
- ½ tsp grated ginger
- Sea salt
- For the rice

- 1 cup of uncooked short-grain white rice
- 2 tbsp rice vinegar
- 1 tbsp sugar
- 1 tsp sea salt
- For the rolls
- 4 nori sheets
- 1 Persian cucumber
- 1 avocado, pitted
- Sesame seeds, for sprinkling
- Tamari, for serving
- Pickled ginger, for serving
- Vegan mayo and sriracha, optional, for serving

INSTRUCTIONS

1. Prepare the beets as follows: Preheat the oven to 400 degrees Fahrenheit. Drizzle olive oil and pinches of salt over the entire beets on a piece of foil. Roast the beets for 46-60 minutes, until they are mushy and fork-tender, on a baking sheet, wrapped in foil. On the basis of the beets' size and freshness, the cooking time will vary. Remove the foil from the beets and take them out of the oven. Peel the skins when they are cold to the touch. I like to hold them under flowing water and use my hands to remove the skins. Cut the beets into 14-inch strips lengthwise.

2. Mix the rice vinegar, tamari, sesame oil, and ginger in the bottom of a small baking dish or shallow basin. Toss in the beets to coat, then set aside to marinade. Toss again after 15 minutes to achieve an equal coating.

3. Make the rice: Follow the instructions in this post to make the rice. Combine the cooked rice, vinegar, sugar, and salt in a mixing bowl.

4. Assemble the rolls as follows: Because your hands will become sticky, have a small basin of water & a kitchen towel near your work area. The bottom two-thirds of one nori sheet should be placed on a bamboo mat with a handful of rice pressed into it. Begin with a row of beets, cucumber, and avocado. Overfilling will hinder rolling. Use a bamboo mat to tuck and roll nori. Once rolled, carefully press and form the roll using the bamboo mat. Invert and roll to the side. Rep the remaining rolls.

5. Sushi should be sliced with a sharp knife. Clean the knife with a wet towel in between cuts to prevent rust.

6. Sesame seeds can be sprinkled on top. If preferred, top with tamari, pickled ginger, and vegan mayo with a dash of sriracha.

48. VEGGIE QUINOA SUSHI

PREP TIME 15 mins
COOK TIME 20 mins
TOTAL TIME 35 mins

INGREDIENTS

- 1 cup of uncooked quinoa rinsed
- 1 and 1/2 cup of water
- 1/2 cup of seasoned rice vinegar
- 5-6 nori sheets
- 1/3 cup of toasted sesame seeds
- 1 cucumber washed, peeled
- 1 avocado washed, peeled
- 2 carrots washed, peeled
- 8 oz cream cheese sliced into strips

INSTRUCTIONS

1. Begin by preparing the quinoa. In a pan over medium heat over high heat, combine the rinsed quinoa and the water. Put on high heat, then turn down to a simmer by covering pan. In 20 minutes, the quinoa will be ready.

2. After 20 minutes, remove the quinoa from the fire and add the seasoned rice vinegar. Gently whisk the quinoa, cover the pot, and set aside to let the quinoa to cool and absorb the rice vinegar.

3. Prepare the fillings and set them out on your work table while the quinoa is chilling to make making the quinoa sushi simpler.

4. To make the quinoa sushi rolls, start by putting a piece of plastic wrap around the bamboo mat. This will keep things tidy and make your job much simpler.

5. Put one nori layer on top of the bamboo mat, flat on your work surface.

6. Fill the nori sheet with 1/3-1/2 cup of quinoa. Spread the cooled quinoa evenly on the nori sheet with the back of a wooden spoon, leaving about a 1 cm border at the edge.

7. Place a couple cucumber slices on top of the quinoa (on the closest side to you). Toss in the carrots. Place the avocado strips on top.

8. Add a dollop of cream cheese and some sesame seeds to the top for garnish.

9. Lift the nearest end of the mat and carefully roll it over the ingredients, pushing as you go to keep your rolls tight. When the quinoa sushi roll is mostly wrapped and only the 1 cm edge piece is visible. Spread a little water on it, then roll it up and lay it aside. This will ensure that it is securely closed. Carry on with the remaining rolls in the same manner.

10. With a moist and sharp knife, cut each roll into 8 pieces. Serve with wasabi and soy sauce.

49. TEXAS SAUSAGE "SUSHI" ROLL

Prep Time 15 minutes
Cook Time 12 minutes
Total Time 27 minutes

INGREDIENTS

- Recipe makes 8 Servings
- 12 Oz H-E-B Texas Heritage Pecan Smoked Beef Sausage
- 6 burrito sized tortillas
- 6 Folios Cheese Tortillas, cheddar or Jarlsberg works well
- 1 cup of(s) H-E-B Specialty Series Bourbon Bacon BBQ Sauce, divided use
- 4 Oz mild hatch diced green chilies

INSTRUCTIONS

1. Set the oven temperature to 351 degrees Fahrenheit.
2. Each sausage should be cut into three equal sections: two straight and one curled. The curved one should be cut in half at the bend.
3. Make a flat surface out of 6 flour tortillas and place them on it. Spread a layer of BBQ sauce and green chilies on top of each flour tortilla.
4. Roll tortillas around sausage, placing it in the center of the roll. Use toothpicks to keep in place.
5. Remove from the oven after 11 minutes of baking. Turn the oven to broil and cook the tortillas for an additional 2 to 3 minutes, just to slightly brown them.
6. Discard toothpicks and cut into bite-sized pieces, much like a sushi roll would be cut for consumption. Add extra BBQ sauce for dipping if necessary.

50. VEGAN SUSHI ROLLS WITH QUINOA STICKY RICE

PREP TIME 20 MINUTES
COOK TIME 20 MINUTES
TOTAL TIME 40 MINUTES

INGREDIENTS

- 1/2 cup of uncooked sushi rice
- 1/2 cup of dry quinoa
- 2 cup of water or broth
- 2 TBSP rice vinegar
- 1/8-1/4 tsp sugar
- 1/8-1/4 tsp salt
- 4 sheets of nori
- 10 spears of asparagus (blanched)
- 1/4-1/2 an English cucumber
- 1-2 large carrots
- 1/2 a large yellow bell pepper
- 4-8 green onions
- broccoli/clover sprouts (as need)
- toasted sesame seeds and chia seeds

INSTRUCTIONS

1. The saucepan should be on medium-high heat.
2. Rinse the quinoa before cooking it. Stir frequently while lightly toasting it for an additional nutty taste after draining it of any moisture.
3. Rice and two cups of water should be added, and the pot should be heated to the maximum setting.
4. Cover and simmer on low heat for twenty minutes once it begins boiling. Season with vinegar, salt, and sugar after it's hot and frothy.
5. Allow to cool in a separate bowl before fluffing with a fork.
6. Whilst the rice and quinoa are simmering, prepare your vegetables:

7. To soften the asparagus, cut off the ends and gently blanch it in boiling water.

8. Then cut the carrots into long strips, then cut the bell pepper and cucumber into long strips.

9. You can snip as many green onion pieces as you like, as well as a large handful of sprouts! As soon as the rice and quinoa are done, I prefer to put all of my ingredients on the counter so that I can quickly assemble the dish and eat it.

10. Place a nori sheet on top of a plastic-wrapped bamboo mat.

11. Spread a thin layer of quinoa and rice over the seaweed sheet using a big spoon.

12. Arrange your vegetables in three tight rows at the very end of the baking sheet to prevent them from wilting.

13. Toss in any additional ingredients, such as fish or cream cheese, now is the time to do so.

14. Sushi-rolling novices? Through get a step-by-step visual guide to the full procedure, [click here].

15. Slice, roll, then sprinkle sesame seeds on top of the rolls!

NOTES

An online recipe nutrition calculator was used to assess the nutritional content of the following recipes. Adjust to your liking and have fun!

51.   TRADITIONAL TUNA NIGIRI SUSHI

INGREDIENTS

- 150 g, Sushi rice
- 150 g, Tuna block
- small portion, Wasabi

STEPS

1. To find out more about sushi rice, enter the numbers below as a search term. 5095927 and 5106970

2. Assemble a sushi kit for nigiri sushi. Amazon US sells it. Use the term "Japan Nigiri Sushi Mold Rice Ball 5 Rolls Maker Press Bento Tool (Style 2)" to find every "Japan Nigiri Sushi Mold Rice Ball 5 Rolls Maker Press Bento Tool (Style 2)". If you're in Japan, Daiso carries it. Wash well and leave moist as part of the preparation.

3. Fill the container with all 150g sushi rice and push down with the lid. Remove the lid and flip the container over on the cutting board. Then, as shown in the photo, cut into half to make little 10 piece rice balls.

4. Cut the tuna block into 10 thin slices. A Japanese chef will use a 10-inch or longer knife and just a stroll to cut a piece. The knife is held slanted to achieve a breadth of one inch. This technique is commonly used when the block lacks sufficient thickness. For 3 sceans strobo motion, see the image.

5. Pinch a piece of tuna, cut.

6. Put a tiny amount of wasabi on top.

7. Place a rice ball on top.

8. Place your thumb in the rice ball. This is the first action.

9. Gently press with your right hand's first and second fingers. This is action number two. Keep in mind that the fingers on both hands are making a box. The upper half of your left hand's fingers, in particular, play a significant function. They are acting as a sidewall.

10. Slowly open your left hand while maintaining the box configuration formed by the upper half of your left hand's fingers and the two fingers of your right hand.

11. The rice ball has rolled for 90 degrees, as seen in the preceding image. Please assist the rice ball roll another 90 degrees by using your thumb and middle finger of your right hand and sliding the entire piece near a bit as shown in the photo. This is the third rice ball rolling movement

12. Gently press with your right hand's first and second fingers. This is action number four.

13. Rotate the entire piece for a half rotation, as seen in the image. This is action number 5.

14. While holding the rice ball in your right hand with your thumb and middle finger, stroke the tuna surface with your left hand's thumb. This is action number six. Finally, softly push again with your right hand's two fingers. This is the seventh action. You've arrived.

52.   SOBA NOODLE SUSHI
INGREDIENTS

- 2 portions of soba noodles
- 2 tbsp rice wine vinegar
- 4 sheets of Nori
- 1 cucumber, thinly sliced
- 1 package of tempeh
- 1 snow peas, thinly sliced
- 1 shredded carrot
- Toasted sesame seeds, soy sauce, pickled ginger and wasabi paste, to serve

STEPS

1. Using a big saucepan, cook the noodles for 4-5 minutes or until they are soft. Drain and rinse with cold water.

2. Add rice wine vinegar to a bowl and toss. Mix.

3. The bottom half of a sushi mat should be covered with a sheet of nori, followed by a little amount of noodles.

4. Add the fillings, then top with noodles. Then, fold up the contents.

5. Serve with soy sauce, wasabi, and ginger and sesame seeds on top.

53.   SUMMER SUSHI
INGREDIENTS

- 100g sushi rice
- 20ml sushi vinegar
- Japanese mayonnaise
- tuna or other seafood of choice
- 2 spring onions
- nori seaweed

HOW TO PREPARE

1. The first step is to prepare sushi rice.

2. Make sure your oven is preheated at 180 degrees Celsius.You should cook any seafood you have now. If you like, you may cut your spring onions thinly.

3. Mix the mayonnaise, tuna, and spring onions in a bowl until well-combined. In our opinion, a 2:1 ratio of mayo to other components is ideal.

4. Just a tiny bit Put a little oil in an oven pan and layout the sushi rice in an even layer. Next, spread the mayonnaise mixture on top of the salad. Cooking time should be about fifteen minutes.

5. Serve it with a dollop of nori seaweed on top after it's been taken out of the oven

54. CRUNCHY CALIFORNIA ROLL SUSHI BOWL

Total Time 40 minutes
Prep Time 15 minutes
Cook Time 25 minutes

INGREDIENTS

- 2 cup ofs water(480 mL)
- 1 tsp kosher salt, + more as need
- 1 cup of sushi rice(200 g), rinsed before the water runs clear
- 1 tbsp sugar
- ¼ cup of rice vinegar(60 mL)
- 1 tbsp canola oil
- ⅓ cup of panko breadcrumbs(15 g)
- ½ tsp pepper, + more as need
- ¼ cup of mayonnaise(60 g)
- 1 tbsp sriracha
- 16 oz crab(455 g), 2 cans, drained
- 1 Persian cucumber, thinly sliced
- 4 raBowles, thinly sliced
- 2 tbspnori, thinly sliced
- 1 bunch scallion
- 1 tbsp sesame seed
- 2 tbsp pickled ginger
- 1 avocado, diced

PREPARATION

1. The water in a small saucepan should be seasoned with a pinch of salt. In a large pot, bring the water to a boil. Then, add the washed rice and bring the mixture back to a simmer. When the water has been absorbed and the rice is soft, cover and decrease the heat to simmer for another 20 minutes.

2. Sugar, salt, and rice vinegar should be mixed in a separate basin before being added to the salad. Take care not to overcook; microwave for two minutes or until the sugar is dissolved.

3. Pour the vinegar mixture over the cooked rice in a medium bowl and stir thoroughly with a wooden spoon.

4. In a saucepan, heat the canola oil to medium-high heat. Stir constantly as you fry the panko until golden brown, about 1-2 minutes into the oil's sizzling. Then switch off the stove.

5. Mayonnaise and Sriracha in a small dish.

6. Rice should be divided into two serving bowls to make bowls. Crispy panko, raBowl, nori, scallions and sesame seeds are placed on top of the crab. Add a layer of Sriracha mayonnaise on the top of the salad

7. Enjoy!

55. QUINOA SUSHI BOWLS WITH ORANGE MISO DRESSING

Prep Time: 10 Minutes
Cook Time: 15 Minutes

INGREDIENTS

- For the Quinoa Sushi Bowls:
- 2/3 cup of Dry Quinoa
- 1/2 tsp Dulse Granules (Optional)
- 1–2 tbsp Rice Vinegar
- 4 small RaBowles, thinly sliced
- 1 1/3 cup of shelled Edamame
- 2 Carrots, cut into matchsticks

- 2–3 Small Seedless Cucumbers, thinly sliced
- 2 Nori Sheets
- 1 Avocado
- Orange Miso Dressing, below
- Sesame Seeds, for garnish
- For the Orange Miso Dressing
- 1 large or 2 small Oranges, peeled
- 1 small Clove of Garlic
- ½" Ginger Root
- 1 tbsp Vegan Mellow Miso
- ½ tbsp Rice Vinegar
- ½ tbsp Tamari
- ¼–½ cup of Filtered Water

INSTRUCTIONS

1. To begin, bring 1 1/3 cups of water and the dry quinoa to a boil in a medium saucepan. Simmer for 17 minutes with the lid on.
2. Wash and chop your vegetables while the Quinoa is cooking.
3. Prepare the Orange Miso Dressing by mixing all the ingredients together in a high-speed blender for 60 seconds, or until they're thoroughly smooth.
4. After 15 minutes, take the Quinoa from the heat and let it rest for 5 minutes before fluffing with a fork. Remove the Quinoa from the heat. Then, add the Rice Vinegar and Dulse Granules, if desired.
5. Combine all of the ingredients in two bowls, then drizzle each one with the Dressing.

NOTES

I would recommend taking a knife to cut the rind off of your oranges and remove part of the pith – almost as if you were going to supreme them – to remove some of the bitter taste the orange peel. For your reference, below is a picture.

It is possible to keep dressing in the refrigerator for a week.

Preparing the Quinoa ahead of time is an option if you like your Quinoa Sushi Bowls to be served cold.

You may make these Quinoa Sushi Bowls ahead of time, but I recommend keeping the Nori separately and adding it shortly before serving.

56. OSAKA-STYLE OKONOMIYAKI RECIPE

Prep Time: 10 minutes
Cook Time: 15 minutes

INGREDIENTS

- 2 cup of flour
- 1 cup of dashi or water, cold or at room temperature
- 1 tsp salt
- 1 tsp baking powder
- 2 tsp sugar
- 1 pound cabbage, coarsely chopped (about 10 cup of)
- 4 eggs
- 1/4 cup of toasted sesame oil
- 8 ounces fresh pork belly, thinly sliced
- Toppings
- Okonomiyaki sauce
- Kewpie or other mayonnaise
- a nori (powdered nori seaweed)
- dried, shaved bonito (katsuobushi)

DIRECTIONS

1. Baking powder and sugar may be combined in one big dish with the flour and dashi to produce the batter. Cook for at least 30 seconds before adding the cabbage and mixing thoroughly. Incorporate the eggs into the cabbage and stir for about 15 seconds, or until the eggs are incorporated into the cabbage but not completely.

2. Pre-heat a nonstick or cast-iron pan over medium heat for at least five minutes. Add one TB of sesame oil to the skillet, making careful to cover the whole thing. Make many okonomiyaki at a time and cook them in separate pans. Make a pancake about 6 inches across and 1 inch thick in the skillet using the cabbage and batter combination. For a light and airy pancake, avoid pressing down too hard on the cabbage. Place a quarter of the pork belly slices over the pancake, being careful not to overlap the pieces.

3. Before serving the pancakes, cook them for about four minutes on each side.. Flip the pancake with a long spatula (a fish spatula is great) so that the pork belly side is now facing down. With the spatula, gently press down on the pancake (don't push too hard, you don't want batter to flow from the edges).

4. Flip the pancake once again, this time with the pork belly side facing up, and cook for another 5 minutes. Use a spatula to reincorporate any stray ingredients back into the pancake if it falls apart when you flip it.) A few more minutes of cooking are needed. The pancake should be gently toasted on both sides, the pork cooked through, and the cabbage within soft when it's done cooking.

5. Add the toppings to the pork side of the pancake before serving. In long ribbons, apply okonomiyaki sauce on pancake, using roughly a tablespoon. Spread roughly 1 tablespoon of mayonnaise across the pancake in long ribbons, and then serve. Sprinkle around 1 tablespoon of aonori on top of the pancake. The pancake should be topped with around 1 tbsp of shaved bonito. (Adjust the amount of any topping to suit your tastes.) Serve the pancake immediately after cutting it into quarters.

6. Repeat with the remaining pancake batter with 3 tbsp oil of olive oil.

57.   OSHI ZUSHI (PRESSED SUSHI CAKE)

INGREDIENTS

- 3.5 oz Raw Salmon Steak Sashimi grade
- 3-4 stalks Broccoli Rabe
- 1 Zucchini
- 2 tsp Yuzu Kosho
- 2 Tbsp Mayonnaise
- 2 pinch Dried Bonito Flakes
- 1/2 tsp Soy Sauce
- Sushi Rice
- ¾ cup of Short-grain Sushi Rice
- ¾ cup of Water
- Sushi Vinegar
- 1 tsp Salt
- 1 ½ Tbsp Sugar
- 2 ¾ Tbsp White Vinegar

INSTRUCTIONS

1. Rice for Sushi

2. Use a strainer to remove any excess water from the sushi rice before drying entirely.

3. Pour water over sushi rice that has been drained. Wait at least 20 minutes before serving.

4. High heat should be used to bring it to a boil. Cover the saucepan with a lid and lower the heat to simmer when it has boiled.

5. Rice should be simmered for about 10 minutes, or until nearly all of the water has been absorbed.

6. After turning off the heat and covering the pan for 10 minutes, remove the lid.

7. Make the sushi vinegar while the sushi rice is cooking.

8. In a small saucepan, combine the sushi vinegar ingredients and bring to a boil. Make sure everything is well-combined.

9. The sugar should be dissolved in 2 minutes, so take it from the fire and let it cool. I recommend making the vinegar ahead of time so you can have a supply on hand when you need it.

10. Take out a bowl and put the rice in it once the vinegar has cooled down a bit. Add the sushi vinegar and blend thoroughly before serving.

11. Make sashimi salmon by slicing the steak as thinly as possible.

12. Rinse the rabe, then cook it in salted water until tender.

13. Using a peeler, slice the zucchini.

14. Mayonnaise and Yuzu pepper paste should be thoroughly mixed.

15. Bonito Pompom: Combine soy sauce and dried bonito flakes.

16. Assemble the various components needed for the recipe.

17. Avoid rice sticking to your hands and Oshibako box by wetting them with water before preparing the meal. A 3.5" x 10" mold is needed for this recipe. The amount of rice and other materials you use will depend on the size of the mold you're using.

18. Make sure the salmon and broccoli rabe are on the bottom of the box. The pressed sushi cake's initial layer will be this. Cut the fish and broccoli rabe to fit in the container.

19. Make sure you're pressing hard and firmly with the lid of the box.

20. Apply the yuzu pepper mayonnaise to the fish before serving.

21. This is followed by a thin covering of sushi rice. Make sure the box is completely filled with rice. Use a quarter of the sushi rice for this recipe.

22. Once more, firmly push down with the lid.

23. The third layer should be zucchini slices. The rest of the rice can be used to finish filling the box. Your sushi mold's size may result in a surplus of sushi rice.

24. Firmly press down with the lid one more time.

25. Remove the fungus from the surface

26. Remove the top cover by flipping the mold over.

27. Using a knife, cut the sushi cake into equal halves.

28. Remove the side of the box from the mold with care.

29. Turn the mold over and remove the top lid once pressing is complete. Slice the cake by inserting a knife into the holes on the mold. Transferring the cake to a dish is as simple as taking the box's side off and placing it on a platter.

30. Serve with soy sauce and a bonito pompom on top.

58.   SPICY PEANUT TOFU POWER BOWL

Prep Time: 30 mins
Waiting time: 30 mins
Cook Time: 10 mins
Total Time: 1 hour 10 minutes

INGREDIENTS

- 1 ½ cup of (280g) uncooked round or sushi rice*
- 14 ounces (400g) super firm tofu
- 2 Tbsp vegetable oil
- 2–4 medium carrots, grated
- ½ English cucumber, sliced
- ½ cup of (80g) edamame
- ½ cup of (125g) creamy peanut butter
- 1 Tbsp agave or maple syrup
- 2 Tbsp fresh lime juice
- 2 Tbsp sesame oil
- 3 Tbsp rice vinegar
- 2 tsp fresh ginger, minced
- 1 to 2 tsp(s) Sriracha or any hot chile sauce
- water
- Lime wedges, for serving
- 2 scallions, thinly sliced
- Fresh mint leaves
- White and/or black sesame, lightly toasted
- Soy sauce, for serving

INSTRUCTIONS

1. To prepare the rice, simply follow the directions on the package. Allow for a little period of cooling.
2. If you need to soften the peanut butter for the sauce, microwave it for 10-15 seconds. The peanut butter, agave syrup, lime juice, sesame oil, rice vinegar, fresh ginger, and Sriracha sauce should be mixed together in a small bowl before being added to the salad. To get the correct consistency, add water one Tbsp at a time.
3. To prepare the tofu, place it on a platter and use a paper towel to dry it. Let it rest for 30 minutes under a cast iron pan or other heavy object.
4. Slice the tofu into small pieces. In a medium cast-iron pan, heat the vegetable oil to medium-high heat. Tofu may be added to a hot pan and allowed to cook for a few minutes before it is well browned on the bottom. Continue cooking until the second side is blackened.
5. Toss the tofu in the spicy peanut sauce and serve.
6. To serve, divide the rice into four bowls and top each with tofu covered in peanut sauce, chopped carrots, cucumber slices, and edamame. Fresh mint, sliced scallions, and toasted sesame seeds accompany the dish. Enjoy!

NOTES

Instead of white rice, try brown rice for a more nutritious option.

There is no need to use all of these toppings, and it is entirely up to your discretion whether or not to use any at all or just a couple. The fresh mint (you may use fresh cilantro instead) and the last drizzle of soy sauce over the bowl upon serving are two of my favorite additions to this dish.

Use gluten-free soy sauce to guarantee that the Bowl is gluten-free from A to Z. If you are not gluten intolerant, regular soy sauce can be used.

59.   PEANUT BUTTER FRENCH TOAST SUSHI ROLLS

Prep Time: 10 mins
Cook Time: 5 mins

INGREDIENTS

- 8 slices sandwich bread, crusts removed
- 1/3 cup of creamy peanut peanut butter
- 2 large eggs
- 1/4 cup of milk
- butter, for greasing the pan

PREPARATION

1. Rolled out sandwich bread pieces should be as thin as possible with the use of a rolling pin.
2. Spread 2 tsp of peanut butter on each piece of bread. The peanut butter will function as glue to keep the slices together when you wrap them up like a cinnamon roll. Cut each slice into six equal pieces (each piece is about 3/4 inch wide).
3. Whisk together the eggs and milk. Dip the pieces into the mixture until they are completely covered in the substance.
4. Pour the melted butter into a sauté pan over medium heat and cook the slices on each flat side for one minute, then on the curved sides for one minute, until the bread is golden brown.

60.   EGG PESTO BREAKFAST WRAP

Prep: 10 mins
Cook: 15 mins
Total: 25 mins

INGREDIENTS

- 2 eggs
- 1 ½ tsp reduced-fat sour cream
- ¼ cup of shredded reduced-fat Cheddar cheese
- 2 tbsp finely chopped onion
- 1 ½ tsp prepared pesto sauce
- 3 grape tomatoes, sliccd
- 1 slice turkey bacon
- ½ ounce marinated artichoke hearts, drained
- 1 10-inch flour tortilla
- salt and pepper as need

DIRECTIONS

1. In a mixing dish, combine the eggs and sour cream before adding the cheese.
2. Using cooking spray, saute and toss the onion and pesto sauce in a pan for about 6 minutes, & until the onion is transparent. Pour in the egg mixture and mix in the tomatoes. For around 3 minutes, simmer and whisk the egg mixture to ensure that the eggs are cooked but not dry. Set aside the cooked eggs in the skillet.
3. The turkey bacon should be fried for about three minutes on each side, in a pan, before it begins to crisp up. The artichokes should be heated for about a minute before the bacon and artichokes are taken out of the pan.
4. To use the tortilla, just coat the pan with cooking spray and set it in the heated pan. Remove the tortilla from the oven when it is pliable and heated.
5. Sprinkle salt and pepper over the eggs, turkey bacon, and artichokes that have been placed in the middle of the tortilla. Fold the bottom two inches of the tortilla up

to completely encircle the filling, and then tightly wrap it around it.

NUTRITIONAL INFORMATION

It has a total of 533 calories, with 27.6 grams of protein, 44.9 grams of carbs, and 26.8 grams of fat.

61. PHILADELPHIA ROLL

INGREDIENTS

- 2 cup of sushi rice(460 g)
- ¼ cup of seasoned rice vinegar(60 mL)
- 4 half sheets sushi-grade nori
- 4 oz smoked salmon(115 g)
- 4 oz cream cheese(115 g), cut into matchsticks
- 1 small cucumber, cut into matchsticks

PREPARATION

1. Before serving, fan and mix the sushi rice before adding the rice vinegar seasoning.
2. Roll a nori sheet with the rough side up on the rolling mat.
3. Then, wet your hands, grab a little amount of rice, and lay it on the nori. Spread the rice uniformly on the nori sheet without squashing it with a spatula.
4. Smoked salmon, cream cheese, and cucumber should be arranged in a horizontal row, 1 inch (2 cm) from the bottom.
5. To construct a tight roll, grab both nori sheets and a mat and roll them over the filling until the additional space at the bottom hits the opposite side. Squeeze the roll as you go to prevent it from retaining its shape.

6. Cut the roll into desired lengths. Using a moist paper towel, wipe the knife on the roll before slicing into six equal pieces.
7. Enjoy!

62. VEGAN KATSU CURRY WITH TOFU

PREPARATION 30 min
COOKING 30 min

INGREDIENTS

- 400 g / 14 oz firm tofu, pressed
- 4 tbsp soy sauce
- all-purpose flour / rice flour for GF version
- salt
- about 1 cup of gelatinous aquafaba**, homemade or from a tin of chickpeas or ½ cup of cornflour mixed in with water
- 100 g / 3.5 oz panko breadcrumbs
- oil for shallow frying
- CURRY SAUCE
- 2 tbsp neutral tasting oil
- 1 white onion
- 5 garlic cloves
- 3 tsp ginger, finely grated
- 2 medium carrots, peeled and sliced
- 1 small Granny Smith apple, peeled
- 4 tsp curry powder
- 1 tsp garam masala
- 1 heaped tbsp white miso paste
- 4 tsp tamari or soy sauce
- 2 tsp rice vinegar
- 2 tsp mirin or maple syrup, as need
- OPTIONAL EXTRAS
- 2 cup of your favourite rice, cooked
- assorted lettuce leaves
- pickled raBowles

METHOD

1. Make four big slices of tofu. Make sure to flip them over from time to time while they're cooking in a shallow bowl with 4 tablespoons of soy sauce (or tamari). Soak the tofu in the soy sauce for a few minutes before serving.

2. In a frying pan with a cover that fits, heat 2 tablespoons of oil. Diced onion should be added and cooked until it is almost transparent. After a few minutes, add the ginger and garlic. Cook for a few more minutes, stirring often, until the meat is no longer pink.

3. Sliced carrots, chopped apples, curry powder, and garam masala are all added. Fry for a few minutes before serving.

4. The miso paste should be dissolved in a cup of warm water before being added to the pan.

5. Cook the carrots and apples until tender, about 10-15 minutes on low heat (with the cover on).

6. If you prefer a richer sauce, use an upright or stick blender. Use tamari or soy sauce, rice vinegar, and mirin to season the food before serving it. To thin down a sauce that has become excessively thick, simply add extra water.

7. Prepare two big plates and a shallow bowl for the meal. On the first plate, sprinkle flour over the bottom. Combine breadcrumbs and 14 teaspoon salt on a second dish and pour the aquafaba into the first. Instead of using aquafaba, you may use 12 cups of cornflour / corn starch and 1 cup of water to make an egg alternative. Keep in mind that cornflour tends to settle at the bottom of the bowl, so give it a good toss before coating each piece of tofu.

8. the bottom of your wok.

9. Every piece of tofu should be coated with flour, aquafaba, and breadcrumbs. Before placing the tofu in the heated oil, remove any extra breadcrumbs by pressing them into the tofu and shaking it slightly. Make sure to coat each item in the cornflour mixture and then breadcrumbs if you're using a cornflour solution.

10. A breadcrumb dropped into the oil should sizzle instantly, so make sure the oil is heated enough before frying each piece of tofu for around 2 minutes on each side - until the coating is golden brown. To remove extra oil from the freshly cooked pieces, spread them out on a dish fitted with a kitchen towel.

11. It's best served with rice, a simple green salad, and a big helping of curry sauce.

NOTES

Using a paper towel and something heavy, set your tofu on a platter and press it down until it's firm (like a can of coconut milk, for example). Replacing a damp paper towel with a fresh one is a good idea. When the paper towel is nearly dry, repeat the process. Tofu that has been pressed is more flavorful because it takes on the flavors of the dish better.

It's best to make your own aquafaba (chickpea brine) or reduce one from a can of chickpeas over a low flame if you're utilizing it for this particular purpose. When I boil my chickpeas, I let them rest in the saucepan for a few hours, which allows the aquafaba to thicken and become almost jelly-like. In this case, I'll put it in a small pot and simmer it over low heat until it's reduced enough.

To make this dish, I've made a few changes to my original recipe for katsu.

63. PEAR AVOCADO SUSHI SALAD WITH PEANUT SAUCE

Prep Time15 minutes
Cook Time45 minutes
Total Time1 hour

INGREDIENTS

- Peanut Sauce
- 1/2 cup of water
- 1/2 cup of natural peanut butter
- 1 clove garlic
- 2 Tbsp. low sodium Tamari
- 1 Tbsp. brown rice vinegar
- 2 tsp. maple syrup
- 1/4 tsp. ground ginger
- 1/8 - 1/4 tsp. crushed red pepper flakes as need
- Salad
- 2 cup of long-grain brown rice or wild rice mix uncooked, I use the Tinkyada brand
- 4 1/2 cup of water
- 1 cucumber peeled
- 2 pears chopped
- 2 avocados peeled
- 1 Tbsp. sesame seeds
- 2 nori sheets
- 2 tsp. lemon juice

INSTRUCTIONS

1. A high-speed blender may be used to combine the following ingredients: 1/2 cup of water; peanut butter; garlic; Tamari; rice vinegar; maple syrup; ground ginger; and crushed red pepper flakes.
2. Blending should begin at a low setting and gradually increase to medium-high (7 on Vitamix). It should take no more than 30 seconds to blend until the sauce is uniformly smooth.
3. Rinse the rice and add 4 1/2 cups of water to a rice cooker, then set the timer for 15 minutes. Set the rice cooker to brown rice mode. Add water to a pot, then stir in the rice and bring it to boil.) Simmer, covered, for 46 to 50 minutes, or until the rice is tender and the liquid has been absorbed.
4. Set aside the cooked rice after fluffing it with a fork.
5. In a very large bowl, mix chopped pears and avocados with lemon juice and toss well.
6. Mix in chopped cucumber and sesame seeds.
7. Stir in a third of the remaining ingredients (cooked rice, peanut sauce, and torn nori) at a time to make mixing go more smoothly. After each addition, thoroughly stir the mixture.

NOTES

Approximately 1 1/2 cups of sauce may be made using this recipe.

64.   FRUIT SUSHI RICE

INGREDIENTS

- 2 cup ofs Carolina® Authentic Short Grain Rice for Sushi
- 1/2 cup of coconut milk
- 2 tbsp granulated sugar
- 1 tsp vanilla extract
- 1 lb strawberries, hulled and sliced
- 2 kiwis, peeled
- 1/2 can mandarin oranges, drained
- 4 tsp black and white sesame seeds
- 1 tbsp grated lime zest

INSTRUCTIONS

1. This Fruit Sushi Rice is the perfect delicious treat for any time of day, whether you're in the mood for dessert or a snack.
2. Package instructions should be followed. Gently whisk in the coconut milk, sugar, & vanilla using a rubber spatula. Allow for thorough cooling.
3. Lay down an 11-by-10-inch piece of plastic wrap on your work area. Spread 1 cup of rice in the center of a 9-by-8-inch plastic wrap rectangle and press with your hands to make a uniform, thin layer. Use water in a dish to loosen up sticky rice if necessary.)
4. Lay fruit over rice in a straight line starting 1 inch from one short edge. When rolling, use the plastic wrap as a guide to make a tight roll by rolling over the filling. Wrap in a plastic bag & other container. You may do this with any remaining rice and fruit.
5. Remove the plastic wrap & cut each roll into 1 1/2-inch pieces. To serve, top with sesame seeds and lime zest.
6. You may also make free-form sushi by forming 2 tbsp of rice into balls, triangles, or squares and rolling or shaping them as

desired. Fill the middle of the top with fruit. To serve, top with sesame seeds and lime zest.

TRICKS

Use different fruits throughout the year. You can also eat star fruit, cantaloupe, pineapple, and mangoes.

Sliced melon and pickled ginger can be used to simulate wasabi and soy sauce, while melted chocolate or fudge sauce can be used as a dip.

65.   PERFECT SUSHI RICE

Prep: 5 mins
Cook: 20 mins
Total: 25 mins

INGREDIENTS

- 2 cup of uncooked glutinous white rice (sushi rice)
- 3 cup of water
- ½ cup of rice vinegar
- 1 tbsp vegetable oil
- ¼ cup of white sugar
- 1 tsp salt

DIRECTIONS

1. Before the water runs clear, rinse the rice in a sieve or colander. combine in a medium saucepan with water For 20 minutes, bring to a boil, then lower the heat and cover. The rice should be soft and absorbed the water. As soon as possible, but not before.
2. Pour the rice vinegar, oil, sugar, and salt into a small saucepan and bring to a boil. Before the sugar is completely dissolved, cook the mixture over medium heat. The rice should be cooled before being mixed in.

This may appear quite moist when added to the rice. If you keep stirring the rice, it will dry out as it cools down and become mushy.

NUTRITIONAL INFORMATION

112 calories; 1.7 grams of protein; 23.5 grams of carbs; 0.5 grams of fat per serving; and 158.2 milligrams of sodium per serving. Full-Flavoured Food

66.   TAMAGOYAKI (JAPANESE ROLLED OMELETTE)

PREP TIME: 5 mins
COOK TIME: 5 mins
TOTAL TIME: 10 mins

INGREDIENTS

- 3 large eggs (50 g every w/o shell)
- 2 Tbsp neutral-flavored oil
- 1 ½ sheet nori
- Seasonings
- 3 Tbsp dashi
- 2 tsp sugar
- 1 tsp soy sauce
- 1 tsp mirin
- 2 pinch kosher or sea salt
- Garnish
- 3 oz daikon raBowl
- soy sauce

INSTRUCTIONS

1. Gather all of the ingredients before starting the cooking process.
2. In a pot, beat the eggs using a whisk. Using chopsticks, "cut" the eggs in a zig-zag motion and avoid over-mixing them.
3. Mix the spices well in a separate dish.
4. Incorporate the spices combination into the egg mixture with a light whisking. Afterwards, transfer the mixture to an easy-to-pour measuring cup (so that you may pour it directly into the frying pan).
5. The Pan Method for Tamagoyaki
6. Apply oil to pan with a folded paper towel soaked in oil. Put a small amount of egg mixture into the pan to test whether it's hot enough.
7. On sizzling, pour a thin layer of beaten egg into the pan, tilting it to coat the bottom.
8. To get the air out, poke the bubbles. When the base of the egg has set however the top is still soft, begin rolling from one side to the other.
9. Add some oil to the pan by wiping a paper towel across the surface of the omelette, making sure it's completely covered in oil.
10. Again, pour the egg mixture into the pan until it covers the bottom. Lift the omelette carefully so that the filling may be evenly distributed below.
11. Starting from one side to the other, roll the egg until the fresh layer of egg has set and is still a little soft.
12. On sizzling, pour a thin layer of beaten egg into the pan, tilting it to coat the bottom.
13. Again, pour the egg mixture into the pan until it covers the bottom. Lift the omelet carefully so that the filling may be evenly distributed below.
14. Starting from one side to the other, roll the egg until the fresh layer of egg has set and is still a little soft.
15. Round 3 has begun. Prick the bubbles.
16. The fourth match. Make careful to cover the whole surface of the rolled egg, including the bottom.

17. Maintain your momentum as you slide down the log. Lifting the frying pan instead of changing the stove heat is a good way to control the pan's temperature. The egg will adhere to the pan if the heat is too low, so be careful.
18. This is the fifth and final round of play.
19. The last round is here, and we're down to the wire...
20. The omelet can be browned a bit.
21. To wrap, remove the omelet from the skillet and set it on a bamboo sushi mat. You can shape your eggs while they're still warm. Stand back for 5 minutes.
22. Using a Round Frying Pan
23. Apply oil to pan with a folded paper towel soaked in oil. Put a small amount of egg mixture into the pan to test whether it's hot enough. On sizzling, pour a thin layer of beaten egg into the pan, tilting it to coat the bottom.
24. To get the air out, poke the bubbles. When the base of the egg has set however the top is still soft, begin rolling from one side to the other. A half-sheet of nori was placed here, and then rolled (optional).
25. Whereas the omelette is still rolling, spread oil in a pan with a paper towel. Again, pour the egg mixture into the pan until it covers the bottom. Lift the omelette carefully so that the filling may be evenly distributed below.
26. Starting from one side to the other, roll the egg until the fresh layer of egg has set and is still a little soft. Before rolling, I add another nori sheet on top. This is optional, but I prefer to do so.
27. Whereas the omelette is still rolling, spread oil in a pan with a paper towel. Afterwards, add another layer of egg mixture to the bottom of the pan. Lift the omelette carefully so that the filling may be evenly distributed below.
28. Starting from one side to the other, roll the egg until the fresh layer of egg has set and is still a little soft. Before rolling, I added another layer of nori. The egg mixture isn't done yet, so keep going until it is.
29. To wrap, remove the omelette from the skillet and set it on a bamboo sushi mat. You can shape your eggs while they're still warm. Stand back for 5 minutes.
30. To serve, cut the omelette into 12" (1cm) slices.
31. Grate the daikon. Squeeze water out of the skin. The daikon should be served with soy sauce drizzled over it.
32. To Preserve or Maintain
33. Tamagoyaki may be stored in the freezer for up to two weeks in an airtight container. Refrigerator or microwave defrost overnight.

67.   SUSHI-STYLE ROLL-UPS

READY IN: 4hrs 35mins

INGREDIENTS

- 2 cup of medium-grain white rice, warm and cooked
- 2 tbsp seasoned rice vinegar
- 1 (3 ounce) package cream cheese, softened
- 1 tsp wasabi paste, as need (or may sub whipped horseraBowl)
- 3 (12 inch) flour tortillas
- 1 cucumber
- 1 red bell pepper

DIRECTIONS

1. Cooked rice and vinegar should be combined thoroughly in a medium basin.
2. Cover and refrigerate for 31 minutes, or until cool.
3. Mix the cream cheese and wasabi paste together in a small bowl.
4. Make 12-inch squares of plastic wrap for each tortilla.
5. To each tortilla, distribute about 2 tablespoons of the cream cheese mixture to the edges.
6. Spoon roughly 1/3 cup of the cooled rice mixture into a 2-inch wide strip in the center of each tortilla.
7. Cucumbers can be quartered in length.
8. 3 portions should be set aside for future usage.
9. Remove the seeds from a quarter of a cucumber and slice it into three long strips.
10. Every rice strip should have one strip pressed into the middle.
11. Slice the pepper into long pieces.
12. Create a long crimson stripe by placing next to the cucumber.
13. Another 1/3 cup of rice mixture should be piled on top of the cucumbers and peppers on each tortilla.
14. Wet your hands and mold rice into firm rolls, covering the cucumber and peppers fully.
15. Every tortilla should be rolled tightly around rice starting from the bottom border.
16. Wrap each roll in plastic wrap so that it is protected.
17. Refrigerate for at least four hours before serving.
18. To serve, trim the rolls' uneven ends and cut them into eight slices 3/4 inch thick.

68.   RAINBOW SUSHI

INGREDIENTS

- cooked rice or quinoa (3 cup of)
- sliced red pepper (1 cup of)
- sliced or shredded beets (1/2 cup of)
- sliced or shredded cucumber or zucchini (1 cup of)
- sliced or shredded carrots (3/4 cup of)
- avocado, sliced or mashed (1)
- nori seaweed (12 sheets)
- sesame seeds (as need)
- hoisin sauce (as need)
- rice vinegar (2-4 tbsp.)
- agave nectar (a few drops)

DIRECTIONS

1. Vegetables should be sliced or shredded into small pieces. Optional: Combine 2 to 4 TBS rice vinegar and agave nectar to season cooked rice (or quinoa).
2. Every nori sheet should have a layer of cooked rice or quinoa on top of it.
3. If using sesame seeds, sprinkle them on top of the avocado and vegetables.
4. Form a log by rolling it up tightly. Repeat. Make smaller pieces of nori by cutting them up. Hoisin sauce may be used as a dipping sauce by diluting it with water.

69. QUICK-PICKLED VEGETABLE SUSHI ROLLS WITH AVOCADO

INGREDIENTS

- 1 1/2 cup of uncooked sushi rice
- 1 cup of plain rice vinegar
- 1 cup of white vinegar
- 1 tbsp sugar
- 1/2 cup of grated carrots
- 1/2 cup of grated daikon raBowl
- 1 1/2 medium avocados (halved, pitted, thinly sliced)
- 2 medium green onions (coarsely chopped)
- 1/2 medium English, or hothouse, cucumber, cut into thin strips
- 4 sheets roasted nori
- 2 tbsp soy sauce (lowest sodium available)

DIRECTIONS

1. To mark a step as completed, simply click on it.
2. Use the instructions on the package to make sushi rice, if necessary.
3. Meanwhile, combine the vinegar and sugar in a larger basin and mix until the sugar is dissolved. Incorporate the carrots and daikon into the mixture and mix well. Allow 15 to 30 minutes for the veggies to stand before serving.
4. Set aside the vegetables in a colander. Drain thoroughly. To remove the leftover liquid, use paper towels to blot.
5. A bamboo sushi mat may be prepared by covering it with plastic wrap before beginning to roll the sushi. (Aluminum foil (3 or 4 sheets) works just as well.) On the bamboo mat, spread out 1 nori sheet. Rice should cover the whole page, leaving a half-inch of space at the top. On top of it, place a single layer of avocados, green onions, and cucumbers. Add 2 tbsp of the quick-pickled veggies to the top. It's important to note that there will be leftover pickled veggies.) Press down once on the nori sheet to roll it up halfway, then lift the mat and repeat. After you've wrapped up the entire sheet, continue to roll. Cut the sushi into six pieces using a moist, sharp knife.
6. The remaining three nori sheets must be used in the same manner (makes 24 sushi rolls total).
7. Soy sauce is a must.

70. TOFU QUINOA SUSHI ROLL RECIPE

INGREDIENTS

- ½ CUP OF White Quinoa
- 1 CUP OF Water
- ¼ TSP Kosher Salt
- 8 OZ High Protein Tofu
- 3 TBSP Soy Sauce
- ½ Red Bell Pepper
- ½ Avocado
- 4 Sushi Nori Sheets
- 2 TBSP Pickled Sushi Ginger (Optional)

INSTRUCTIONS

1. Pour in the water and salt into a small saucepan and bring to a boil. After bringing the water to a boil, lower the heat. Simmer on low for 16 minutes or until the water is absorbed, whichever comes first.

2. The strips of tofu should be 12 inches broad. Pour soy sauce on top of the noodles in a shallow dish.
3. Five minutes in soy sauce is all it takes to tenderize the meat.
4. Slice the bell pepper into long strips.
5. Slice the avocado into small cubes using a mandoline.
6. Lay a towel on the floor, then cover it with a plastic wrap sheet. Spread quinoa on top of a nori sheet. Make a roll out of the tofu, bell peppers, avocados, and then slice it up.
7. Serve with more soy sauce and sushi ginger if desired.

71. VEGGIE QUINOA SUSHI
PREPARATION 30 min
COOKING 20 min

INGREDIENTS

- SUSHI
- 6 nori sheets
- 1½ cup of quinoa (I used black)
- 3 tbsp white miso paste*, adjust as need
- 1 flax or chia egg
- FILLING & CONDIMENTS
- 1 small avocado, peeled
- 1 carrot, peeled
- 1 beetroot, peeled
- 1 small daikon, peeled & julienned
- wasabi
- tamari
- pickled ginger, store-bought or homemade

METHOD

1. Rinse the quinoa thoroughly. A half-cup of water should be used to dissolve the miso paste. Rinse the quinoa and place it in a saucepan with a transparent top. Miso paste and 1 and 34 cups of additional water should be added to the saucepan once it has been dissolved. Bring quinoa to a boil by putting the cover on the pot. Make sure it's boiling before lowering the temperature to simmer. Before you start simmering, wait until the water has evaporated (with the cover on). Immediately after the quinoa has absorbed all the water, turn off the heat and leave the pot on a hot stove (DO NOT LIFT THE LID) for around 5-10 minutes to finish cooking in its own steam. Before constructing sushi rolls, make sure the nori sheets have totally cooled down.
2. Your sushi rolls are now ready: (If you are new to sushi making, see this recipe for step-by-step photos) Wrap a wide sheet of cling film around your sushi mat (or folded kitchen towel, if you're using bamboo). A nori sheet with its glossy side down is placed on top of the mat. Evenly distribute the quinoa on the nori sheet. leaving a 1 cm space at the very top for sealing with a spoon. In addition to distributing the quinoa evenly, use the back of a spoon to push it into the mat.
3. Slices of avocado, beets, carrots, and diakon should be scattered throughout the baking sheet.
4. Squeeze the roll tightly with both hands as you gently roll it on the mat. Regularly check in with your youngster to verify all is well.
5. The next step is to brush water on the edge of the roll with your finger in order to seal it. Set the roll aside after you're done rolling. Repeat the previous processes with the remaining nori sheets.

6. After you've completed rolling all of the sushi, use a sharp knife to cut it into 1-centimeter pieces. Tamari, wasabi and pickled ginger are all that's needed to accompany this dish (or soy sauce).

NOTES

Sushi rolls will not come apart if you add miso paste to the boiling water before adding quinoa. A few tsp. of flax or chia egg can be added to quinoa that isn't sticky enough to attach to nori sheets, if you don't have miso on hand.

72. QUINOA SUSHI SALAD
35m prep
05m cook

INGREDIENTS

- 2 x 250g pkts Coles Microwave Brown Rice & Quinoa
- 2 tbsp mirin seasoning
- 1 tbsp white vinegar
- 1 tbsp soy sauce
- 425g tuna in oil, drained, flaked
- 1 avocado, peeled, stoned, thinly sliced
- 1 large carrot, cut into matchsticks
- 1 Lebanese cucumber, seeded, cut into matchsticks
- 1 sheet nori, cut into thin strips
- 1 tsp sesame seeds, toasted
- Extra soy sauce, to serve
- Pickled ginger, to serve
- Wasabi, to serve

STEPS

1. Quinoa is ready to be cooked.
2. In doubt about how much you'll need?

3. By clicking on the highlighted ingredients, you can find out how much of each component there is. Flipping back and forth is a waste of time!
4. Follow the mixing instructions on the packet. Pour into a heat-resistant bowl. Toss together the mirin, vinegar, and soy sauce. Allow 15 minutes for cooling.
5. Serve the quinoa mixture in individual serving dishes. Avocado, carrots and cucumber go well with the tuna. Add nori and sesame seeds to the salad. Extra soy sauce, pickled ginger, and wasabi are all that is needed for this dish.

73. PRESSED SUSHI WITH SMOKED SALMON
Cook Time: 10 minutes
Total Time: 15 minutes

INGREDIENTS

- 2 full-sized rolls Sushi Rice
- 3.5oz/100g thinly sliced smoked salmon
- 1/2 avocado sliced
- 1 tbsp Japanese mayonnaise
- garnish with tiny shiso leaves and white sesame seeds
- wasabi
- Soy sauce for dipping
- Sushi ginger

INSTRUCTIONS

1. Gather and prepare all of the materials you will be pressing.
2. Under running water, wet the "Osinbajo" pressing mold. *6

3. Start with the bottom base, and then add the outer box on top.
4. At the bottom of the mold, place slices of smoked salmon.
5. Spread a layer of mayonnaise on top, followed by slices of avocado.
6. Place half of the sushi rice evenly into the mold, ensuring sure the corner is especially full. *8
7. Use some force to firmly compress with the mold's top.
8. Do not use the outside box. Remove the outer box now. Slide the outer box up while keeping your thumbs on the pushing lid.
9. Carefully remove the pressed lid. *9
10. Flip the pressed sushi over onto a serving or chopping board that has been turned upside down.
11. Sushi should be sliced roughly 1.2 inches (3cm) apart with a sharp knife once the bottom is removed.
12. Use a moist towel to clean the sharp knife after each use. *11
13. Sesame seeds and tiny shiso leaves can be used as a garnish.
14. Eat with wasabi and soy sauce if desired.

NOTES

1 Calculate how much sushi rice you'll need with the help of the Sushi Rice Calculator. Two full-sized sushi rolls will yield two rectangle pressed sushi. The mentioned cooking time does not include the time it takes to create sushi rice.

There is no need to provide the following: 2-5 are optional. 2 Watercress may be used in place of the shiso leaves if you can't find them, and *3 Wasabi can be used if you want your food spicy.

You may not be able to get fresh wasabi in Bowle, but you can buy Wasabi Paste online.

See this post for a five-step recipe for making sushi ginger at home.

6 Alternatively, cling wrap can be used to create a second layer if desired. Sushi rice will not adhere to the mold as a result of this procedure.

7 Place the sushi items that you wish on top of the sushi first. Make sure the toppings are placed towards the bottom of the mold, as the bottom layer is what ends up on top of the sushi. Also, make certain that any gaps and crevices are adequately sealed.

8 There is a tendency for corners to be unevenly occupied. To avoid causing the sushi to crumble, ensure that all of the corners are correctly filled.

As you press down on the lid, check to see that nothing comes off.

A serving plate is needed to serve the sushi if you cut it on a chopping board instead of a serving board.

11 Sushi won't fall apart because of this step's clean sliced surface.

NUTRITION

Calories: 368kcal, 59g carbs, 11g protein, 1g saturated fat, 6mg cholesterol, 251mg sodium, 322mg potassium, 5g fiber, 0g sugar, 100IU vitamin A, 5mg vitamin C, 11mg calcium, 0.9mg iron.

74. FUGU KIMBAP

Total: 2 hr 45 min

INGREDIENTS

- Sesame Rice:
- 2 cup of cooked rice
- 3 tbsp toasted sesame oil
- 1 tbsp toasted sesame seeds
- Dash cooking oil
- 4 eggs
- 1 tbsp mirin
- 1 tsp sugar
- 1/2 tsp salt
- 2 pounds thinly sliced beef
- 3 tbsp soy sauce
- 1 tbsp toasted sesame oil
- 1 tbsp sugar
- 1 tsp minced garlic
- 1/2 tsp ground black pepper
- 4 ounces thinly sliced onion
- 4 sheets seaweed
- 1 carrot, thinly sliced and sautéed
- 1 cucumber, thinly sliced
- 1 pickled raBowl, sliced into strips

DIRECTIONS

1. Sushi rolling mat made of bamboo
2. To cook the rice: Mix the sesame oil and seeds into the rice. Save and reheat at a later date. Set aside.
3. For the egg sheets, use: The nonstick pan should be heated to medium-high heat, and a paper towel soaked in oil should be used to lightly lubricate it. The eggs, mirin, sugar, and salt should be whisked together in a bowl. Swirl a quarter of the mixture into the pan and cook to a medium brown. To avoid any discoloration, flip the egg sheet as soon as it has finished setting. Re-do this process for the remaining eggs. Four to six thin egg sheets should be formed from the mixture.
4. In a small basin, combine all marinade ingredients and marinate for two hours. In a heated pan, cook the mixture. Wait until it has cooled down before serving at room temperature.
5. Each seaweed sheet should be coated with half a cup of the seasoned rice. Then add some of the meat mixture, carrots, cucumbers, and rabies to the egg sheet. On top of a bamboo mat, wrap up the seaweed and rice mixture with the addition of the various fillings. Serve each roll by slicing it into eight equal pieces.

75. SAKE ONIGIRI (SALMON RICE BALLS)

Prep Time15 minutes
Cook Time0 minutes

INGREDIENTS

- 20 grams (Scant 3/4 ounce) broiled salmon flaked
- 1 1/2 tbsp(27 grams) sea salt
- 2 tsp (10 grams) butter
- 2-3 cup of (400-600 grams) Steamed Japanese-Style Rice or Sushi Rice freshly cooked
- 2 sheets nori halved

INSTRUCTIONS

1. Salt, butter and rice are all mixed together in a big basin.
2. Make a ball out of half of the mixture, or whatever shape you choose, with your hands wetted with water to avoid the rice sticking to your palms.

3. To prevent your fingers from coming into contact with the sticky rice, wrap a nori sheet around the onigiri and use it like a tortilla.

4. Onigiri number two may be made the same way. So that the nori stays beautiful and crisp, you should serve it as soon as possible.

76. SALMON & AVOCADO SUSHI ROLLS

INGREDIENTS

- 2 cup of sushi rice, cooked according to package directions
- 6 Tbsp. rice wine vinegar
- Bamboo mat or plastic wrap for rolling
- 6 sheets nori
- 6 Tbsp. Hellmann's® or Best Foods® Avocado Oil with a hint of Lime Mayonnaise Dressing
- 1/2 Tbsp. wasabi
- 8 ounces salmon fillet, cut into strips
- 1 avocado, peeled, pitted and sliced

METHOD

1. Follow the package instructions for making sushi rice. Add vinegar and let cool on a baking sheet.

2. One nori sheet should be laid out on a bamboo mat or plastic wrap. Leave a 1/2-inch border all the way around the nori after pressing a thin layer of cooled rice on top of it. blend avocado oil with a touch of lime mayonnaise, such as Hellmann's® or Best Foods® Spread a thin coating of wasabi dressing on top of the rice.

3. On top of the salmon, place a 1-inch border of avocado and sprinkle some salt and pepper. The nori's top edge is somewhat moist. Assisting yourself with a mat, tightly roll the mat from the bottom to the top. Slicing into eight sections Repeat to make six rolls. If desired, top with more mayonnaise dressing and soy sauce for dipping.

77. SMOKED TOFU & VEGETABLE SUSHI ROLL

Active: 10 mins
Total: 10 mins

INGREDIENTS

- 1 sheet toasted nori
- 1 ounce sliced baked smoked tofu
- ¼ sliced ripe avocado
- 4 thin slices red bell pepper
- 4 matchsticks cucumber

DIRECTIONS

1. Using a cutting board, lay nori shiny side up, ready to be sliced into little pieces. Layout the nori so that the bottom third is covered with tofu, avocado, bell pepper, and cucumber. Seal the nori roll by moistening the last inch of the roll. Slicing into eight sections.

78. QUINOA, SMOKED SALMON AND SHREDDED VEGETABLE SUSHI ROLLS

Time to make: 40 mins ,
+ 30 mins

INGREDIENTS

- 1 cup of (190g) quinoa, rinsed, drained (we used a blend of red, white and black quinoa)
- 1 ½ tbsp rice wine vinegar
- 1 tbsp toasted sesame seeds
- 2 tbsp white vinegar
- 4 sheets nori
- 2 tbsp pickled ginger and 2 tbsp reduced-salt soy sauce, to serve
- Filling
- ½ medium ripe avocado, seeded, peeled, sliced
- 100g smoked salmon, sliced
- 1 large carrot, peeled, shredded
- 1 red capsicum, seeded, thinly sliced
- 1 large Lebanese cucumber, trimmed, seeded, cut in thin matchsticks

INSTRUCTIONS

1. Add 2.2 cups of water to a medium pot and bring to a boil. Cook, covered, for 12-15 minutes or until all the water has been absorbed, on low heat. Steam for 5 minutes after removing from heat and covering with a lid. Quinoa is supposed to be sticky or gummy when cooked.

2. Gently whisk in sushi seasoning and sesame seeds into quinoa. Apply foil to a large baking pan. Quinoa should be spread out evenly on a tray and left to cool before being stored in an airtight container.

3. Add 1 cup of cold water to a small dish of white vinegar. Count out four equal servings of quinoa and do the same thing. You may use a baking sheet or a bamboo mat to place one nori sheet with the glossy side facing you, with the longest side facing you.

4. Spread 14 of the quinoa equally over the bottom of the nori sheet, leaving a little border around the nori's edge, then moisten your palms with the vinegar mixture.

5. Stack the avocado, salmon, and carrots on top of the quinoa and garnish with some cucumbers. To construct a full roll, lift the end of the mat nearest to you and roll it over the contents to surround them. Keep on with the rest of the nori, quinoa, and fillings. Refrigerate the rolls for 30 minutes before serving. Pickled ginger and soy sauce should be served with each roll.

6.

79. TEMAKI SUSHI

Prep Time: 10 minutes
Total Time: 10 minute

INGREDIENTS

- 1 batch sushi rice
- 1 packnori (full-size sheets cut in half)
- tuna
- ikura
- salmon
- lettuce
- kaiware sprouts
- green shiso
- mayonnaise

STEPS

1. Place a big spoonful of sushi rice on the left half of a sheet of nori with the rough side facing you.
2. Temaki Sushi may be made by sprinkling some rice on the nori's rough side.
3. Spread the rice evenly on the left half of the nori by dipping your fingertips in water first.
4. Half of the nori should be covered with a triangle of rice.
5. On top of the rice, layer your filling ingredients, working your way to the top.
6. Prepare your hand roll fillings.
7. Using your fingers, create a cone-shaped cylinder out of nori by rolling its bottom left corner up until it reaches the center of its uppermost edge.
8. Temaki sushi should be rolled starting from the leftmost corner of the bottom sheet.
9. Continue rolling until the nori is no longer able to be rolled any farther. Consume right away.

80.   CUCUMBER WRAPPED SUSHI

PREP TIME: 45 mins
TOTAL TIME: 45 mins

INGREDIENTS

- 2 Persian/Japanese cucumbers
- 3-4 cup of sushi rice (cooked and seasoned)
- Toppings of your choice:
- 4 oz sashimi grade salmon
- 4 oz sashimi-grade yellowtail
- 4 ozsalmon roe sashimi grade tuna
- 4 Tbsp ikura (salmon roe)
- 10 sashimi-grade shrimp (amaebi)
- For Garnish
- 10 shiso leaves (perilla/ooba)
- 1 green onion/scallion
- 1 lemon
- 1 bunch kaiware daikon raBowl sprouts

INSTRUCTIONS

1. Gather all of the ingredients before starting the cooking process. I also use a round cookie cutter with a diameter of 1 3/8 inches (4.5 cm).
2. Fillings to be Made
3. Scallion, soy sauce, and sesame oil are combined with diced tuna in a mild marinade.
4. Slice the cucumber into long, thin strips using a peeler.
5. To Put Together
6. Serve the shiso leaves on a dish. Place a shiso leaf on top of a cookie cutter dipped in water (to prevent rice from sticking). Once you've stuffed the cookie-cutter halfway with sushi rice, gently lift the cutter out of the sushi. Measure the circumference of the sushi cylinder by rolling a cucumber slice around it.
7. Slit the end of a cucumber slice using a knife as shown below. The strip is now ready to be interlocked around the rice.
8. Fill the cucumber-wrapped sushi with any of your favorite toppings.. I lay a few pieces of amaebi (sweet shrimp) from the outside borders to the center of the cucumber cup to make it seem like a flower.
9. Cucumber cups are a great way to serve sashimi-grade fish. Slice the fish perpendicular to the muscle (the white line you see in the fish).

10. Put the tuna mixture in the cucumber cup and serve immediately. The dish is completed with the addition of fresh lemon and daikon raBowl sprouts. Serve at once.

TO RETAIN

Sashimi-grade fish and shrimp should not be stored for more than 24 hours. Before serving, keep them in the refrigerator.

81.   CALIFORNIA ROLL + SPICY CALIFORNIA ROLL

prep time: 25 MINUTES
total time: 25 MINUTES

INGREDIENTS

- 4 cup of sushi rice – visit my post on how to make sushi rice
- 1/4 English cucumber
- 1 avocado, peeled, pitted
- 1/4 pound imitation crab
- 3–4 Nori sheets
- 2 tbsp sesame seeds
- For the spicy mayo
- 2 tbspmayonnaise
- 2 tbsp sriracha sauce
- Pinch ichimi (optional)

INSTRUCTIONS

1. Place a bamboo mat on a level surface or a chopping board and cover it with plastic wrap. Place a small basin next to the bamboo mat filled with water and rice vinegar.
2. Nori sheets with the glossy side facing down on a bamboo mat should be placed in the center of the nori sheet, with roughly half a cup of rice.
3. With your fingers dipped in vinegar water, spread the rice out over the nori paper until it is completely covered.
4. Evenly spread out sesame seeds on the rice (about 1 tsp).
5. Carefully push the nori sheet close to the bottom border of the bamboo mat after flipping it over the rice is facing down.
6. Layout the nori sheet with the cucumbers, imitation crab, and avocado at the bottom of the dish.
7. Spicy mayonnaise (approximately 1 Tbsp or more if you want more taste) is put on the bottom of the nori sheet, followed by cucumbers, imitation crab meat, and avocado.
8. Grab the mat's bottom borders with your thumbs while keeping the toppings in place with the rest of your hand. Tuck the contents tightly into the cylinder and elevate the bamboo mat's edge slightly to form a cylinder.
9. The filling will not leak out if you gently roll it forward while applying slight pressure. When reach the opposite end of the mat, let go of it.
10. In order to divide the roll into thirds, cut the roll into thirds.
11. Soy sauce and wasabi should be served alongside the dish.

82.   BEER AND GOUDA AND SOUP

Prep:15 mins
Cook:40 mins
Total:55 mins

INGREDIENTS

- 1 tsp butter
- 1 sweet onion (such as Vidalia), minced
- 1 clove garlic, minced
- 1 can or bottle light beer
- 4 cup of chicken broth
- 2 cup of milk
- ¼ cup of butter
- ¼ cup of all-purpose flour
- 1 cup of shredded Gouda cheese
- ½ cup of shredded sharp white Cheddar cheese
- ½ tsp ground black pepper
- 4 slices cooked bacon, crumbled
- ¼ cup of chopped fresh chives

DIRECTIONS

1. Sweet onion and 1 tablespoon butter in a large pot over medium heat for 4 minutes or until softened. Cook and mix the onion and garlic together for approximately a minute until the garlic is aromatic. Simmer the onion in a pot of light lager for approximately 10 minutes, until it's soft and mushy.
2. Add the chicken broth a spoonful at a time, and bring the mixture to a boil.Simmering while stirring, slowly pour the milk into a pot to make the soup foundation.
3. In a microwave-safe bowl, microwave 1/4 cup of butter for 30 to 60 seconds until melted and heated. Pour the roux into the soup while the combination is still a liquid.

Cook and stir the soup for 7 to 10 minutes until it starts to boil and thicken.

4. Remove the soup from the heat. Add a handful of grated Gouda and/or Cheddar cheese to the soup at a time, stirring well after each addition; season with freshly ground black pepper. Serve the soup garnished with bacon and chives in individual dishes.

83.   UNAGI ROLL (BROILED FRESHWATER EEL)

INGREDIENTS

- 8 ounces sushi rice
- Sushi Su seasoning, recipe follows
- 1 full sheet nori (roasted seaweed)
- 1-ounce cucumber, julienned
- 1/2-ounce kaiware (daikon sprouts), juilienne
- 4 ounces Unagi (broiled freshwater eel)
- 1 pinch sesame seeds
- 1 ounce Unagi Glaze, recipe follows
- Gari (pickled ginger), as need
- Wasabi (Japanese horseraBowl), as need
- Soy Sauce, as need
- Sushi Su seasoning:
- 3 tbsp sugar
- 1 tbsp salt
- 1 cup of rice vinegar
- 1- ounce sea kelp
- Unagi Glaze:
- 4 ounces sake
- 4 ounces mirin
- 1-ounce sugar

- 1-ounce water
- 1/2-ounce soy sauce

DIRECTIONS

1. Makisu, a piece of specialized gear (bamboo rolling mat)
2. Cooking the sushi rice is as simple as washing, draining, and letting it sit in a colander for 30 minutes. It's best to use less than a cup of water per cup of rice while making rice in the rice cooker. To hasten the chilling process of the rice, transfer it to a large mixing bowl after 45 minutes of cooking (plastic or wood are preferred; metal is OK as well). Mix in 1 ounce of sushi su seasoning to the rice and combine thoroughly. Allow for cooling on a stand. To ensure consistent cooling, rotate your rice every few minutes. Take a break for around 21 to 30 minutes, then re-enter the water.
3. Place a nori sheet (rough side up) on the bamboo rolling mat and roll it out to the desired thickness. Using wet hands, press the rice into a uniform layer over the whole sheet, excluding approximately 7/8-inch at the far end. From left to right, sprinkle sesame seeds over the rice. Nori should be garnished with strips of Unagi, cucumber, and kaiware sprouts. Once you've completed the first section, gently wrap the second section up and away from you, tucking in any loose ends. Assuring that all components are properly attached during rolling will aid in the preservation of the contents during cutting. The bamboo mat may be used to compress the roll. It's up to you whether you want to make your roll somewhat circular or square. In order to serve, cut the bread into 12 equal pieces. Serve with Unagi glaze in a bowl or on a platter. As a final touch, drizzle wasabi and pickled ginger over the top of the sushi. Soy sauce is a good accompaniment.
4. Sushi-related tidbits: Nori has a rough and sparkly side to it. Both sides of the rice bowl have advantages and downsides. Sushi preparation needs a lot of water. Hands should be kept slightly damp while handling rice to prevent the rice from sticking. You need to maintain your knife moist at all times when cutting sushi rolls in order for it to slide through the rice.
5. A saucepan with all the ingredients is brought to a boil, and the mixture is ready. Cook before the sugar is completely dissolved, then remove from the heat. Remove the food from the heat and allow it to cool to room temperature.
6. Set aside after combining all ingredients.

84.   VEGAN 'TUNA' ONIGIRAZU SUSHI SANDWICH

INGREDIENTS

- 150 g sushi rice
- 1 Tbsp rice vinegar
- 4 sheets nori seaweed
- 4 Tbsp vegan sriracha mayonnaise
- 1 pack Good Catch Naked in Water plant-based tuna
- 2 Tbsp pickled ginger
- 3 spring onions, finely sliced
- 0.50 avocado, sliced
- 0.50 carrot, finely shredded
- 3 raBowles finely shredded
- wasabi
- soy sauce

- pickled ginger

METHOD

1. The rice should be cooked according to the package directions. Serve on a platter with rice vinegar sprinkling it on top.
2. Clean and dry a piece of nori seaweed before using it. The rice should be divided into eight equal amounts. Shape a bit of rice into an about 8cm square and lay it in the middle of the nori sheet, wetting your palm a little.
3. Spritz some siracha mayonnaise on top of the rice and spread it out in a thin layer. Toss in a quarter of the carrots, raBowl spring onion, pickled ginger, and avocado.
4. Another square of rice should be put on top of the first one. Wrap the rice and filling in a tight square by folding the nori sheet's edge inward. Seal everything in place with a damp finger dipped in water.
5. Wrap and refrigerate before consuming!
6. Thevenin Supermarket and Debenhams are great places to shop for vegan pantry supplies and kitchenware, respectively.

85.   KAWAII SUSHI ROLL
INGREDIENTS

- 1 Roll
- 3 bowls cooked rice
- 1 stick cheese
- 1/2 cucumber
- 1 tbsp Sakura Denbu (dried fish flakes stained pink)
- 1 tbsp Sushinoko(Sushi powder)
- 2 sheets Nori

STEPS

1. Cucumber should be cut into slices. Put Sakura Denbu in a bowl of sushi rice after you've mixed the powder and rice together.
2. Place 1/6 of a Nori sheet on 1 tbsp. of pink Sushi rice.
3. Rice should be spread out evenly.
4. Tighten the ties.
5. Produce 5 mini buns with the ingredients listed above.
6. Rice should be adhered to 1/6 and 1/2 Nori sheets. Place Nori on a bed of white rice.
7. Three pink buns with stick cheese on them.
8. in which chopped cucumbers should be positioned
9. Tightly rolled
10. Wrap the item in a couple minutes of film.
11. Dissect Sushi Roll

86.   EASY-TO-MAKE KIMCHI
INGREDIENTS

- 10 pounds baechu (napa cabbage)
- 1 cup of kosher salt
- ½ cup of sweet rice flour
- ¼ cup of sugar
- water
- 1 cup of crushed garlic
- 1 to 2 tbs ginger, minced
- 1 cup of onion, minced
- 1 cup of fish sauce
- salty, fermented squid (see FAQ, above)
- 2½ cup of Korean hot pepper flakes (gochugaru) (as need)
- 2 cup of leek, chopped
- 10 green onions (diagonally sliced)

- ¼ cup of carrot, julienned
- 2 cup of Korean raBowl, julienned

DIRECTIONS

1. Remove the cabbage's discolored outer leaves.
2. Remove the cores and quarter the cabbage lengthwise. Make it easy to eat by chopping it up into little pieces.
3. Put the soaked cabbage into a big bowl and cover it with a lid. Sprinkle with salt.
4. Turn the cabbage over after 30 minutes to ensure that the salt is distributed evenly.
5. After 112 hours, carefully clean the cabbage by rinsing it three times in cool water.
6. Set aside a second bowl to hold your cabbage.
7. How to make a bowl of oats:
8. Bring 3 cups of water and 3 tablespoons of sweet rice flour to a boil, stirring constantly. Keep stirring until bubbles form in the porridge (about 5 minutes).
9. Add a quarter cup of sugar to the mixture. Stirring often, cook until transparent, then remove from heat.
10. Take a breather.
11. Make a paste out of the kimchi:
12. Cold porridge should be placed in a big bowl. You'll now add each ingredient one at a time.
13. Incorporate fish sauce, hot pepper flakes, chopped ginger, and minced onion.
14. Using a food processor makes things so much simpler!
15. Drain the salty squid and rinse it. Make a paste by chopping it and adding it to the kimchi.
16. a hint: a recipe for salty squid may be found in the FAQ up above!
17. Toss in green onions, sliced leeks, Korean raBowl, and carrots, and serve
18. Your kimchi paste is ready after you've incorporated all of the ingredients into a smooth mixture.
19. Action! Mix the kimchi paste into the cabbage!
20. Add all of the cabbage to a large bowl with the kimchi paste. Hand-mixing the ingredients yields the best results.
21. If you don't have a big enough basin, start with a little and work your way up.
22. Put the kimchi in a glass or plastic jar with a tight-fitting lid.
23. You may consume it straight away, or you can wait until it's fermented before doing so.
24. Except for a tiny amount stored in a small container, I store most of my kimchi in the refrigerator. Keeping the larger container in the fridge for a longer period of time allows me to enjoy fresh kimchi, whereas the smaller container ferments quickly and becomes sour. To make kimchi jjigae, for example, I prefer to use sour kimchi. After that, I replenish the little container with kimchi from the larger one. If you try it and experiment, you'll get the hang of it!

87. KOREAN SUSHI ROLLS WITH WALNUT-EDAMAME CRUMBLE

Active: 1 hr
Total: 2 hrs

INGREDIENTS

- 2 cup of sushi rice, rinsed well
- 2 cup of water

- 1 tbsp canola oil
- 2 cup of coarsely chopped walnuts
- 1 cup of (4 ounces) shelled edamame
- 3 tbsp molasses
- 1 ½ tbsp soy sauce, + more for serving
- 1 tbsp toasted sesame seeds
- 10 sheets of nori, see Note
- 20 shiso leaves, see Note
- 10 nori-length pieces of pickled daikon
- Note
- 2 large carrot

DIRECTIONS

1. In a separate pan, bring the rice and water to a boil. When the water has been absorbed, cover and simmer for another 15 minutes on low heat. Allow the dish to rest for ten minutes, covered, once you have turned off the heat. Put the rice in a bowl when it's been scraped out. Allow 30 minutes for the dish to cool enough to handle under a kitchen towel.

2. Meanwhile, heat the oil on medium-high in a nonstick skillet. A high-heat pan should be used to fry the walnuts for around 3 minutes. Toss in the soybeans and simmer for 5 minutes with molasses and 1 1/2 tbsp of soy sauce over a medium-high heat. Add the sesame seeds to the mixture and mix well. Allow to cool in a basin.

3. On the sushi mat, place one nori sheet. 2/3 cup sushi rice is patted onto the nori sheet in a rectangle that covers the lower two-thirds, about 1/3 inch thick, with lightly moistened hands To serve as adhesive, press two rice grains together in the corners. Over the rice, place two shiso leaves. Place a slice of daikon, two tablespoons of carrots, and two tablespoons of the walnut-edamame combination in the center of the shiso. Tuck in the filling by lifting the end of the bamboo mat nearest you and pushing it into a cylinder. Roll the fillings up very tightly. Make nine more rolls by repeating the process. Put six pieces of each roll on a serving dish. Soy sauce is a good accompaniment.

NOTES

Many Asian marketplaces sell nori, shiso, and pickled daikon.

88. KOREAN DEEP-FRIED SEAWEED SPRING ROLLS

Prep Time: 20 minutes
Cook Time: 10 minutes
Total Time: 30 minutes

INGREDIENTS

- 8 dried seaweed sheets , cut into halves
- 1 fistful Korean glass noodles , boiled and cut into little finger size
- 1/3 carrot , julienned,
- 10 stalks garlic chives , chopped little finger lengths
- some cooking oil for deep frying
- SAUCE – MIX THESE IN A BOWL
- 1 Tbsp soy sauce
- 1 tsp fine sea salt
- 1/4 tsp sesame oil
- A few sprinkles ground black pepper
- BATTER – MIX THESE IN A BOWL
- 1/2 cup of all-purpose flour , sifted
- 1/2 cup of potato starch, sifted
- 1/4 tsp fine sea salt , sifted
- 3/4 cup of water

INSTRUCTIONS

1. Noodles, carrots, and garlic chives may all be mixed together in a single dish. Using your hands, incorporate the sauce into the mixture and thoroughly coat the meatballs.

2. The glass noodles and vegetable combination from step one should be placed on the seaweed sheet in a little amount. The seaweed should be rolled up like a cigar. It will stick better if the seaweed is brushed with a bit of water after rolling it. Carry on with the remainder of the ingredients in the same manner.

3. Roll seaweed into the batter and coat it well. Each time, I use four rolls.) Every other can be squashed by too many at the same time.)

4. Add a 6 drops of oil to a wok. Toss in the battered seaweed rolls once the water comes to a boil. Before they're done cooking, fry them (about 2 to 3 mins).Place the oiled spoons on a kitchen towel to absorb the excess oil.

5. Once the seaweed rolls have cooled, cook them again for added crispness.

6. Serve. If you like, you can eat them alone or with Tteokbokki and Rabokki.

NUTRITIONAL ADVICE

This meal has 47 calories per 1 gram of carbohydrate, 1 grams fat, and a sodium-potassium ratio of 251 milligrams to 60 milligrams per serving.

89.   LATIN SUSHI
Prep 25 MIN
Total 45 MIN

INGREDIENTS

- 1 cup of sushi rice
- 1 ½ cup of water
- ½ cup of rice vinegar
- ½ tsp of salt
- ¼ tsp of sugar
- ½ mango cut into small cubes
- ½ jalapeño
- 3 sheets of nori seaweed
- 1 fried plantain, julienned
- 1 avocado, finely sliced
- 4 fresh cheese, cut in strips

DIRECTIONS

1. Start by heating a saucepan
2. of water until it is boiling.
3. Reduce to a low heat, cover the saucepan, and cook until the rice grains have fully opened.
4. In a cup, combine the vinegar, salt, and sugar. Shortly heat this combination in a microwave or on the stove. Only bring it to a boil for a short period of time to properly combine the ingredients.
5. Put the rice in a jar with half of the vinegar mixture, salt, and sugar. The remainder can be put aside.
6. Mix thoroughly and allow to cool before serving.
7. The sauce may be made while you wait. Toss the mango cubes and jalapeño slices together. The balance of the rice vinegar mixture should be poured over these items. Before serving, remove the sauce from the heat and set it aside.
8. Add some sushi rice on a nori sheet on a sushi mat. Using a wooden spoon, flatten it into the shape of a tennis ball and set it in the centre of the mat. When you're trying to

level out the rice, you may also use your fingertips.

9. Place slices of plantain, cheese and avocado on the rice.
10. With the aid of the mat, roll it up into a cylindrical shape before squeezing it.
11. Serve the sushi with the mango and jalapeño sauce cut into pieces.

90.   MAKI SUSHI RECIPE

Prep Time: 1 hr
Cook Time: 20 mins
Total Time: 1 hr 20 mins

INGREDIENTS

- Roasted Shiitakes
- 6 ounces shiitake mushrooms
- 1 tbsp extra-virgin olive oil
- 1 tbsp tamari
- Carrot ginger dipping sauce
- ½ cup of chopped roasted carrots, about ¾ cup of raw carrots
- ⅓ to ½ cup of water
- ¼ cup of extra-virgin olive oil
- 2 tbsp rice vinegar
- 2 tsp minced ginger
- ¼ tsp sea salt
- Sushi rice
- 1 cup of short-grain brown rice, rinsed well
- 2 cup of water*
- 1 tsp extra-virgin olive oil
- 2 tbsp rice vinegar
- 1 tbsp cane sugar
- 1 tsp sea salt
- For the rolls
- 3 nori sheets
- 1 cup of thinly sliced red cabbage

- 3 long thin strips of cucumber
- ½ avocado, sliced into strips
- Sesame seeds, for sprinkling
- Tamari, for serving
- Pickled ginger, optional, for serving

INSTRUCTIONS

1. Shiitake mushrooms should be grilled. Line a big and a small baking sheet with parchment paper before placing them in the oven. Combine the tamari and olive oil and coat the shiitake mushrooms. On a large baking sheet, spread the mixture evenly. Roast for about 26 to 31 minutes, or until the edges are browned. Roast the carrots for the dipping sauce on the second sheet.

2. This is how you make the carrot-ginger sauce: A blender is all that is needed to combine the roasted carrots and water with the olive oil, rice vinegar, ginger and salt. Set aside the shiitake mushrooms before you begin cooking.

3. Prepare the sushi rice by following these directions: Bring rice, water, and olive oil to a boil in a medium saucepan. Simmer covered for 45 minutes at a lower temperature. Remove the rice from the fire and allow it to cool for another 10 minutes before serving. Fluff with a fork, then add the rice vinegar, sugar, and salt and mix thoroughly with a spoon. Before using, cover the container.

4. Set up the sushi maki rolls. Keeping a small basin of water nearby, as well as a kitchen towel, will help you keep your hands clean as you work. Lay down a nori sheet with the shiny side down on a bamboo mat, then press a handful of rice into the lowest two-thirds of the nori sheet. Your toppings

should be placed at the bottom of the rice (see picture). Trying to roll anything that's too full will make it more difficult to do so. Tuck and roll the nori with the help of the bamboo mat. The bamboo mat may be used to shape and press the roll once it's been rolled. The cut side of the roll should be on the side. Repeat with the rest of the dough.

5. Sushi should be sliced using a chef's knife that is as sharp as possible. Between each cut, use a moist cloth to wipe the blade clean.

6. If desired, sesame seeds can be sprinkled over the top.If desired, garnish with tamari and pickled ginger.

NOTES

You may skip the olive oil if you're using a rice cooker.

Preserve uncut rolls in the fridge overnight by covering them tightly with plastic wrap. Using this method helps to protect the rice from drying out. To eat, slice when you're ready.

91.   KANI MAKI (CRAB STICK SUSHI ROLL) RECIPE
Prep Time: 15 mins

INGREDIENTS:

- 1/2 cup of Japanese short-grain rice + sushi vinegar (as need)
- 3 pieces 19x10cm nori (seaweed) sheet
- 4 crab sticks microwave for 2 mins; peel every crab stick to half (lengthwise)
- Japanese mayonnaise as need
- pickled ginger, shoyu (Japanese light soy sauce) & wasabi

DIRECTIONS:

1. Take a look at the sushi rice directions and follow them to the letter. Make three equal servings.

2. Rough side up, lay nori sheet on bamboo mat. A 5cm space should be left at the top of the nori, where one quantity of rice should be placed.

3. Line the crab sticks across the mayonnaise, then spread a thin layer of mayo over the center of the rice.

4. Using a strong grip, roll the bamboo mat securely halfway through the maki, then continue rolling until the maki is complete.

5. Prepare your sushi by trimming the maki's ends and cutting through the center with a sharp knife dampened with water. Three equal halves may now be made out of each half. The pickled ginger, soy sauce, and wasabi should be served on the side with the maki.

92.   SMOKED MACKEREL MAKI ROLLS
Prep:20 mins
Cook:25 mins

INGREDIENTS

- 150g sushi rice
- 2 tsp rice wine vinegar
- 4 nori sheets
- 1 red chili, deseeded
- ½ carrot, peeled and cut into matchsticks
- ¼ cucumber, cut into matchsticks
- 100g smoked mackerel, skin removed, torn into small pieces
- soy sauce, for dipping

METHOD

1. Remove the starch from the rice by squeezing the grains with your hands in a basin of cold water. Until the water is clear, drain and repeat the process until it is clean.

2. Set up a small pot with a tight-fitting cover to cook the rice. For 10 minutes, bring 2.5cm of cold water to a boil, cover, and simmer on a medium heat. Leave the cover on for another 15 minutes after removing the heat. Pour the vinegar into the mixture, then allow it to cool fully.

3. Make sure you have a sushi mat (around $1 from any big supermarket) and a small bowl of cold water. Placing a nori sheet on top of the sushi mat so that the shiny side is facing up is recommended. Leave a 1cm border at the top when spreading out a quarter of the rice on the nori.

4. Stack the rice with about a fourth of the chilies and carrots. A quarter of the cucumber and mackerel should be placed in a strip along the middle.

5. To help seal the roll, apply a small amount of water to the top of the roll. Roll up the maki by folding the bottom edge of the seaweed over the first layer of filling, then using a sushi mat to do so. Make four more rolls by repeating the process. Each roll should be divided into eight equal pieces using a serrated knife. Serve with a dipping sauce of soy sauce.

6.

93.   ALASKA ROLL SUSHI
Prep Time: 10 minutes
Cook Time: 30 minutes

INGREDIENTS

- Sushi Rice
- 1 cup of small or medium-grain white rice
- 1 cup of + 1 tbsp water
- 2 tbsp seasoned rice vinegar
- 1 tsp salt
- Alaska Roll Sushi
- 1 sheet nori (seaweed paper)
- 6 oz 6 thin slices Sushi-Grade Salmon
- ¼ cup of imitation crab meat or real Alaskan crab meat
- 1 tbsp mayonnaise (optional)
- ½ tsp sriracha (optional)
- 2-3 slices cucumber (cut into matchsticks)
- 2-3 slices avocado
- pickled ginger (optional)
- wasabi (optional)
- Optional Sauces and Toppings
- spicy sriracha mayo
- bang bang sauce
- eel sauce
- white or black sesame seeds

INSTRUCTIONS

1. Sushi rice: a basic recipe
2. In order to Take the excess starch from the rice, a fine mesh strainer is ideal (water should run clean). Excess water should be shaken out.
3. Add salt and washed rice to the Instant Pot. Activate. Add a little bit of water. Add 2 tsp of salt to the mixture.
4. minutes of high pressure cooking in an instant pot (with full natural release).
5. Toss rice into a serving dish. Distribute the rice vinegar in a uniform layer on top of the grains.

6. Don't crush the grains of rice when you gently fold them in the vinegar.
7. spicing up the crab combination
8. Shred Alaskan or imitation crab flesh.
9. Mix mayonnaise and sriracha with fake or Alaskan crab meat.
10. Learn how to make Alaskan Sushi Rolls.
11. Using plastic wrap, cover a sushi rolling mat made of bamboo.
12. The mat should be covered with a nori sheet.
13. To eliminate surplus moisture, wet hands and clap. Keep a small bowl of water and a towel on hand in case you need them in an emergency.
14. Cover nori with a layer of rice. Approximately 1 cup of cooked rice is required for each nori sheet.
15. Cover the entire nori sheet with rice (no gap). Spread salmon slices equally over half of the surface.
16. Nori should be turned over (rice/salmon side down, nori up)
17. 2 tablespoons of crab mix, 2 slices of avocado, and 3-4 long cucumber strips are all that's needed to make this rice dish a little more interesting. Ideally, the rice paper should be placed about an inch from the bottom. The sushi roll will not seal properly if you put too many ingredients in it.
18. Use a bamboo mat to raise up and overfill the borders of the dish. To tuck the roll, use your fingers.
19. Pull back and tighten the mat once it has been rolled up so that only the nori and no rice are visible.
20. Squeeze and shape the mat as you move it around.
21. Make sure your knife doesn't become too sticky by wiping it off with a moist cloth after each slice.
22. Cut each half into three equal pieces.

NOTES

A risk of foodborne disease might be increased by eating raw or undercooked meats and seafood as well as eggs. Contact the Food and Drug Administration (FDA) and/or the relevant regulatory agency for food safety guidance.

NUTRITION

Thirteen hundred and ninety-nine kilocalories, 173 grams of carbohydrates, 55 grams of protein, 8 grams of saturated fat, 98 milligrams of cholesterol, and 2494 milligrams of potassium.

94. HOMEMADE AVOCADO SHRIMP SUSHI ROLLS

PREP TIME 45 mins
TOTAL TIME 45 mins

INGREDIENTS

- 1½ cup of arborio rice
- 3 cup of water
- pinch salt
- 2 tbsp rice wine vinegar
- 2 tsp sugar
- 1 medium avocado peeled, pitted
- 10 large cooked shrimp peeled, deveined
- 2 tbsp sesame seeds
- Make Recipe
- Powered by
- Chicory logo

INSTRUCTIONS

1. Start by heating a saucepan of water until it is boiling.
2. In a fine-mesh sieve, rinse the rice several times under running water until the water runs clear.
3. Simmer the rice for about 12 minutes or until all the water has evaporated and the grain is soft. Take the skillet from the heat and fluff with a fork.
4. As soon as the rice has finished cooking, transfer it to a baking sheet and spread it out to cool.
5. Toss the rice vinegar and sugar into a small saucepan and bring to the boil. Pour the vinegar over the rice as it cools down. Continue to chill the rice while you prepare the filling.
6. Wrap a sushi mat with plastic wrap and set it aside.
7. Lay a nori sheet across the sushi mat in the same direction as the sushi rice.
8. Spread at least half a cup of the cooled rice on the nori sheet, being sure to wet your hands well.
9. Flip the rice and nori sheet over so that the rice is now on the bottom and the nori sheet is on top.
10. Sliced avocado and shrimp should be placed on the nori sheet in a horizontal position.
11. If desired, sesame seeds can be sprinkled over the top.
12. When just the rice is visible after rolling, use the mat to firmly roll the sushi (adjust the mat as necessary).
13. Continue with the other ingredients and the roll once the first one has been set aside.
14. Slice the rolls into 1-inch pieces with a sharp knife.
15. Before serving, put the food in the fridge to keep it fresh.
16. If desired, top with teriyaki sauce, wasabi sauce, and/or soy sauce.

NOTES

Equipment and tools:

Sushi mat, plastic wrap, fine mesh colander, cutting board, chef's knife, baking sheet, saucepan, wooden spoon, tiny bowls, and a basin of water to keep rice from sticking to hands are all necessities for this recipe..

NUTRITION

Single-Serving 52 kcal is the caloric intake. 8 grams of carbohydrate 1g of protein 1g of fat 0g of Saturated Fat The following is the cholesterol level: 5 milligrams (mg). Amount of sodium in a serving: 17 mg 44mg of potassium 0 grams of fiber It has zero grams of sugar per serving. ten IU of Vitamin A 0.7 milligrams of vitamin C 10 milligrams of calcium 0.6mg of iron

95. MALIBU BAY BREEZE

Prep: 2 mins
Total: 2 mins

INGREDIENTS

- 2 jiggers coconut flavored rum
- 4 fluid ounces pineapple juice
- 1 tbsp cranberry juice

DIRECTIONS

1. Blend the coconut rum, grapefruit juice, and cranberry juice

2. in a large glass filled with ice.

96.   VEGAN AVOCADO MANGO CUCUMBER SUSHI

Total Time30m
Prep Time10 m

INGREDIENTS

- 1/2 cup of soaked rice
- 10 green grapes
- 2 cup of milk
- 2 tbsp water
- 4 large mango
- 4 strawberry
- 8 tbsp sugar

STEPS

1. To begin, combine milk, sugar, and rice in a medium saucepan. Cook until the mixture is just thickened, whisking continuously to avoid lumps. Add more water to bring back the moisture, then give the mixture a last whirl to combine. Once it's done, Take it from the heat and allow it to cool.

2. Mangoes should be washed, peeled, and then sliced into thin strips. Gather your fruit and lay it aside for later. Spread the rice mixture equally over the mango strips on a platter once they've been arranged. Next, place the sliced grapes and sliced strawberries on top of this layer of fruit.

3. Using a cling wrap cover for every roll, gently roll up the mango strips once they've been filled. For best results, keep the packed strips in the fridge for a few hours. Take a bite and enjoy it!

97.   AVOCADO AND MANGO SUSHI ROLL

Prep Time: 20 minutes
Total Time: 20 minutes

INGREDIENTS

- 1 large California Avocado thinly sliced
- 1 large Cucumber thinly sliced
- 1 head cauliflower riced
- 1 head Purple Cabbage thinly sliced
- 1 large Mango thinly sliced
- 1 large Carrots thinly sliced

INSTRUCTIONS

1. A thin coating of cauliflower rice should cover roughly two-thirds of your nori wrap.

2. Lay your cabbage, carrots, cucumbers, California avocado, and mango approximately three-quarters of the way down the nori sheet.

3. To begin with, begin by rolling the nori firmly from the edge closest to you. Apply a small amount of water to seal the nori roll. To wrap it up, (if you have one, you may use it as a sushi mat).

4. Gently slice the sushi into quarters with a very sharp knife. Add some low-sodium soy sauce or coconut amino acids to the plate, and then dig in!

98.   SPICY TUNA HAND ROLLS

PREP TIME: 0 hours 30 mins
COOK TIME: 0 hours 20 mins
TOTAL TIME: 0 hours 50 mins

INGREDIENTS

- FOR THE SUSHI RICE:
- 1 3/4 c. Water

- 1 tsp. Kosher Salt
- 1 1/2 c. Short Grain Rice
- 1 tbsp. Rice Wine Vinegar
- 8 oz. weight Sashimi Grade Raw Tuna
- 1 tsp. Sambal Or Chili-garlic Sauce
- 1 tsp. Sriracha
- 1 1/2 tsp. Fresh Ginger, Minced
- 1 tbsp. Sesame Oil
- 2 tbsp. Coconut Amino Acids
- 2 tbsp. Rice Wine Vinegar
- FOR THE HAND ROLLS:
- 6 Sheets Nori, Cut In Half
- Black Sesame Seeds
- Avocado
- Shikoku Mushrooms
- Cucumber
- Fresh Cilantro

DIRECTIONS

1. To make the sushi rice, combine the water and salt in a small saucepan before adding the rice. Add a cover and bring the heat down to low after 1 minute of boiling. Simmer for around 15–17 minutes, until all the liquid has evaporated.
2. Using a fork, stir in the rice wine vinegar, then return the cover to the saucepan and cook for another 3 minutes.
3. For the tuna with a kick:
4. Cut the tuna into bite-sized pieces on a chopping board. Take a big, sharp knife and mince the tuna, then set it aside.
5. Mix the sambal, sriracha, ginger, sesame oil, amino acids, and rice wine vinegar together in a medium-sized dish. Toss the tuna into the sauce and mix it up. Set aside for at least 31 minutes to let the flavors blend.
6. Assemble hand rolls by following the steps below:

7. A nori sheet should be laid out flat. Use a sharp knife & scissors to cut 2 inches off the edge of the sheet. One tablespoon of rice should be placed at one end of the nori. Wet your fingers and flatten the rice with them. Top the rice with 1 tbsp of the spicy tuna mixture and a sprinkling of sesame seeds.
8. Top the tuna with avocado, mushrooms, cucumber, and cilantro. The nori should be rolled into a cone. Use a few drops of water to brush the edge of the nori to seal the cone. Serve as soon as possible with the remaining ingredients.

99. MAZESUSHI
INGREDIENTS

- 11 oz uncooked Japanese sushi rice
- FOR THE SUSHI DRESSING
- ½ cup of rice vinegar unseasoned
- 2 Tbsp superfine sugar
- 1-1 ½ tsp salt
- FOR THE MAZESUSHI:
- Small carrot about 3 1/2 oz, peeled
- 1 cup of mushrooms finely sliced
- 3 Tbsp dashi stock
- 1 Tbsp soy sauce
- ½ Tbsp superfine sugar
- ½ Tbsp mirin
- 12 large peeled raw shrimp more if you want more shrimp
- 1 Tbsp sake
- Juice of 1/2-1 lemon
- Nori seaweed-to garnish
- FOR THE KINSHI TAMAGO CREPES:
- 4 medium eggs
- 1 ½ Tbsp superfine sugar
- 2 tsp sake

- Salt-to season
- Sunflower or vegetable oil

INSTRUCTIONS

1. Drain and let the rice stand for 10 to 15 minutes after properly rinsing it in cold water.
2. To prepare the sushi dressing: In a small saucepan, bring the rice vinegar to a boil. Add the sugar and salt when the mixture is hot. Remove off the heat and allow it cool down to room temperature.
3. Slice the carrot into julienne strips using a mandolin. 1 and a half inches in length
4. In a saucepan, mix combine the dashi stock, soy sauce, sugar, and mirin. Simmer the mixture until the carrot is barely cooked, then add the julienned carrots. Drain
5. A little boiling water combined with sake is all that is needed to devein the shrimp. Then cover the pot and let it to cool. They will cook slowly in the liquid's heat. Put something aside for when you want to add it.
6. Add 1 2/3 cups of water to a large pot and cook the rice until it is tender. To start, bring the water to a boil. Then turn the heat down to low and let the water simmer for 10 to 12 minutes. For another 10 minutes, do not remove the cover from the pot.
7. Sushi dressing should be poured over the cooked rice and mixed in gently. Put in the carrots and the mushrooms. To re-heat the mixture, add the drained shrimp and lemon juice.
8. To create the kinshi tamago crepes, combine the eggs, sugar, sake, and salt in a basin and whisk until smooth. To achieve a uniformly colored crepe, strain the batter. A thin layer of oil and egg mixture should be applied to the pan's bottom before baking. Keep an eye on the crepe while it cooks since it will be done very soon. Once the crepe is done, lay it aside and continue the process until all of the mixture is gone. In a 7-inch skillet, around 8-10 crepes may be produced.
9. Make thin strips out of the cooked crepes, then use your fingers to loosen the pile. You'll be shocked at how much the crepes expand.
10. Sprinkle nori seaweed over the rice mixture and top with kinshi tamago crepe strips before serving on a large serving platter.

100. SPICY SHIITAKE MUSHROOM ROLL

INGREDIENTS

- 1 cup of sushi rice
- 2 cup of water
- 1 TB rice vinegar
- 1 TB sugar
- 1/2 TB salt
- 5–7 big dried shiitake mushrooms, steeped for 31 minutes to an hour in boiling water
- 1 1/2 teaspoon Ener-G, mixed with 5 quarts of water
- 1 cup of cornstarch
- vegetable oil
- 2 nori sheets
- 1–2 tablespoons sriracha, plus 1-2 tablespoons Vegenaise
- to serve: crushed red pepper, pickled ginger, and soy sauce

INSTRUCTIONS

1. The rice should be soaked for 31 minutes in cold water. In a rice cooker, add 2 cups of water and thoroughly rinse under fresh, cold water.

2. The vinegar, sugar, and salt may be added to a big glass dish and microwaved for 10-15 seconds once the rice has been cooked. Stir the cooked rice into the glass basin. Set away for later.

3. Add the oil to a small pot and bring it to a boil over medium heat. After draining and de-stemming the mushrooms, cut them into strips. As soon as the oil is heated enough, add a few mushroom slices and coat them in Ener-G before adding them to the pan. When the oil bubbles up, you're ready to fry. Then drain on a couple sheets of paper towel after being cooked for only a few seconds.

4. TO PUT YOUR SUSHI TOGETHER

5. The shiny side of a sushi mat should be facing down. Place a nori sheet on the mat. Spread rice on the sheet with a sushi paddle. To prevent the rice from adhering to your fingers, spread the rice out evenly using your fingers.

6. Spread out half of the mushrooms on the nori sheet's shortest side. Roll the sriracha-Vegenaise mixture into a cylinder, making sure to keep the sriracha-Vegenaise mixture as close to the cylinder as possible. Make eight rolls by cutting the roll in half with a very sharp knife.

7. Serve with soy sauce and ginger pickles.

101.   SPAM MUSUBI

INGREDIENTS

- 12 ounces Spam
- 1/4 cup of oyster sauce
- 1/4 cup of soy sauce
- 1/2 cup of sugar
- Nori roasted seaweed used for sushi, cut into halves or thirds
- 6 cup of cooked sushi rice

INSTRUCTIONS

1. Put the SPAM in a Ziplock bag and cut it into 8-10 slices, depending on your preference for slices that are thin or thick. Add the oyster sauce, soy sauce, and sugar to a bowl and whisk to combine before adding to the SPAM bag. Marinate for 15 minutes before serving.

2. Remove the SPAM from the marinade and cook it over medium heat, flipping once, until crispy and cooked through, as desired. After frying, some people prefer to coat the SPAM in the marinade/sauce. Either way, it's delicious!

3. Place a nori strip on a cutting board or other clean surface and cut it into desired lengths (shiny side down). You should place the Musubi mold in the middle of the nori sheet, as shown. The mold should have around 1-1 1/2 inches of Sushi Rice pressed down firmly and evenly. The mold and your fingers can be kept from adhering by dipping them in water as you go.

4. Remove the mold from the rice after that. You'll be able to see the rice right there on the nori. Cooked spam can be sprinkled on top. Wrap the nori in one end and adhere it to the top of the SPAM before re-wrapping the other end. As though you're putting the

finishing touches on a cute little box. If necessary, apply a small amount of water to your finger to seal. Serve hot.

5. Some like soy sauce, some prefer ketchup, while yet others prefer it as is.

NOTES

A lot of money is saved when you make a lot of money. Wrap each piece in plastic and store in the refrigerator for up to a week. Unwrap and microwave for 15-20 seconds when you're ready to eat it.

102. BEST HOMEMADE NIGIRI SUSHI

Prep Time: 15 minutes
Cook Time: 45 minutes
Total Time: 1 hour

INGREDIENTS

- Nigiri-Making Staples
- Sushi Rice
- Sushi Vinegar
- Wasabi
- Pickled Ginger
- Soy Sauce
- Eel Sauce
- Nori Seaweed Sheet
- Sharp Knife
- Most Popular Topping Ingredients: Choose Your Favorite
- Salmon
- Tuna
- Shrimp Ebi
- Tamago Egg
- Yellowtail Hamachi
- Eel
- Octopus
- Uni

INSTRUCTIONS

1. Prepare the Sushi Rice: Take a bucket of cold water, and rinse the rice.Fill the rice cooker halfway with water, then add the rice. Please follow the recipe's instructions.

2. Rice should be seasoned with salt and pepper: Let the rice cool down a bit before transferring it to a big bowl. Stir in the sushi vinegar while it's still heated (or the mixture of rice vinegar and sugar).

3. Preparation of the Topper: If you're using raw fish, cut it at a 30- to 45-degree angle against the grain. Cut it into 3-inch-long, 1-inch-wide, and 1/4-inch-thick pieces for optimal flavor and texture. At times you'll have to change this angle to achieve the right length and thickness. Cooking the egg is a must for tamago nigiri. For further information, please see this post.

4. Place roughly 3 tablespoons of rice in your hand and form it into a ball. Before it becomes a definite oval shape, squeeze it together tightly. Create a flat bottom and a rounded top for the bottom. (You can use tezu water to keep your hand from sticking.)

5. Your fingers should be placed at the base of your fingers when you are preparing the Nigiri. In the centre of the slice, spread a pea-sized quantity of wasabi. Turn over and cover both pieces with your fingertips, making sure the rice is well covered. Press down on the rice with the index finger of the other hand. Let the topping slice rest on top of the rice before turning the dish over.

6. For some nigiri sushi, such as Tamago, you can bind the topping to the rice by wrapping a thin nori strip around the nigiri.

Pickled ginger and wasabi may be served on the side.

103. EASY VEGAN SUSHI

total time: 35 minutes

INGREDIENTS

- 2 cup of uncooked sushi rice*
- ¼ cup of soy sauce
- 2 tbsp of maple syrup
- 1 tbsp of cornstarch
- ½ tbsp of grated ginger
- 1 clove of garlic, minced
- 2 tbsp of water
- 1 tbsp of oil
- 1/2 block of extra firm tofu
- 1 large carrot, thinly sliced
- ½ of a cucumber
- 1 Avocado
- 2 tbsp of rice vinegar
- 2 tbsp of white wine vinegar
- 5–6 Nori sheets

INSTRUCTIONS

1. Cooking rice should be done according to the package guidelines.Refrigerate in a large basin after finished.
2. In a large bowl, combine water, ginger and garlic with the soy sauce and maple syrup. Whisk together until well combined. Set away for later.
3. 1 tbsp. oil in a big nonstick pan, on medium, is plenty. Sauté the tofu for 5 minutes without moving it once the pan is heated. For a total cooking time of around 12 minutes, flip the chicken over and cook it for a few minutes on each side. When the sauce has thickened, continue cooking for a few more minutes. Tofu should be well covered in the sauce before serving. Allow to cool before storing.
4. Set aside the rice vinegar and white wine vinegar when the rice has cooled down.
5. Using a sushi mat*, place a nori sheet on top. Using a nori sheet, spread 2/3 cup of the cooked rice over the nori, leaving approximately 2/3 of an inch clean on the other end (see video). Two slices of avocado and some cucumber are all that is needed on top of the salad. Continue softly and *tightly* rolling the nori sheet before it's completely folded up over the contents. Continue the process with the remaining components (I end up with 5-6 rolls depending on how I filled them).
6. ENJOY! Slice into 1-inch chunks. Adding a little of sliced ginger and soy sauce to mine is my favorite way to eat it.

NOTES

Short-grain Japanese rice is what you need. To make sushi, you need a substance with an unique stickiness to it. This recipe does not work with long grain rice, such as basmati (I tried it!).

Tofu that has been firmed up will also work.

A sushi mat isn't necessary for this recipe.!

104. CURED HAM SALAD SUSHI ROLLS

INGREDIENTS

- 1 bowlful Sushi rice
- 1 1/2 sheet Nori seaweed
- 2 slice Sliced cheese

- 4 slice Cured ham
- 1 egg's worth Scrambled eggs
- 1/4 Avocado
- 1 Lemon juice , grainy mustard

STEPS

1. Place the entire nori sheet on the makisu and cover it with sushi rice as thinly as possible. On the close side, leave approximately 1 cm uncovered, and on the far side, leave about 2 cm uncovered. The use of a rubber spatula is recommended.
2. Add sliced cheese, nori and half nori.
3. Sandwiches with Salad and Cured Ham Sushi Rolls
4. Top with a generous portion of smoked ham
5. Wrap it up with scrambled eggs and avocado slices.
6. Citrus juice and grainy mustard should be added to the dish.

105.   HAM, CHEESE AND AVOCADO SUSHI ROLLS

15 mins preparation
15 mins cooking

INGREDIENTS

- 1 1/2 cup of (300g) sushi rice
- 2 tbsp rice wine vinegar
- 4 nori sheets, cut in half
- 1 1/2 tbsp sesame seeds, toasted
- 2 tsp black sesame seeds, toasted
- 1 small avocado, mashed
- 12 slice shaved leg ham
- 1 small carrot, grated
- 50 gram low-fat cheddar cheese, cut into 1/2cm-thick strips

METHOD

1. Rice should be rinsed and drained before the water clears out. Take a strainer or colander and let it drain for 15 minutes. To cook the rice, combine 1 1/2 cups water and the rice in a saucepan over medium-low heat. Bring to a boil, covered.
2. Reduce the temperature. 12 minutes of simmering should be enough time to see holes emerge on the surface. Remove from the heat. For ten minutes, keep your head covered. Using a fork, mash the potatoes.
3. Rice should be spread out over a big, shallow bowl of glass or porcelain. Break up any lumps by stirring the rice with a spatula. Lift and flip the rice as you gradually add vinegar. Wrap a tea towel in a moist paper towel. Take a break and allow the food to cool down before serving.
4. Nori should be placed on a bamboo sushi mat with the glossy side down. With wet hands, distribute a fourth of rice over nori with your fingertips. In a dish, combine the sesame seeds. Sprinkle 2 tsp of sesame mixture over the rice.
5. Wrap the rice with plastic. Using a mat, turn the nori over so that it is facing up. Slide plastic, nori-side up, onto mat after removing it.
6. Place a quarter of the avocado on top of the nori and serve immediately. Along the edge closest to you, place a quarter of the ham, carrots, and cheese mixture. Take care not to roll plastic wrap into sushi by using the rolling mat as a guide.
7. Unroll the sushi mat while keeping the sushi in the plastic bag.. Slice the sushi roll into six equal pieces using a sharp knife. Dispose of any plastic items.

8. To produce 24 pieces, repeat the process with the remaining ingredients.

106.   HAM 'SUSHI' RECIPE
INGREDIENTS

- 1 slice granary bread, crusts removed
- 1 tbsp soft cheese
- 1 slice wafer-thin ham
- 1 thin cucumber stick, trimmed to length of bread

METHOD

1. Flatten the bread gently using a rolling pin. Using a sharp knife, cut a thin slice of ham and spread a layer of soft cheese on one side of it.
2. One end of the bread should have a cucumber stick. A little additional soft cheese is all that is needed to secure the bread around the cucumber. Prior to serving, refrigerate any rolls that have been made ahead of time, if possible.
3. Make 'sushi' rounds out of the roll and put them in a lunchbox.

107.   HAM & TURKEY "SUSHI ROLLS"

PREP: 25 minutes
COOK: -1 minutes

INGREDIENTS

- 2 slices King's Hawaiian Sliced Bread
- Mayo
- Sliced Ham
- Sliced Turkey
- Cheddar Cheese Slice
- Avocado Slice
- Rolling Pin
- Sushi Mat

PREPARATION

1. Two slices of King's Hawaiian Sliced Bread are used to make a sandwich. To remove the crust, use a knife to cut it off.
2. Roll out a single piece of bread using a rolling pin on a cutting board. On a sushi mat, place the flattened piece (if you prefer to tuck and roll by hand, sushi mat is not needed).
3. Then, add a slice of avocado, a slice of cheddar cheese, and some mayo to the middle of the slice.
4. The bottom half of the bread slice should be carefully picked up, rolled over, and tucked into the top half of the bread. The bottom half of the sushi mat should be rolled up and tucked beneath the bottom half of the sandwich before you begin making the sushi (see illustration).
5. Slice into "1" rolls using a sharp knife.

108.   KETO CHEESEBURGER SUSHI
PREPARATION

- 16 ounce ground beef
- Salt and pepper as need
- 2 ounce cheddar cheese
- 10 slice bacon
- 1/2 medium red onion, sliced
- 2 medium dill pickle, diced
- 1/4 cup of mayonnaise
- 2 tbsp low-carb ketchup
- 1 tbsp yellow mustard

- 2 tbsp unsweetened dill pickle relish

EXECUTION

1. Prepare all the ingredients by gathering them and putting them in a bowl. Pre-heat the oven to 375F.
2. Lay the bacon pieces out on a piece of plastic wrap so that they are slightly stacked on top of one another.
3. Then, on top of the bacon, add the ground beef. To ensure that it cooks thoroughly, spread it out in a thin layer. Add salt and pepper to taste.
4. On top of the ground beef, arrange the sliced cheddar cheese, red onion, and dill pickles. A clear line will make it easier to roll the dough.
5. Use toothpicks if necessary to keep the bacon coiled securely, encasing everything inside.
6. Bake the roll for 41 minutes, or until it's cooked all the way through. Make the dipping sauce while the cheeseburger sushi is cooking. Dill pickle relish, yellow mustard, and mayonnaise are mixed together in a bowl. Set aside this mixture before it is completely absorbed.
7. Cut the sushi into rolls and serve one per person after it has somewhat cooled. Serve the sauce on the side.

NOTES

A serving of Keto Cheeseburger Sushi is enough for four people. The calories in each serving are 602 calories, and the fat content is 50.8 grams. The net carbs are 3.45 grams, and the protein content is 30.7 grams.

109.   HAND ROLLS (TEMAKI SUSHI RECIPE)

PREP: 30 MINS
COOK: 20 MINS
TOTAL: 50 MINS

INGREDIENTS

- TEMAKI
- 2 c sushi rice cooked and seasoned
- 1 pack nori (sheets of seaweed) gold or silver grade preferred
- FISH
- 2 oz salmon sushi-grade & cut into strips
- 2 oz yellowtail sushi-grade & cut into strips
- 1.5 oz tuna sushi-grade & minced
- ¼ tbsp sriracha Huy Fong Foods
- 1 tbsp Kewpie Japanese mayonnaise
- 2 oz scallops sushi-grade
- roe
- FILLINGS
- raBowl sprouts
- Persian or Japanese cucumbers
- shiso leaves
- avocado sliced
- toasted sesame seeds
- Kewpie Japanese mayonnaise
- sriracha
- SIDES
- soy sauce
- wasabi
- gari (pickled ginger)

INSTRUCTIONS

1. Take care of sushi rice.
2. Prepare the spicy tuna filling and the scallops by cutting them in half or into bite-sized pieces, then cut the fish into strips. A

spicy filling is possible by mixing the scallop pieces with Kewpie and sriracha.

3. Make thin slices of the vegetables by cleaning and slicing them into long strips.

4. Cut a nori sheet in half horizontally using one sheet.

5. Stack rice on the left-hand side of the nori sheets.

6. Vegetables should be arranged diagonally from the upper left corner to the lower center.

7. The fish should be placed on top of the vegetables or any fillings you've chosen.

8. Fold the left side of the bottom corner over the fish.

9. Make a half-moon shape by folding one side of the nori over the other and then rolling it back to the front. Seal the open fold with a piece of rice.

10. Make sure you eat it all before creating any additional rolls so that you may enjoy the crunchy nori as much as possible.

110. PINEAPPLE MUSUBI ROLLS

Hands-On: 34 mins
Total: 59 mins

INGREDIENTS

- ¾ cup of uncooked short-grain rice
- ¾ cup of + 1 tbsp water
- 3 tbsp rice wine vinegar
- 1 tsp mirin (sweet rice wine)
- 1 tbsp + 2 tsp sugar, divided
- ½ tsp kosher salt
- 1 tbsp lower-sodium soy sauce
- Cooking spray

- 4 ounces Spam Lite, cut into 2 (3/4-inch-thick) pieces
- 2 nori (seaweed) sheets
- 4 (4-inch) julienne-cut pieces fresh pineapple
- 2 (8-inch) pieces green onions
- ½ tsp Sriracha (hot chile sauce, such as Huy Fong)

DIRECTIONS

1. Use a fine-mesh strainer to strain the rice. The rice should be rinsed under cold water and stirred until the water clears (about 1 minute). In a small saucepan, combine 3/5 cup + 1 tbsp water with the mix rice and bring to a boil. Reheat on low for one more minute after bringing to a boil. Simmer for 5 minutes on low heat. Cook for 30 seconds on high heat. Remove from the heat. Before usage, remove the cap and allow it to settle for five minutes.

2. Using a microwave-safe bowl and 30 seconds on HIGH, whisk together rice wine vinegar, mirin, 2 tbsp sugar, and salt. Cool.

3. Put the rice in a bowl with the vinegar mixture and stir. Keep it covered with a paper towel that has been soaked in vinegar.

4. Whisk the remaining sugar and soy sauce in a separate bowl. The skillet should be preheated to a medium-high temperature. Apply cooking spray to the pan. When the Spam begins to brown, remove it from the pan and set it aside. Toss in the soy mixture. For 5 minutes, let it stand. Using a knife, slice the soy mixture into two equal halves lengthwise. Set aside the leftover soy mixture.

5. Every nori sheet should have the top fourth of the short end cut off. The glossy side of a

nori sheet should face you on a sushi mat wrapped in plastic wrap. A wet hand pats approximately 3/4 cup of rice mixture evenly over nori and leaves about a 1-inch border on the long end. Along the top third of the rice-covered nori, arrange 2 slices of Spam, 2 pineapple chunks, and 1 green onion chunk. Add 1/4 tsp. Sriracha and half of the remaining soy mixture to the top of the salad. Fold the nori over the filling, lifting the edge closest to you. Squeeze tightly as you roll from one end to another on a sushi mat that's been lifted from the bottom edge. Once you've reached the top of the sushi roll, seal it tight with the mat. Remain with the seam down for five minutes. Slice the roll in half horizontally into 10 pieces. Make a second batch using the leftover rice, nori, spam, pineapple, onion, sriracha, and soy mixture.

111.   VEGAN CARROT SALMON

Preparation Time: 15 minutes
Cooking Time: 10 minutes
Total Time: 20 hours 25 minutes

INGREDIENTS

- 4 carrots large
- 2 tbsp vinegar (rice or apple cider)
- 1 sheet nori
- 1 tbsp salt
- 1 tbsp liquid smoke
- 300 ml water cold
- 3 tbsp olive oil
- 2 drops liquid smoke
- salt as need

INSTRUCTIONS

1. Cook or steam carrots for five minutes by using a potato peeler to make long strips.
2. Gather all of the ingredients into a sealable container, including vinegar, nori, salt, and 1 teaspoon of liquid smoke.
3. Toss in the carrot strips and refrigerate overnight (or for at least 2–3 days) before serving.
4. Salt and two additional drops of liquid smoke can be added to the oil before you coat the carrots and fish with the mixture.

112.   CUCUMBER AVOCADO SUSHI ROLLS

PREP TIME 15 mins
TOTAL TIME 15 mins

INGREDIENTS

- 1 English cucumber
- 1 avocado mashed
- 1/2 lemon juiced
- 1/4 cup of fresh mint and basil rough chopped
- 2 tbsp hemp seeds
- salt and pepper as need

INSTRUCTIONS

1. To finely slice the cucumbers, use a vegetable peeler.
2. Add salt, pepper, and lemon juice to a bowl and mash the avocado with a fork.
3. Spread some avocados thinly from one end of the cucumber strip to the other.
4. Roll up and decorate with hemp seeds and fresh herbs.
5. Keep on and have fun with the remainder of it.

113. VEGETARIAN SUSHI GRAIN BOWL

INGREDIENTS

- 2 tbsp rice vinegar
- 2 tbsp reduced-sodium tamari
- 2 tbsp avocado oil
- 2 tsp toasted (dark) sesame oil
- 2 tsp grated fresh ginger
- 2 cup of cooked brown rice
- 1 cup of shredded carrot
- 1 cup of diced cucumber
- 1 avocado, diced
- 1 cup of frozen shelled edamame, thawed
- 1 cup of chopped toasted nori
- Sesame seeds for garnish

DIRECTIONS

1. A small bowl is all that is needed to combine the ingredients for the marinade.
2. Serve brown rice in four separate dishes. Equal portions of carrots, cucumbers, avocados, edamame, and nori should be placed on top. Sprinkle sesame seeds on top if preferred and drizzle with 2 tbsp dressing each serving.

114. VEGAN SUSHI

Prep Time: 30 mins
Cook Time: 20 mins
Total Time: 50 mins

INGREDIENTS

- For the sushi rice:
- 2 cup of Japanese sushi rice
- 1/4 cup of rice vinegar
- 2 tbsp sugar or maple syrup
- 1 tsp salt
- nori sheets
- For the vegan sushi filling:
- 7 oz firm tofu
- 1 avocado
- 1 cucumber
- 2 carrots
- soy sauce

INSTRUCTIONS

1. Under running water, rinse sushi rice using an ultrafine mesh strainer.
2. The rice may either be cooked in an Instant Pot or on the stove. Use the rice setting if you have an Instant Pot (low pressure for 12 minutes). Allow the stress to go on its own. As a rule, the rice should be well-cooked and the water should have been absorbed. The rice and water should be brought to a boil, then reduced to a simmer, covered, and cooked for 20 minutes on the stovetop. When it comes to making sushi rice, I generally like to use my Instant Pot.
3. A bowl with rice vinegar, sugar, and salt in it is the best way to mix them. Combine the vinegar, sugar, and cooked rice in a large bowl. Take a breather. Before using the rice, dampen a napkin or kitchen towel and place it over the bowl.
4. During this time, thinly slice the cucumbers, the carrots, the avocados, and the tofu in half. Tofu strips should be crisped up on a flat pan with a little oil over high heat for about 4 minutes. During the cooking process, add one tablespoon of soy sauce.
5. Bamboo rolling mat with glossy side down: Place nori sheet lengthwise on mat. Wet your hands in a basin of cold water. Place a little amount of rice in the middle of the

nori sheet and press it down firmly. Discard the nori sheet, leaving a 3/4 inch wide border exposed.

6. A nori sheet should have a line of thin strips of cucumbers, carrots, tofu, and avocados on the near side. Don't load the nori up too far.

7. Hold the ingredients in your hands by tucking your thumbs under the bamboo mat. Then, gently roll the bamboo mat and nori sheet toward your fingertips. Make sure the rice and nori sheet are covering all of the ingredients. Slowly roll the sushi to ensure that it is evenly rolled.

8. Wet your fingers again in the small bowl of water and moisten the nori sheet's exposed portion. Then use the bamboo mat to thoroughly fold up the nori sheet.

9. Cut the sushi roll in half with a sharp knife on a cutting board. Before and after chopping, put the knife in a bowl of iced water. Slice the sushi into tiny pieces by placing the two sides side-by-side.

10. Sesame seeds and soy sauce should be sprinkled on the vegan sushi rolls before serving. Wasabi and pickled ginger are optional extras.

NOTES

To roll sushi, you'll need a bamboo mat (also known as a masiku). Ordering it online or in an Asian market is also an option. It's possible to find it in the grocery store at times.

Slowly roll the sushi to make sure it's all folded up evenly.

Before and after cutting the sushi, run the knife under cold water. Always use an extremely sharp knife.

Gluten-free versions of this recipe can be prepared by replacing tamari for the soy sauce.

Ensure that the sushi rolls aren't overstuffed.

For the rice vinegar, salt, and sugar combination, maple syrup might alternatively be used in place of the sugar.

NUTRITION

Four hundred and thirty-seven calories, eleven grams of protein, eleven grams of carbohydrates, three grams of fat, six hundred and thirteen milligrams of sodium, two hundred and twenty-nine milligrams of potassium, four grams of fiber, & eight grams of sugar make up this meal.

115. SPICY SALMON MAKI

Prep: 20 mins
Cook: 25 mins
Additional: 30 mins
Total: 1 hr 15 mins

INGREDIENTS

- 1 cup of glutinous white rice (sushi rice)
- 1 ½ cup of water
- ¼ cup of rice wine vinegar
- 2 tbsp white sugar
- ½ tsp salt
- 1 (1 ounce) package nori (dry seaweed)
- 1 medium avocado, thinly sliced
- 1 (8 ounce) farmed Atlantic salmon
- 3 stalks green onions, halved lengthwise
- ¼ cup of sriracha mayonnaise (Kikkoman)
- 2 tbsp hoisin sauce

- 2 tsp black sesame seeds
- 2 tsp toasted sesame seeds
- ½ tsp wasabi paste, or as need
- 1 tbsp pickled ginger, or as need

DIRECTIONS

1. A sieve and flowing water is all that's needed to rinse rice. In a saucepan, bring the water and rice to a boil. Reduce heat to low, cover, and cook for about 20 minutes on medium-high heat. Remove from the heat.
2. Meanwhile, in a small pot, combine wine vinegar, sugar, and salt. Before the sugar dissolves, cook on medium heat. Remove and let cool before serving. Cooked rice will dry out as it cools, so add vinegar mixture to it. Allow the rice to cool down for about 30 minutes before eating it.
3. Put the nori on a sushi mat and roll it up. Spread roughly half a cup of rice onto the nori sheet with a rice paddle.
4. Overturn the nori so that the rice is on the bottom. Stack 3 to 4 avocado slices, 2 ounces of salmon, a strip of green onion, and 2 tbsp of Sriracha mayonnaise on the nori sheet in a criss-cross pattern.
5. Closely roll nori into a roll by squeezing the materials together. Hoisin sauce and additional Sriracha mayonnaise should be drizzled on each roll and sesame seeds should be sprinkled on top.
6. Using a knife, cut each sushi roll into eight slices. Wasabi and pickled ginger can be served as an accompaniment.

116.   SKIRT STEAK WITH SHISO-SHALLOT BUTTER

Active: 45 mins
Total: 2 hrs 30 mins

INGREDIENTS

- Steak
- ½ cup of hoisin sauce
- ¼ cup of light brown sugar
- ¼ cup of soy sauce
- 3 garlic cloves (very finely chopped)
- 2 tbsp finely grated fresh ginger
- 2 tbsp rice vinegar
- 1 tbsp sambal oelek or other Asian chili paste
- 4 pounds skirt steaks
- 2 tbsp extra-virgin olive oil
- 5 medium shallots (thinly sliced)
- ¼ cup of soy sauce
- 14 medium shiso leaves (coarsely chopped (about 2/3 cup of) or 1 tbsp chopped tarragon)
- 1 tsp crushed black peppercorns
- 1 stick unsalted butter (4 ounces softened)
- 3 bunches of scallions

DIRECTIONS

1. Blend all of the ingredients (except the steaks) in a large mixing bowl and thoroughly combine them. An oven pot big enough to hold the steaks should be used. Pour the marinade over the meat and flip it to coat it with the flavorful marinade. Refrigerate for two hours before serving.
2. A medium-sized skillet should be preheated with olive oil. Add the shallots and simmer for approximately 10 minutes, stirring occasionally, until tender and

gently browned. Allow 2 minutes for the soy sauce to evaporate before removing from heat and allowing to cool.

3. Shallots, shiso leaves, and peppercorns go into the butter in a separate bowl. Place in the refrigerator to cool.

4. Set up a charcoal barbecue. For medium-rare meat, cook the steaks over a hot fire for 3 to 4 minutes on each side. Take the meat from the pan and let it rest for 5 to 10 minutes on a carving board. During this time, carefully brown the onions on the grill, flipping once, for about 2 minutes total. Transfer the steaks and scallions to a serving plate and garnish with thinly sliced steaks cut against the grain. Serve the steaks right away with the shish butter on top.

5. Refrigerating or freezing the shish butter keeps it fresh for up to one month.

6. The herbal shish butter on this grilled steak pairs nicely with a Shiraz with a touch of Viognier that has been created in recent years by ambitious Australian winemakers who have taken their cues from the traditions of the northern Rhône.

117.   RAW VEGAN SHIITAKE MUSHROOM SUSHI

Prep Time:30m
Total Time:30m

INGREDIENTS

- For the Mushrooms
- 8 shiitake mushroom caps, sliced into strips
- 1 garlic clove, minced
- 1/4 c filtered water
- 2 tbsp. coconut aminos
- 1 tbsp. green onion, diced
- pinch cayenne pepper
- For the Jicama Rice
- 6 c jicama, roughly chopped
- 1/2 c raw almonds
- 1/4 c raw apple cider vinegar
- 3 tbsp. raw agave nectar
- 1 tsp. sea salt
- For the Sushi Rolls
- 8 nori sheets
- 1 cucumber, cut into strips
- 1 avocado, pitted, peeled, and thinly sliced

INSTRUCTIONS

1. For the Mushrooms' sake

2. Toss the ingredients together in a medium-sized mixing basin.

3. For 30 minutes, cover the mushrooms in plastic wrap and allow them to absorb the aromas of the marinade. Wait for the rice to cook as you set this aside.

4. The Jicama Rice calls for

5. Once you've processed the jicama until it resembles rice, remove it from the processor and set it aside to cool. Incorporate the almonds by pulsing until they are finely minced.

6. Squeeze excess moisture from the mixture using a cheesecloth.

7. Fold the apple cider vinegar, agave nectar, and sea salt into the rice mixture that has been mixed in a medium bowl. Taste and adjust spices if necessary, after mixing everything together.

8. When it comes to sushi rolls

9. To begin rolling your sushi, place a sheet of nori on a cutting board or a sushi mat. Make

sure to leave a half-inch margin around the borders of the nori sheet when spreading the rice.

10. Along the nori sheet closest to you, arrange some mushroom, cucumber, and avocado slices in a row.

11. Apply pressure to the wet surface of the nori sheet after wetting the other end with your finger. When you roll it up, it will be easier to keep it together if you do this.

12. Once you've completed the roll, press it firmly. The process should be repeated until all the rolls have been made before moving on.

13. Simply slice the rolls into the appropriate size and enjoy. Dip in coconut aminos, if desired.

118.   HOT DOG SUSHI

PREP TIME: 0 HOURS 10 MINS
TOTAL TIME: 0 HOURS 35 MINS

INGREDIENTS

- 1/2 16-oz. bag frozen Tater Tots
- 8 slices white sandwich bread
- 1/2 c. mayonnaise
- 1/2 c. shredded Cheddar
- 1/3 c. thinly sliced pickles
- 1 package mini hot dogs
- Ranch dressing, for serving

DIRECTIONS

1. 425 degrees Fahrenheit is the recommended temperature for cooking them.

2. Roll out the bread pieces with a rolling pin until they are extremely flat. Top each slice of bread with cheese after spreading it with mayonnaise. Stack on top of the bread tater tots, then slam the bread down with a fork. Roll up firmly and serve with pickles and small hot dogs on the side. Slice into four or five pieces.

3. Ranch dressing is a great accompaniment.

119.   MACKEREL PRESSED SUSHI (SABA OSHIZUSHI)

PREP TIME: 40 mins
COOK TIME: 40 mins
TOTAL TIME: 1 hr 20 mins

INGREDIENTS

- 2 rice cooker cup of uncooked Japanese short-grain rice
- 1 frozen marinated mackerel fillet
- 6 shsio leaves
- 4 Tbsp Kikkoman® Seasoned Rice Vinegar
- Homemade Sushi Vinegar Seasonings
- 4 Tbsp rice vinegar
- 2 Tbsp sugar
- 1 tsp kosher or sea salt

INSTRUCTIONS

1. Gather all of the ingredients before starting the cooking process.

2. Use a rice cooker cup to measure out the rice and rinse it under cold water by gently massaging the rice with your hands in a circle motion. Drain the starchy water from the rice after it has been submerged in it for a few minutes. Rinse and re-rinse until the water clears up.

3. The water should be able to soak the rice for 20-30 minutes at a time.

4. Take 10 minutes to thoroughly drain the water. Do your best to shake off any

remaining water if you are pressed for time. Place the rice in the rice cooker after removing it from the bag.

5. Prepare "Sushi Rice" by adding 2 cups of water (or slightly less if "Sushi Rice" is not an option) and then starting the cooking process. Use less water than you would normally since you will season the rice after it has been cooked if you don't have a rice cooker. Then follow my instructions for making rice in an Instant Pot or a conventional pot on the stovetop instead.

6. With a rice scooper or paddle, fluffing the rice is the final step. If you are using a big bowl, be sure to wet it with water first to prevent the rice from sticking to the oke/hangiri. Cool rice faster by spreading it out evenly in the sushi oke after it's been cooked.

7. Make homemade sushi vinegar or Kikkoman® Seasoned Rice Vinegar and stir it into the heated rice while it's still hot. You have complete control over the dosage. A rice paddle can help you separate the rice grains by cutting them at a 45-degree angle. You'll need a fan to keep the rice glossy and prevent it from going mushy as it cools.

8. In between each slice, carefully turn the rice. Prevent the rice from cooling completely before repeating this step. A moist cloth or paper towel can be used to keep the rice from drying out before cooking.

9. For Mackerel Preparation

10. Cut the marinated mackerel fillet in half lengthwise once it has been opened and defrosted.

11. You may butterfly the fillet by starting from the long edge you just cut. As a visual aid, please check out the accompanying video. Repeat the other half of it.

12. For a great char taste, carefully sear the skin on a ceramic dish using a kitchen torch.

13. Making pressed sushi is a simple process

14 Tbsp Kikkoman® Seasoned Rice Vinegar, prepared as directed, and water in a small basin (or rice vinegar). Your hands will not adhere to the rice if you dampen them.

14. Using the bottom foundation and side pieces, construct the Oshibako mold to leave the top open. Vinegar water can be used to keep the rice from sticking to the surface.

15. Put the skin side down of the mackerel fillet on the bottom. The fillet should be sliced in half if it's larger than the box, and any gaps filled in.

16. Atop the mackerel, place shiso leaves.

17. Continue adding rice from one side to the other. Use your fingers to fill the corners and attempt to maintain the rice level even across the dish.

18. Fill the mold to the rim with rice, if required.

19. Use the mold's top piece to firmly push down on the rice.

20. Once you've turned 180 degrees, press down firmly with your entire body weight once more.

21. It's time to do a little mold flipping. Slide down the mold's walls.

22. This item can be disassembled. Use a knife to separate the fish from the top piece if it's stuck. Make a slit in the sidewall and insert the bottom piece.

23. It is currently on the bottom section of the oshizushi. Detach the bottom piece by inserting a knife.

24. Cut each side of the oshizushi into three pieces. Garnish with pickled ginger before serving. For a second piece of mackerel, you may do the same thing. Before producing the second batch, wash and wet the mold. Instead of cleaning every time, you may wrap your food in plastic.

120.   INARI SUSHI

PREP TIME: 30 mins
TOTAL TIME: 30 mins

INGREDIENTS

- For Sushi Rice
- 2 rice cooker cup rice
- 1½ cup of water
- 1 piece kombu
- 4 Tbsp rice vinegar
- 2 Tbsp sugar
- 1 tsp kosher or sea salt
- For Inari Sushi
- 1 tbsp toasted white sesame seeds
- 12 Inari age
- For Garnish
- sushi ginger
- 5 shiso leaves

INSTRUCTIONS

1. In order to Prepare Sushi Rice
2. Gather all of the ingredients before starting the cooking process. Make sushi rice in advance.
3. Make circular motions with your fingertips as you wash the rice with your fingers. Rinse many times before the water is clear. To remove any remaining water, strain through a fine-mesh sieve.
4. After draining the rice, place it in the rice cooker pot and fill it up to just under the 3-cup mark with water. If you have a "Sushi Rice" setting in your rice cooker, pour water to the line. Let rice soak in water for 20 to 30 minutes before cooking, then remove kombu and begin cooking. For those who don't own a rice cooker, you can follow the recipe in an Instant Pot or heavy bottomed pot on the stove.
5. To prepare sushi vinegar, combine vinegar, sugar, and salt in a small dish and stir until smooth. The sugar should be thoroughly dissolved after 30-40 seconds in the microwave. Instead, warm the sushi vinegar over low heat.
6. Remove the kombu from the rice and set it aside to cool. If you're using a wooden sushi oke (also known as a hangiri), wet it thoroughly and then dry it thoroughly. Cooked rice should be transferred to the sushi oke, a big dish, or a baking sheet coated with parchment paper when it has cooled. The rice will cool more quickly if it is spread out evenly.
7. Slowly drizzle sushi vinegar over the rice while it is still hot. Keep it at room temperature or lukewarm at most. To include the sushi vinegar mixture and separate the rice bits, use a rice paddle to gently "slice" the rice at a 45-degree angle. The rice will turn mushy if you stir or mix it, so don't do it. Using a paddle fan or similar form of fan, rapidly fan the rice while slicing it. This reduces the temperature of the rice and removes the extra moisture. Fanning enhances the rice's appearance and prevents it from getting soft. A moist cloth (or paper towel) can be

used to keep the sushi rice at room temperature for a few hours.

8. For the Making of Inari Sushi

9. Prepare to create Inari Sushi, shall we? The inari age may be found in the refrigerator.

10. Gently "slice" the sushi rice to include the sesame seeds. Cut the sushi rice in half (make 3 Inari sushi pieces with every quarter of sushi rice).

11. Inari ages may be drained and the juice/cooking liquid can be saved. Place a tiny handful of sushi rice (about 14 cups) in the palm of your hands to moisten them.

12. Shape the sushi rice into an oval. ' Repeat with the remaining sushi rice. 12 rice balls should be possible.

13. Carefully separate the skin from the bottom of the Inari age pockets (be gentle as the skin is thin). On the top, make a fold outward from the skin.

14. Inari age should be stuffed with every rice ball you can find. The sushi rice should be loaded to the brim to give it a smooth and round appearance on the two corners when served.

15. Fold both corners of the Inari age inward to seal the age's end..

16. Then seal the rice ball by folding the remaining edges inward. Continue with the remainder of Inari's life by placing the seam side down.

17. Kansai-style: Inari Sushi can be decorated with brightly colored toppings in this manner. Keep the top of the bag open & tuck the edges of the Inari age into the pocket for a lovely smooth round-edged. The top is yours to adorn as you choose. Cooked salmon flake and egg crepe (kinshi tamago) were combined with cucumber slices in this dish.

18. Room temperature is ideal for serving Inari Sushi. Serve it with shiso and sushi ginger as garnishes.

TO RETAIN

While the leftovers can be stored for many hours in a cool location, they should be consumed as soon as possible. They'll keep for up to a day in the fridge.If possible, refrigerate in an airtight container or on a platter wrapped with a thick kitchen towel for the best results. In this method, the food is kept chilled and safe, but the cold air in the refrigerator does not cause the rice to harden.

121. TERIYAKI CHICKEN SUSHI BURRITO (VEGAN)

INGREDIENTS

- 1 cup of sushi rice
- 1/4 cup of rice vinegar
- 1/4 cup of sugar
- 1 tsp. salt
- 1 tsp. vegetable oil
- 2 tsp. sesame seeds, optional
- 2–3 thin pineapple spears
- 1 pkg. vegan chicken strips
- 1 cup of teriyaki sauce
- 1 sheet nori

INSTRUCTIONS

1. The rice should be cooked according to the instructions on the packet. Pour in the vinegar, sugar, salt, vegetable oil, and sesame seeds and stir well.For at least 30 minutes, allow it cool before serving.

2. Pour the teriyaki sauce over the pineapple spears and vegan chicken in a shallow bowl.

Set aside for at least 31 minutes to let the flavors blend.

3. Use a sushi mat or plastic wrap to lay down the nori sheet lengthwise with the dull side up. A 1-inch strip at the top of the sheet should be left uncovered by a layer of rice.

4. Layer on top of each other: Pineapple and vegan chicken; carrots, bell pepper, and avocado. The sheet should be rolled up from the bottom up. Seal the roll by moistening the nori strip at the top with water.

122. INSIDE-OUT SUSHI ROLLS

INGREDIENTS

- 50g Thai fragrant long grain rice
- 1 tsp rice vinegar
- 1 large cucumber, peeled into 10 ribbons, core discarded
- 100g soft cheese
- 200g smoked salmon, sliced
- 1 tsp wasabi paste
- For the dipping sauce
- 3 tbsp light soy sauce
- ½ tsp freshly grated ginger

METHOD

1. Cook the rice in 150 ml of cold water in a saucepan. Cook for 10 minutes with a lid partially on, at a low simmer.

2. take from the heat, cover, & and allow it to rest for 5 minutes. Pour the mixture onto a platter and put it in the fridge to chill down completely before serving.

3. Spread out the cucumber slices on a big piece of paper. Using a kitchen towel, pat the ribbons dry, then sprinkle a little

amount of soft cheese over each of them. Make a slit through the middle. Every end should have a slice of salmon on it, with approximately an inch of empty space on the other side. The salmon should be dotted with a little amount of wasabi, then a thin covering of rice. Start at the salmon end and roll-up.

4. Serve the sushi rolls with a dressing made from the following ingredients: Serve at once.

5. See more recipes for healthy snacks.

123. KIMBAP (KOREAN SUSHI ROLLS)

Prep: 30 mins
Cook: 8 mins
Total: 38 mins

INGREDIENTS

- For the Rice:
- 2 cup of cooked short-grain white rice
- 2 tsp sesame oil
- 2 tsp kosher salt
- For the Filling:
- 1 medium carrot, peeled and julienned
- Kosher salt, as need
- 1 medium cucumber, peeled, seeded, and julienned
- 2 large eggs, beaten
- 4 sheets dried nori
- Optional: 8 ounces cooked beef bulgogi
- 1 package frozen spinach, cooked and squeezed dry
- 1/2 cup of pickled raBowles, drained and julienned
- Optional: 12 ounces imitation crab

PREPARE

1. Gather the materials.
2. In a mixing bowl, combine the rice, sesame oil, and salt. The combination can be saved for later.
3. Stir-fry the carrot in a nonstick skillet over a high heat for 2 or 3 minutes, then Take from the bowl and set aside. Keep a portion aside for later use.
4. Stir-fry the cucumber for 2 or 3 minutes, then remove it from the pan and set it aside. Keep a portion for later.
5. Eggs in a small dish, whisked to a froth For one minute, cook the eggs in a flat omelet in a nonstick skillet.
6. After a minute on one side, gently turn the burger over and finish cooking it for a further 30 seconds.
7. The omelet is ready to be sliced into long pieces when it is removed from the pan. Keep a portion for later.
8. Using a rolling pin, flatten the Kimbap.
9. Lay a piece of dried seaweed shiny side down on a bamboo sushi roller or an aluminum foil sheet.
10. Leave the top third of the seaweed exposed and spread roughly half a cup of the cooked rice on it. The rice will not adhere to your hands if you have a bowl of water nearby to wet them, which will assist seal the rolls.
11. The bulgogi should be laid down approximately a third of the way up from the bottom of the seaweed, if you're using it. Roll out a long piece of meat horizontally and remember that too much stuffing might make the rolls difficult to handle or cut.
12. Add a quarter of each filling: carrots, spinach, cucumber, raBowles, egg, and imitation crabmeat, if using.
13. Firmly push down on the contents to hold them in place as you securely roll from the bottom
14. , much as you would when rolling a sleeping bag.
15. As you continue to roll, lower the roll toward the end of the bamboo mat. Apply a tiny quantity of water to the top seam of the roll to seal it.
16. Assemble the remaining dried seaweed sheets in the same manner. Before serving, place the rolls in the refrigerator.
17. Serve with 7 to 8 pieces cut from each roll. Enjoy.

124.   CHICKEN TERIYAKI RECIPE

INGREDIENTS

- 2 Tbs. Soy sauce
- 2 Tbs. Mirin
- 2 Tbs. Sake
- 1 Tbs. Sugar
- 1 tsp. Fresh ginger juice, grated garlic or finely chopped green onion
- 2 chicken thighs boneless, skin on
- 1 Tbs. Cooking oil

INSTRUCTIONS

1. Add the soy sauce, miring, sake, sugar, and ginger/garlic/green onion juice to a small mixing bowl and stir well. Set away for later.
2. Add cooking oil to a medium-sized pan and stir to coat. After 7 to 8 minutes in a heated skillet, remove from heat when the skin is golden brown and crispy.

3. Turn the chicken over & cook for a further 2 to 3 minutes, or until the meat is well cooked.

4. After removing the chicken from the pan, wipe the skillet clean with a paper towel to remove any remaining oil.

5. Heating to medium-low temperature. For 3.5 minutes or until it thickens, add the teriyaki sauce to the skillet.

6. Stir in the cooked chicken to the skillet and heat through, then turn the heat down to medium-low and stir in the sauce until well combined. Let it simmer for a few minutes.

7. 3 to 5 minutes of cooling time is recommended before serving this dish.

8. If you want to serve with chopsticks, cut the chicken into bite-sized pieces.

9. Serve the chicken with the leftover sauce overheated short-grain rice, soba noodles, or salad greens.

125. QUINOA AVOCADO SUSHI

Prep Time 30 mins
Cook Time 15 mins
Total Time 45 mins

INGREDIENTS

- 3 sheets of Nori, sushi paper
- bamboo rolling mat
- plastic wrap
- 1 cup of Quinoa
- 1 1/3 cup of water
- 1/2 cup of rice vinegar
- 2 tbsp sugar
- 2 tsp salt
- 1 ripe California Avocado, pitted, peeled and sliced
- 1/2 cup of oil, drained
- 3 strips of bacon, crispy
- For the Spicy Mayo:
- 2 tbsp Japanese Mayo
- 2 tsp Sriracha Hot Sauce
- dash of Sesame Oil

INSTRUCTIONS

1. For Quinoa, use the following:

2. In order to eliminate any soap residue, rinse the quinoa in a bowl of lukewarm water. Mix up water and quinoa and bring to a boil in an oven-safe pan.Before it reaches a boil, turn the heat up to high and whisk often. Cook for 12-15 minutes on low heat with a lid on.

3. Meanwhile, combine the vinegar, sugar, and salt in a small saucepan and bring to a simmer. It's time to dissolve the sugar and salt in the water, turn off the heat and allow the mixture to cool completely. When the quinoa is done cooking, scoop it into a bowl using a wooden spoon. (Avoid using a metal dish; the vinegar will react badly with metal). Toss quinoa with vinegar mixture before folding it in. Reheat the quinoa, if necessary.

4. When it comes to the Sushi Roll,

5. The bamboo mat should be placed on a level surface, with a layer of plastic wrap on top, followed by a sheet of Nori.

6. Spread the cooled quinoa evenly over the Nori using the back of a wooden spoon (approximately a 1/4" thick). Leave a sliver of Nori exposed at the end furthest away from you, approximately a quarter inch.

7. A few pieces of sun dried tomato and a few slices of crispy bacon should be placed on top of the quinoa (the side nearest to you).

8. Lift the end of the mat and roll it carefully over the ingredients, pushing a little to ensure even coverage. To complete a roll, roll it forward. Continue with the rest of the ingredients.
9. To cut into 1" pieces, use a moist knife and a sharp one.
10. If you're using Spicy Mayo, follow these instructions.
11. Small bowl: combine the Japanese Mayo with Sriracha and sesame oil. Prepare sushi rolls by drizzling the sauce on top of them, or serve it as a dip.

NUTRITION

There are 251kcal in this meal, with 28 grams of carbohydrates, 7.5 grams of protein, 12.4 grams of fat, and 5.7 grams of cholesterol. There are also 1059.4 milligrams of sodium and 4.5 grams of sugar.

126. SABAZUSHI – MACKEREL SUSHI WRAPPED IN KOMBU

INGREDIENTS

- MARINATED KOMBU
- 4 sheets of shiraita-konbu
- 108g of rice vinegar
- 24g of sugar
- SUSHI RICE
- 250g of sushi rice
- 300ml of water
- 1 small piece of kombu, approx. 3x3cm
- SUSHI VINEGAR (FOR 500G COOKED RICE)
- 30ml of rice vinegar
- 8g of salt
- 18g of sugar
- 1 small piece of kombu
- TO CURE THE MACKEREL
- 2 large mackerel fillets
- 1 tbsp of sugar
- 1 tbsp of salt
- MACKEREL MARINADE
- 40g of sugar
- 270g of rice vinegar
- 41g of usukuchi soy sauce
- 5g of kombu
- TO SERVE
- 20g of pickled myoga
- 16g of tobiko

METHOD

1. The first step is to marinade the kombu. Before the sugar completely dissolves, combine the vinegar and sugar in a dish and whisk well. Overnight, soak the kombu sheets in the marinade before serving.
2. For best results, let it the rice sit for a few minutes before cooking.Use your fingers to stir the rice before the water becomes milky white. Return the rice to the bowl after draining in a colander. Before the water is clear, repeat this cleaning and draining operation four or five times.
3. a pound and a half of rice
4. A dish of rice should be filled with water and left to soak for 20 minutes at this stage
5. In a saucepan, combine the rice, 300ml of water, and a tiny piece of kombu. Stir to combine. Using a high-heat pan, cook for 5 minutes with the lid on, then lower the heat to medium and continue cooking for another 21 minutes.
6. In a saucepan, combine all of the ingredients except the sugar and salt and

boil until the sugar and salt have dissolved. Vinegar should be kept warm.

7. Gather your ingredients in a bowl and stir the rice thoroughly. Add the sushi vinegar to the rice while it's still hot, being careful not to break too many grains with the edge of the paddle.

8. Transfer the rice to a dish or tray, cover with a wet kitchen towel, and allow to cool for a few minutes once the vinegar has been integrated.

9. Begin prepping the mackerel by placing each fillet skin side down on the cutting board. Bones should protrude from the centre of a fillet with your finger. Every side of the bone line should have an incision made down the length of the bone.

10. Remove the boney meat from the fillet and dispose of it.

11. 20 minutes before it's lovely and hard, sprinkle the fillet with a little sugar and leave aside. Dry the fillets with kitchen paper after washing them. Wash and dry with kitchen paper after salting and setting aside for 30 minutes.

12. Add the mackerel fillets to a shallow bowl and mix the marinade ingredients together. One hour of marinating is plenty.

13. Take the mackerel from the marinade and pat it dry before serving it

14. Gently remove the fillet by pinching the skin on the head side and pulling it apart.

15. Maintaining your knife at an angle to the chopping board, carefully cut away at the fillet's top to flatten it. The trims will be used to patch in any holes in the roll.

16. Line a bamboo mat with cling film and place the cling film skin-side down on the bamboo mat. The trimmings may be used to fill up any holes in the mackerel flesh so that you end up with a lovely uniform rectangle.

17. Take around 100 grams of rice and wet your hands. Spread it out equally on top of the mackerel. Keep the mackerel in place as you wrap the rice and mackerel together.

18. Once again, use the sushi mat to push down on the marinated kombu sheets to cover the mackerel and rice.

19. Then cut each roll into eight pieces, arrange on a serving platter and serve with a wet knife between each slice. Make a second roll using the remaining ingredients.

20. Use little bits of myoga to decorate the sushi. Finally, garnish the dish with fresh nasturtium leaves and tobiko.

127.   SALMON SKIN ROLL
INGREDIENTS

- Sushi Rice
- 1 1/2 cup of short-grain sushi rice
- 1 1/2 cup of water
- 1 tbsp rice wine vinegar
- 1 1/2 tsp sugar
- 1/4 tsp sesame oil
- 1 tbsp sesame seeds
- Salmon Skin Roll
- 1/2 pound salmon skin
- 1/2 tsp salt
- 1 tbsp tamari (or soy sauce)
- 1 tbsp brown sugar
- 2 tbsp mirin
- 2 mini cucumbers, julienned
- 1 avocado, sliced
- 1 bunch watercress
- 4 to 6 sheets nori

DIRECTIONS

1. Rinse the rice twice or three times under cold water to eliminate part of the starch. Before serving, leave rice to rest for a few minutes after it's been cooked in a rice cooker or on low heat (about 10 to 12 minutes on the stovetop).

2. Using a big bowl, fill it up with rice. Pour the vinegar, sugar, and sesame oil into a small bowl and then add the rice and sesame seeds. To season the rice, gently mix it (so as not to crush the rice grains).

3. The skin of the salmon can be rolled into a sushi

4. Rinse and dry the salmon skins well. Bake for 4 to 7 minutes on a parchment-lined sheet pan over high heat until crispy and golden. Cut into strips after cooling on a wire rack after removing from the oven.

5. Mix tamari, brown sugar, and mirin in a small pot and bring to a boil. Low-heat cooking is the way to go when you've reached half-thickness of the original sauce and the sugar has dissolved.

6. Sushi is ready to be served. Spread a thin layer of nori on top of the rice, then cover it with another piece of nori. One side of the plate should have salmon skins, cucumber, avocado, and cress. Slice into bite-sized pieces when the roll has been securely sealed. Drizzle the pieces with eel sauce at the end. Once the rice is laid down on the nori, sesame seeds are sprinkled and then the nori is flipped onto a sheet of clingfilm so that the contents may be added to the nori-side and rolled up.

128. SMOKED SALMON AND AVOCADO SUSHI

INGREDIENTS

- salmon uramaki:
- 250g of sushi rice
- 2 tbsp of rice vinegar
- 1 tsp caster sugar
- 4 sheets of nori seaweed, square
- 1/4 cucumber, sliced into thin strips
- 1 handful of coriander leaves
- 1/2 avocado, small and ripe, thinly sliced
- 4 tbsp of mascarpone
- 200g of smoked salmon
- to serve:
- 2 tsp wasabi paste
- 3 tbsp of soy sauce

HOW TO PREPARE

1. In a large bowl, add the rice. Using your hands, swirl the rice in the water until it becomes hazy. After draining the water, continue the process until the water is nearly clear – about 4–5 times.

2. Drain the water and add 285ml of water to the pan after it is nearly clear. Add a pinch of salt, cover, and come to a boil. Bring water to a boil, lower the heat, and simmer for 10 minutes.Immediately remove from heat and allow it cool before serving. For an additional 10 minutes, keep the cover on the pot, then remove.

3. During the time the rice is cooking, combine the rice wine vinegar with caster sugar and stir until the sugar is completely dissolved. In a large bowl, fluff the cooked rice. Before adding the sushi vinegar, allow the mixture to cool for a few minutes.

4. Your bamboo mat is the first step. The mat should be covered with cling film, with a nori sheet placed on top of the cling film. When the rice is moistened, press a quarter of it onto two-thirds of the nori, leaving about a 2cm strip exposed. Rice-side down on the nori sheet, flip it over.

5. Spread a little mascarpone in a line at the base of the nori that hasn't been coated with rice. Avocado, cucumber, and coriander are arranged in a ring on top.

6. Roll the nori that hasn't been wrapped in rice into a Bowle and use the bamboo mat to push it together tightly.

7. Spread a little mascarpone on the sushi roll before serving it (to ensure the smoked salmon will attach). Flatten the salmon with your hands as you lay it over the sticky rice.

8. Using a very sharp knife, cut the meat into approximately 2cm circles. Add Any extra wasabi or soy sauce can be put on the side.

129.   SHRIMP TEMPURA ROLL

Prep Time25 minutes
Cook Time15 minutes
Total Time40 minutes

INGREDIENTS

- For the sushi rice:
- 2 cup of uncooked sushi rice
- 2 cup of water
- 2 tbsp rice vinegar
- 2 tbsp sugar
- 1/2 tsp salt
- For the sushi rolls:
- sheets of nori
- pre-cooked tempura shrimp
- strips of cucumber
- slices of avocado
- 2 tbsp black

INSTRUCTIONS

1. Rinse the rice with running water in a colander.

2. Over high heat, combine the rice with the 2 cups of water in a medium saucepan. Cover and bring to a boil. The water should boil before the heat is reduced to a simmer. Allow the pot to rest for ten minutes with the lid on after removing it from the heat.

3. In a small dish, combine the rice vinegar, sugar, and salt; microwave for 20-30 seconds until warm. In a large bowl, combine the vinegar mixture with the rice. To get a complete blend, give the ingredients a good stir. Wait until the rice has cooled down to room temperature before serving.

4. Spread 1/3-1/2 cup of rice on the nori's surface, going all the way to its edges, and pressing it down firmly. If your fingers are somewhat wet, this is the best way to do it.

5. Invert a sushi mat so that the seaweed side is up and place a piece of plastic wrap over the rice-covered nori.

6. Lay down two shrimp, two cucumber strips, and two avocado slices on the nori.

7. Roll the sushi tightly starting with the edge of the mat closest to the shrimp mixture.

8. Sesame seeds, about 2 tablespoons, should be pressed into the sushi rice.

9. Slice the sushi and serve it right away with a sharp knife.

130. DRAGON ROLL WITH SHRIMP TEMPURATOTAL: 45 MIN

Active: 45 min

INGREDIENTS

- Tempura:
- 2 cold large eggs, lightly beaten
- 1 2/3 cup of ice water
- 2 cup of all-purpose flour
- 3 tbsp cornstarch
- Canola oil, for frying
- 4 extra-large shrimp, peeled and deveined
- Kosher salt
- Spicy Mayonnaise:
- 1/2 cup of Japanese mayonnaise, such as Kewpie brand, or regular mayonnaise
- 2 tbsp sriracha
- 2 tsp dark soy sauce
- Zest and juice of 1/2 lime
- Assembly:
- 2 sheets toasted nori
- 1 cup of cooked sushi rice, warm
- 1 Persian cucumber, peeled
- 2 to 4 ounces tobiko wasabi
- Freshly grated wasabi and pickled ginger
- Soy sauce

DIRECTIONS

1. A deep-fry thermometer and a bamboo sushi mat are required tools.
2. For the tempura, use the following as a guide: A large bowl should be placed inside an ice-filled larger bowl before the top bowl is cold to the touch. The eggs and ice water should be added and whisked briskly until they are incorporated. Only a few quick stirs are required after sifting the flour and cornstarch over the wet ingredients. Even if the batter contains some lumps, it's just OK.) Overworking the gluten in the wheat will cause the batter to be heavy.)
3. A deep, heavy-bottomed pot with a 4-inch-thick layer of oil should be heated to 360 degrees Fahrenheit. Paper towels and a slotted spoon are needed for this task.
4. Each shrimp tail should be cut a few times along the internal length to relax, straighten out, and stop curling. Indulge in a pinch of salt
5. To coat the shrimp, dip them into the batter. Transfer to the heated oil with care, carefully swirling the oil to ensure equal cooking on all sides. For 2 to 3 minutes, cook the shrimp until they are golden brown and crispy on the outside. Sprinkle salt on paper towels as soon as you take it from the pan using a slotted spoon.
6. When it comes to the spicy mayonnaise, combine the mayonnaise, lime zest and juice and sriracha in a medium-sized bowl. Taste and adjust the seasonings. Remove from consideration.
7. Plastic wrap should be tightly wrapped around a bamboo sushi rolling mat for the sushi roll. Rolls won't cling to the mat if you do this.
8. Wrap the bamboo mat with a nori sheet, shiny side up. After carefully pressing and spreading 1/2 cup sushi rice into a shape that matches the nori, leave a half-inch border around the borders.
9. Starting at the end closest to you, spread a thin coating of spicy mayonnaise on the rice. Lay two cucumber slices on top of the spicy mayo, and then add another drizzle.

The shrimp tempura should be topped with two pieces of it. Tuck the clean edge of the nori beneath the fillings to thoroughly encapsulate them. Gently press the bamboo mat on top of the roll, curling your fingers as you go, to secure it.

10. It is best to cut the roll into eight even pieces with a serrated knife, but do not split them. The pieces should be slightly overlapping on the plate. Tobiko wasabi is topped on each piece of sushi and the roll is drizzled with spicy mayonnaise.

11. Using the remaining ingredients, continue to roll the dough.Soy sauce and ginger pickle sauce should be offered with the rolls as a condiment.

COOK'S MENTION:

Keep the batter ingredients as cold as possible to ensure the lightest, crispiest tempura possible.

131.   DRAGON ROLL RECIPE

Prep Time: 15 minutes
Cook Time: 45 minutes
Total Time: 1 hour

INGREDIENTS

- For the Sushi Rice
- 1 ½ cup of sushi rice (uncooked short-grain sushi rice)
- 1 ½ cup of water
- 2 tbspsushi vinegar (or mixing 1 tbsp rice vinegar, 1/2 tbsp sugar)
- For the Dragon Roll
- 8 shrimp tempura
- 1/2 cucumber
- 2 avocados
- 2 sheets nori
- Lemon optional
- Optional for Serving
- unagi sauce
- masago

INSTRUCTIONS

1. Preparation of Sushi Rice and the rest of the food
2. Rinse sushi rice. Rice and water should be added next. Move the meal to a large dish once it cools. Add sushi vinegar while the mixture is still hot (or the mixture of rice vinegar and sugar).
3. The rice may be cooked while the cucumbers are sliced. If necessary, prepare shrimp tempura. Baked shrimp tempura from frozen was all I had to work with, so I followed the directions and incorporated them in the sushi.
4. Make the Dragon Rolls.
5. Plastic wrap should be laid over the bamboo mat before it is placed on a level surface.
6. Split the nori sheet in half with a pair of scissors after folding it in half.
7. Place the glossy side of half of the nori sheet down on the bamboo mat.
8. Then, using your hands, distribute about 3/4 cup of cooked rice over the nori sheet. Dip your hands in Tezu vinegar water* to keep them from sticking.
9. Make a U-turn, so the rice is on the bottom.
10. On top of the nori, place two pieces of shrimp tempura and two strips of cucumber.
11. Lift the bamboo mat's edge up and over the filling with your thumbs below the mat.
12. It's time to tighten the bamboo mat by rolling the surface away from you. You'll get there if you keep going till the finish. Get rid

of the bamboo mat and the plastic wrapping. Place the rolls in a separate container and set aside.

13. Make the Avocado Topping and put it all together.

14. Cut the avocado in half lengthwise. The pit and skin can then be removed.

15. Each component should be cut into half-moon-sized pieces. Slice it into extremely thin pieces so that the toppings may be shaped more quickly.

16. It's time to get down to business!

17. Using a large knife and avocado slices, top your sushi roll.

18. It's important that the avocado layer covers your roll correctly. Then cover the sushi mat with plastic wrap and press down firmly. Gently squeeze the avocado into a roll form.

19. Using the plastic wrap, remove the mat from the roll, but save the mat itself. Cut the roll into bite-sized pieces using a sharp knife. Start by taking the plastic wrap off of the meat.

132. KING PRAWN NIGIRI

PREP TIME 20 mins
COOK TIME 5 mins

INGREDIENTS

- 6 Large King Prawns (Shrimp) - raw, deveined and peeled
- 1 tbsp Ginger Paste
- 1 tbsp Sea Salt Flakes
- 200 g Cooked Sushi Rice
- 12 Chive Stems - optional garnish

INSTRUCTIONS

1. Turn on a full pot of water.

2. Small skewers or cocktail sticks can be used to skewer six Large King Prawns along their whole length. This will prevent them from curving while they cook.

3. To remove the remaining vein, cut the front of each shrimp with a sharp knife.

4. Salt and Ginger Paste should be added to a small saucepan half-full of the now-boiled water. Bring the liquid to a rolling boil.

5. Cook for 2 minutes before adding the king prawns to the pot.

6. Prawns should be rinsed under cold water once the pan has been taken from the heat. Let the prawns cool before drying them.

7. Dish out the cooked sushi rice, around 200 grams.

8. Using cold water, moisten your hands and shape the rice into a long and thin rectangle. Cut the rectangle in half twice with a sharp knife. Make 12 portions by dividing each of those quarters into three equal halves. If you've changed the recipe's serving size from the customary 12, work in portions.

9. Pick up a piece of rice with your wet hands and squirt some water over it. Make sure the rice is tightly packed together using your hands, and then gently round the rectangle's corners. To mimic the prawns' slightly curved shape, I bend my knees slightly.

10. The remaining pieces of rice should be treated in the same way. Remove from consideration.

11. Remove the skewer from each of the cooled prawns.

12. Remove the tails and legs of prawns and place them on top of each rice piece.

13. Every 12 Chive Stems, tie a knot and clip the long ends using scissors. (optional)

14. Serve the prawns with a chive knot on top.

133. EGG AND EDAMAME BROWN RICE BOWL

Prep: 45 mins
Cook: 5 mins
Total: 50 mins

INGREDIENTS

- 2 cup of cooked Rice
- 4 scallions, thinly sliced
- ½ cup of edamame
- 1 tsp red wine vinegar
- Kosher salt and freshly ground black pepper
- 3 tbsp olive oil
- 4 large eggs
- 1 avocado, chopped
- Optional:
- Sriracha hot sauce
- Thai basil

DIRECTIONS

1. Combine the rice, edamame, and scallions in a small dish with the vinegar. Season to taste with salt and pepper
2. Medium-high heat works best for heating oil in a nonstick skillet. Eggs should be cracked into a pan and seasoned with salt and pepper before they begin to set around the edges, approximately one minute. For runny yolks, fry the eggs for 30 seconds after flipping them.

134. EASY AVOCADO EGG ROLLS

Prep Time: 5 minutes
Cook Time: 5 minutes
Total Time: 10 minutes

INGREDIENTS

- 3 avocados halved, peeled and seeded
- 1/2 cup of tomatoes diced
- 1/3 cup of diced onion
- 2 tbsp chopped fresh cilantro leaves
- salt and black pepper as need
- Juice of 1 lime
- 12 egg roll wrappers
- 1 cup of vegetable oil for frying
- For the cilantro dipping sauce
- 1/2 cup of fresh cilantro leaves loosely packed
- 1/4 cup of sour cream
- 1 tbsp mayonnaise
- 1 jalapeno seeded and deveined
- Juice of 1 lime
- 1 clove garlic
- Salt and freshly ground black pepper as need

INSTRUCTIONS

1. Add all of the ingredients for the cilantro dipping sauce to the bowl of a food processor and process until smooth. Add salt and pepper to your preference. Remove from consideration.
2. Medium-high heat a big pan or Dutch oven with the vegetable oil.
3. Gently mash avocados with a fork in a medium bowl. Sprinkle with salt and pepper and gently toss with the diced onions, tomatoes, cilantro, lime juice, etc.

4. Place the avocado mixture in the middle of each wrapper. Alternatively, one at a time. Wrap the filling in the bottom of the wrapper, tucking in the sides as you go. Do not stop rolling until the wrapper's top has been r everyed. The edges of the wrapper should be rubbed with water and pressed to seal. Before you're through, go through the rest of the wrappers.

5. Place the egg rolls in batches and cook until they are golden brown and crispy, about two to three minutes. Pat dry on a paper towel-lined plate.

6. Serve with dipping sauce as soon as possible. Enjoy!

135.   CHICKEN AND EGG SUSHI ROLL BENTO

Prep Time 30 mins
Cooking Time 5 mins

INGREDIENTS

- rice
- egg, hardboiled
- 2 to 3 pieces chicken sausage
- 5 sheets nori (dried seaweed)
- 1 sheet nori (dried seaweed)
- 1 piece cheese
- Japanese mayonnaise
- cabbage salad
- broccoli

HOW TO COOK

1. Separate the yolk from your hard-boiled egg. Mix 2 cups of rice with one egg yolk. Before the rice becomes golden, mix. Divide into five equal halves. Save the white of the egg for salad.

2. One portion of the egg yolk rice may be scooped into the bag using a sandwich bag. Form into a long rice roll when you've packed it all up (about the thickness of a pinky finger). Take a roll out of the package and place it on the counter. Remove from consideration. Repeat to produce five long rice rolls with egg yolks.

3. Place an egg yolk rice roll on the edge of a 2" x 8" nori sheet and cover it with nori. Seal the nori around the rice roll with a little water or Japanese mayo. Repeat the process with the remaining four egg yolk rice wraps. Remove from consideration.

4. The ends of your chicken sausages should be trimmed off before cooking. Make a long sausage out of them by putting them all together.

5. CONTINUE READING BELOW THE ADVERTISEMENT

6. Layer your egg yolk rice rolls around the chicken sausage, like a flower. You may bind the pieces together by using Japanese mayonnaise.

7. A thin coating of white rice should cover about three-quarters of a nori sheet. Assemble your chicken sausage flower on top of the nori sheet and white rice, and then coil up. Seal the ends with water or Japanese mayonnaise.

8. Lunchboxes can be stuffed with 1-inch-thick pieces of meat.

9. Fill the remaining space with a salad consisting of broccoli and cabbage.

136. EGG SUSHI ROLL

Prep Time 10 MIN
Cook Time 10 MIN

INGREDIENTS

- 1 cup of prepared sushi rice seasoned with rice wine vinegar
- 2 Eggland's Best eggs (large)
- Pinch of sugar
- Pinch of salt
- 1 tbsp oil
- 1 avocado, sliced or mango
- ½ of a cucumber, cut into long, ¼ wide strips
- 1 carrot, cut into long, ¼ wide strips
- To serve (optional) -
- Sriracha mayo
- Soy sauce
- Pickled ginger
- wasabi

PREPARATION

1. A non-stick pan should be heated to medium-high heat.
2. Add the sugar and salt to the eggs and whisk until smooth.
3. Coat the pan with a few droplets of oil
4. by swirling about in it.
5. After a few more minutes of cooking, add the other half of the egg mixture to the pan and stir. Tilt the bowl so that the egg covers the whole surface. A few more seconds of cooking are needed for the egg to be rolled up and placed in the pan.onds.
6. Re-use the other half of the egg mixture.
7. Slice the tomato (egg roll) into quarters.
8. A nori sheet is laid out on a mat, then the rice and the contents, including the egg, are placed on top of the nori sheet.
9. As you roll, be sure to push hard down on the roll to keep it together.
10. It's best served with sriracha mayo or soy sauce as a condiment.

137. EGGPLANT SUSHI

PREPARATION 45 min
COOKING 30 min

INGREDIENTS

- SUSHI
- 4-5 nori sheets
- 2 cup of sushi rice*
- 3 tbsp rice vinegar
- 1 tbsp maple syrup or sugar
- ½ tsp fine sea salt
- FILLING
- 2 tbsp sesame seeds
- 1½ tsp toasted sesame oil
- 2 tbsp tamari (for GF version) or soy sauce
- 1 tbsp maple syrup
- 4 tsp rice vinegar
- ½ tsp spicy chilli sauce (I used sambal oelek)
- 2 small eggplants / aubergines
- approx. 30 g / 1 oz baby spinach leaves
- 1 carrot, peeled and julienned
- 1 Lebanese cucumber, cored and julienned
- CONDIMENTS
- wasabi
- tamari (for GF version) or soy sauce
- pickled ginger, store-bought or homemade

METHOD

1. The rice is SUSHI RICE

2. Do not stop rinsing sushi rice until the water is completely clear before using. I prefer to rinse in a glass bowl since it's easier for me to tell when it's done.

3. Cover 2 cups of washed rice with 2 cups of water in a medium saucepan with a glass top. Cover the bowl and bring it to a boil. Rice will not be fully cooked if the water is left unattended once it has reached a rolling boil (about 10 minutes). To complete cooking, turn off the heat but don't remove the lid; instead, let the covered pot rest on a warm burner for another 5-10 minutes to finish cooking.

4. Gather your ingredients for a small dish of seasoning by combining rice vinegar, maple syrup, or sugar, and salt. It's up to you how sweet and salty it is.

5. Season the cooked rice with the mixture you produced earlier by gently mixing the seasoning into the rice with a spatula on a large baking sheet (being careful not to squash the grains). Allow the rice to cool fully; if you have the opportunity, you may speed up the cooling process by fanning it.

6. FILLING

7. Sesame seeds should be lightly toasted in a hot pan until fragrant and golden. Use a pestle and mortar to break them up.

8. Combine sesame oil, tamari (or soy sauce), maple syrup, rice vinegar, and sambal oelek in a small basin to make the marinade for the eggplant. Set aside smashed sesame seeds.

9. Using a knife, cut eggplants into 112 cm (0.5") long slices. Remove any bitterness by salting the eggplant slices on both sides and letting them soak for about an hour or so. Remove the salt off the slices and pat them dry.

10. Place the griddle pan over medium-high heat and begin cooking. Pour some olive oil on the pan before sprinkling the eggplant slices on it and letting them cook for a few minutes. To achieve the desired char, grill them for about six minutes on each side.

11. Remove the slices from the heat and let them cool down. It's best to cut each piece into three long strips, then cover them in the marinade (don't throw away the marinade, it makes an excellent dipping sauce).

12. ASSEMBLY

13. Prepare a small basin of water and your sushi mat (either a bamboo mat or a folded kitchen towel). A nori sheet with its glossy side down is placed on top of the mat. You'll need a 1 cm margin at the top of the nori sheet to seal it, so grab some cold sushi rice. With a spoon, push the rice into the mat until it is equally distributed.

14. To make this dish, lay down a long strip of nori sheet with a long line of fresh vegetables along its bottom border, leaving a little room below so that you may fold the nori sheet over the filling.

15. Squeeze hard with both hands while gently rolling the roll on the mat.Six minutes on either side should do the trick.

16. The next step is to brush water on the edge of the roll with your finger in order to seal it. Set the roll aside once you've finished rolling it. The remaining nori sheets can be used to repeat procedures 4 through 6.

17. Cut the sushi rolls into 1 cm slices with a sharp knife once you've rolled all of them. With a side of tamari, pickled ginger, and wasabi (or soy sauce).

NOTES

If you're a novice sushi chef, check out this recipe for detailed instructions.

*You could use brown rice for this, despite the fact that it goes against tradition. For brown rice, use 3 cups of water and cook it in the same manner as white rice.

138.   SPICY EGGPLANT SUSHI

Prep Time 15 minutes
Cook Time 30 minutes
Total Time 45 minutes

INGREDIENTS

- For the Rice
- ⅔ cup of sushi rice
- ¾ cup of + 2 tbsp. water
- ½ tbsp. salt
- ½ tbsp. rice vinegar
- For the Filling
- 2 tbsp. vegetable oil
- 1 garlic clove minced
- 2 tbsp. Asian chili paste
- 1 scallion
- ½ medium eggplant sliced into thin strips
- For Finishing and Serving
- 2 nori sheets
- sesame seeds
- soy sauce or tamari
- wasabi
- pickled ginger

INSTRUCTIONS

1. Rice is ready.
2. Using a sieve, pour the rice into the flowing water and let it soak for 1-2 minutes.
3. Stir in the other ingredients for the rice in a small saucepan and bring to a boil. Continue to simmer for another 21 minutes or more, or until the liquid has been absorbed
4. .Allow it cool for another 10 minutes, covered, before serving.
5. Cook the Eggplants.
6. Set up a medium pan with the oil and bring it to a medium-low simmer. Onion powder and chili paste can be added now. Remove from fire and
7. put aside after a few seconds of cooking.
8. Place the eggplant slices in a single layer. Make sure the beef is fork-tender and well-browned on both sides, which takes approximately 5 minutes each side.
9. Sushi is rolled.
10. Using a pair of scissors, cut roughly a third of the nori sheet's length and discard or store for another dish.
11. Bamboo mats may be used to place one of your sheets on.
12. Keep a small bowl of water beside you at all times. Wet your hands and spread a thin coating of rice over the nori.
13. Make a line of half of your eggplant down the nori's width, approximately an inch from you. Then, along with the eggplant, arrange half of the onion stalks.
14. Roll your filling securely in the bamboo mat and nori end nearest to you. Continue rolling the nori, using the mat to press it tight as you do so.
15. Slice the rolled dough into eight equal pieces. Use the second nori sheet and the leftover rice and filling to repeat the process.
16. Top with sesame seeds and soy sauce or tamari, wasabi, and pickled ginger.

139. SPICY TUNA ROLL

Prep Time: 15 minutes
Total Time: 15 minutes

INGREDIENTS

- For Spicy Tuna
- 360 gramstuna
- 2 tbsp sriracha
- 1 tbsp soy sauce
- 1 tspugar
- 1 tsp toasted sesame oil1scallion
- 2 tbspstobiko (use sesame as an alternative)

STEPS

1. Tuna with a kick.
2. You'll need some green scallions for garnish.
3. Scallion greens, chopped.
4. Chop the tuna into small pieces by slicing it into thin strips and then turning the strips 90 degrees. You may stop here if you like your spicy tuna chunky, or you can keep chopping the tuna until it is smaller. I like to cut up the scallion stems with the tuna and add them to this mixture.
5. Making spicy tuna buns using tuna minced
6. Mix the chopped tuna with the sriracha, soy sauce, sugar, sesame oil, and tobiko in a dish before serving.Refrigerate the mixture until you're ready to use it, then cover and store it.
7. In a glass bowl, combine the tuna and spices.
8. Add a couple tbsp of rice vinegar to a small bowl of water, and you'll have some Tezu in no time.
9. Gunkan
10. The diagram in the headnotes above shows how to cut the nori for the Gunkan.

11. Grab roughly 2 tbsp of rice and wet your hands with the tezu. Do not shatter the individual grains, but gently flatten the rice into a rectangle with your hands.
12. To make spicy tuna gunkan, you'll need to shape sushi rice.
13. To make the gunkan, use the nori strips you cut for the rice rectangles.
14. Making a Gunkan roll by wrapping sushi rice with nori.
15. To make the rice fill out the nori wrapper, press the center of the rice.
16. Using to hold hot tuna indented sushi rice.
17. Every cup of nori should have a dollop of spicy tuna. Add scallion greens as a garnish.
18. The addition of spicy tuna to the gunkan roll
19. Hosomaki
20. The diagram above shows how the nori sheets should be sliced in half for Hosomaki.
21. Place the glossy side of the nori on the bottom edge of a sushi mat.
22. You'll need a tiny amount of rice, so dip your hands in the Tezu first. Working from one side of the nori's top edge, lay the rice in a line. Nori should be left at the top, so be sure to do so.
23. Spread the rice to the bottom edge of the nori with a plucking and pushing motion, if necessary. The rice should not be smashed or smeared.
24. Sushi rice on nori for creating spicy tuna hosomaki.
25. In the lower half of the rice, spread a thin stripe of spicy tuna.
26. Rice and nori topped with spicy tuna.
27. It is important that you roll the spicy tuna hosomaki with the use of a mat to ensure

28. Using a sushi mat to roll out hosomaki sushi.

29. Pull the edge of the mat away from the nori and press the rear of the mat forward so that the seam rolls to the bottom of the mat..

30. Make a roll by pressing three of the roll's sides against the cutting board with your fingers.

31. Pressing the sushi roll's form using a sushi matt is a good idea.

32. To learn how to cut a roll, refer to the notes or watch the video.

33. Uramaki

34. If you're making Uramaki, you'll need to use a sushi mat that's coated with plastic wrap since the rice will adhere to the mat if you don't.

35. A nori sheet and a handful of rice should be placed on the mat's bottom edge. Because there is no need to leave a border, you'll need to use a little more rice than you would for hosomaki.

36. Spread a thin, even layer of rice down the bottom border of the nori, taking care not to shatter the rice as you go.

37. To make a uramaki-style spicy tuna roll, place the rice on nori.

38. Toss the rice with some sesame seeds in a dark brown color.

39. Black sesame seeds are scattered over a bed of rice.

40. A cucumber strip should be positioned in the bottom half of the nori, and the rice should be flipped over.

41. From one end to the other, create a line of spicy tuna.

42. Nori-wrapped sushi with spicy tuna and cucumber.

43. Prior to the rice touching the nori on the opposite side, flip the mat bottom edge up and overfilling.

44. Using a sushi mat to create a spicy tuna roll.

45. To roll the seam to the bottom, pull the mat's edge away from the rice and push the mat's back.

46. To form the roll, gently press the mat on the top, sides, and bottom of the roll.

47. To cut the spicy tuna roll, follow the directions in the headnotes.

140. KANIKAMA SUSHI (NIGIRI)

Prep Time: 15 minutes
Cook Time: 1 hour
Total Time: 1 hour 15 minutes

INGREDIENTS

- For Sushi Rice
- 1 cup of sushi rice short-grain sushi rice
- 1 cup of water
- 1 ½ tbspoptional sushi vinegar or mixing 1 tbsp rice vinegar, 1/2 tbsp sugar, and 1/2 tsp salt
- For Kanikama Sushi
- 8 kanikama sticks
- 1 sheet nori seaweed

INSTRUCTIONS

1. Cooking sushi rice is as simple as washing and adding water to a rice cooker. Once the food has cooled down, move it to a big bowl. Stir in the sushi vinegar while the mixture is still extremely hot (or the mixture of rice vinegar, sugar, and salt).

2. The rice should be shaped into an oval shape approximately 1 12 inches long by taking 3/4 of the cooked rice and doing so. Gently flatten the bottom of the rice by squeezing it. In order to avoid getting your hands stuck, you can dip them in vinegar water.

3. The kanikama sticks should be sliced in half. Every stick should be cut into smaller chunks (about 2 inches).

4. Use your fingers to press down hard enough to secure it to your rice, making sure that it doesn't fall off. You may hold the nigiri sushi with one hand and press it with the other. You can "glue" the crab stick to the rice by sprinkling a small amount of wasabi on top of the rice.

5. Use 1/4-inch strips of seaweed to wrap the nigiri to hold the crab stick in place on the rice.

6. The nigiri is ready to be served. It's time to eat!

NUTRITION

calories 43kcal, 10g carbs, 1g protein, 1g fat, 1g saturated fat, 1mg cholesterol, 4mg sodium, 9mg potassium, 1g fiber, 1g sugar, 1mg calcium, 1mg iron.

141.   EASY PARTY SUSHI ROLLS

INGREDIENT

- 2 sheets nori, halved
- 2 c. prepared Sticky Sushi Rice, divided
- Sesame seeds, as needed, divided
- Roe (Tobiko, flying fish egg), as needed, divided
- 1 large cucumber, sliced, divided
- 1 avocado, peeled, pitted and sliced, divided
- 4 oz. Hy-Vee FishMarket imitation crab meat, divided

DIRECTIONS

1. Turn over a nori sheet and put the shiny side down on a sushi rolling mat. Spread half a cup of rice evenly on the nori with your fingertips wet with water. If desired, top with sesame seeds and serve with roe that has been spooned out. The sesame seed side of the nori should face up.

2. Make a horizontal line across the centre of the sheet with 1/4 of each of the cucumber, avocado, and crab. Keep the contents in place with your fingers while you roll the mat into a tight cylinder, using the mat to form the cylinder. Wrap the meat in plastic and remove it. Continue with the rest of the ingredients.

3. Remove the plastic wrap before serving. Using a pair of scissors, slicing each roll in half, divide each half into three equal pieces. To prevent the knife from sticking, use a wet cloth to wipe it down.

4. TIP:

5. Use a gallon-sized plastic bag to keep your sushi rolling mat clean. Make sushi in the bag; then toss it.

142.   MAKI SUSHI WITH BAKED FISH

Preparation: 40 min.

INGREDIENTS

- 2 ounces sushi-grade salmon
- 1 avocado
- 1 nori seaweed
- 6 ounces cooked sushi rice
- 1 tsp wasabi
- soy sauce (as need)
- 6 ounces ready to cook, skinless mackerel
- salt
- rice flour
- sesame oil (for frying)
- 2 lettuce (such as lollo biondo)
- chili sauce
- black and white sesame seeds (for garnish)

PREPARATION STEPS

1. Remove the pit from the avocado by slicing it in half. A spoon works well for scooping meat from the peel. Slice into quarter-inch wide strips.. Slice the fish into strips of a comparable width.
2. Organize the nori by laying it out on a work area (a plastic-wrapped sushi bamboo mat if available). On top of sushi rice, spread out the nori sheet equally. A 1/4-inch-wide border should be left open at the top of the image. Spread a thin strip of wasabi over the middle of the rice using your finger. Place the avocado slices on top of the Wasabi, then the salmon. Sprinkle a little water on the nori that has been left exposed. The nori should be rolled around the filling from the bottom up. Gently seal the wet edge by pressing it. Cut the salmon wrap into 12 equal-sized portions.
3. Wash and pat dry the mackerel, then cut it into 12 equal pieces. Dredge in rice flour and season with a little salt. In heated sesame oil, cook until golden brown, only a few seconds. Top the salmon wrap with lettuce, then mackerel. Sesame seeds and soy or chilli sauce are excellent dipping accompaniments.

143.   FRESH FRUIT SUSHI

INGREDIENTS

- 1 ½ cup of short-grain rice(300 g)
- 2 cup ofs water(480 mL)
- 3 tbsp sugar
- ¼ tsp salt
- 1 cup of coconut milk(240 mL)
- 1 ½ tsp vanilla
- A VARIETY OF FRUIT
- pineapple
- strawberry
- mango
- kiwi
- 1 pt blackberry(475 g)
- raspberry

PREPARATION

1. Mix the rice, water, sugar, and salt in a medium saucepan. On a low heat, cook the rice for about twenty minutes, or before it has absorbed all of the liquid.
2. Coconut milk and vanilla extract should be added. Moldability is a must. If it's too runny, cook it for a few more minutes.
3. Carve a wide swath of the fruit of your choosing.

4. To thinly slice the mango, use a potato peeler.

5. On a counter top, place a wax paper rectangle on top of a wooden rolling pad.Over the paper, create a 7x5-inch (17x12-cm) rectangle by spreading the rice out to a thickness of about 12 inch (1 centimeter).

6. 3 minutes of toasting 14 cup (25g) coconut shreds.

7. Carefully roll the rice with fruit bits on it. Try spreading the rice a bit thicker if it's sticking to the paper too much.

8. The mango slices or the toasted coconut can be used to coat the rolls.

9. Cut each roll into six equal pieces.

10. Roll the remaining rice into little balls (like nigiri).

11. A half-blackberry on top of kiki or strawberry slices makes it seem like fish eggs.

12. Make a dipping sauce by combining 14 cups of (25 g) raspberries with 1 cup of (60 ml) water.

13. Enjoy!

144.   TUNA NIGIRI RECIPE

Prep Time: 15 minutes1 hour
Total Time: 1 hour 15 minutes

INGREDIENTS

- For Sushi Rice
- 1 cup of sushi rice uncooked, it's best to use Japanese short-grain sushi rice
- 1 cup of water
- 1 tbspsushi vinegar or mixing 1 tbsp rice vinegar, 1/2 tbsp sugar, and 1/2 tsp salt
- For Tuna Nigiri

- 8 oz sashimi-grade tuna
- 2 tsp wasabi optional
- Optional for Serving:
- soy sauce
- wasabi
- pickled ginger

INSTRUCTIONS

1. Make Sushi Rice by following the instructions below: The rice should be well rinsed in cold water until the water flows clear. After that, fill the ice maker with rice and water. Prepare the food in accordance with the recipe's directions.

2. To cool the rice down a bit, move it to a big bowl and allow it to sit for a few minutes. Stir in the sushi vinegar while it's still heated (or the mixture of rice vinegar, sugar, and salt).

3. Tuna is ready: Cut at a 30 to 45 degree angle perpendicular to the grain. Thinly slice your tuna before cooking it. 3 inches long, 1 inch broad, and 1/4 inch thick is the ideal size.

4. In your right palm, place roughly 3 tablespoons of rice. To form a "log"-sized oval shape, squeeze it together before it hardens. The bottom should be level with the rounded top. As long as you don't squeeze it too hard, and the rice still has some air, you should be fine.

5. When it's time to put the Nigiri together, start by placing a piece of tuna on the tips of your fingernails. Then put a pea-sized quantity of wasabi on top of the fish.

6. Fold your fingers to form a seal around the tuna and the rolled sushi rice. The index finger of the opposite hand should be used to press down on the rice.

7. Make sure that the tuna slice sits on top of the rice when you turn the fish and rice over. Serve the tuna nigiri with pickled ginger and wasabi, if desired.

NOTES

Wet your hands with tezu water before handling rice to prevent it from sticking. Simply combine 1/4 cup water with 2 teaspoons of rice vinegar to produce tezu water.

Because the raw fish will lose flavor the next day, it's recommended to consume tuna nigiri right away.

NUTRITION

It has 64 calories, 10 grams of carbohydrates, 4 grams of protein, 1 gram of fat, and 1 gram of sugar in total. It also contains 309 IU of vitamin A, 1 mg of vitamin C, and 1 gram of iron, making it a complete meal.

145.   SWEET CHILLI CHICKEN SUSHI

50m prep
20m cook

INGREDIENTS

- 1 cup of sushi rice
- 1/4 cup of Obento mirin seasoning
- 4 chicken tenderloins, cut into strips lengthways
- 1/4 cup of sweet chilli sauce
- 2 tsp rice bran oil
- 2 tbsp Kewpie mayonnaise
- 4 nori sheets
- 1/2 medium avocado, thinly sliced
- 1/2 Lebanese cucumber

- 4 green oak lettuce leaves, torn

STEPS

1. Sushi rice is made by preparing sushi rice: Rinse and drain rice three times, or until the water is clear, whichever comes first. Set up a sieve with a bowl of rice inside. Drain for ten minutes before using.

2. Place 1 cup of water and 1 cup of rice in a pot and bring to a boil. Cover. Bring the water to a rolling boil. Reduce the temperature to a comfortable level. Cook for 12 minutes with the lid on, or until the water has been absorbed. Remove from the oven. Cover yourself and stay there for a full ten minutes.

3. Then, add the rice to a large ceramic bowl. Stir the rice to break up any lumps with a spatula. Lift and flip the rice as you gradually add spice, before the rice has cooled.

4. Add 2 tbsp of sweet chilli sauce to a small dish of chicken. Turn to your coat.

5. Medium-high heat a small frying pan with the oil. Then, throw in some chicken. Cook for 5 minutes or until the meat is done. Pour remaining sweet chilli sauce into a small dish, then add mayonnaise.

6. The glossy side of a nori sheet should be facing down on a sushi mat. Wet your fingers and distribute 1/4 of the rice mixture over the nori, leaving a 2cm strip at one long end. Rice should be covered with about a fourth of the mayonnaise mixture. Rice should be topped with a quarter of a chicken, avocado, cucumber, and lettuce.

7. Form a roll by rolling up tightly on a mat. Slice the roll into six equal pieces. Re-use the leftover nori sheets, rice mixture,

mayonnaise mixture and the rest of the ingredients to produce 24 pieces. Serve.

146. SHRIMP SPRING ROLLS

Prep: 45 min. Cook: 5 min

INGREDIENTS

- 1/2 cup of packed brown sugar
- 1 tbsp cornstarch
- 1/4 tsp chicken bouillon granules
- 1/2 cup of cold water
- 1/2 cup of red wine vinegar
- 1/2 cup of finely chopped green pepper
- 1 jar (2 ounces) diced pimientos, drained
- 1 tbsp reduced-sodium soy sauce
- 2 garlic cloves, minced
- 1/2 tsp minced fresh ginger root
- spring rolls:
- 2 tsp cornstarch
- 1/2 tsp sugar
- 1/4 tsp salt
- 2 tbsp reduced-sodium soy sauce
- 3/4 pound medium peeled, deveined, and chopped uncooked shrimp
- 2 garlic cloves, minced
- 4 tsp canola oil, divided
- 2 cup of finely shredded cabbage
- 1 cup of finely chopped fresh mushrooms
- 1/2 cup of finely chopped water chestnuts
- 1/2 cup of shredded carrot
- 4 green onions, thinly sliced
- 12 egg roll or Chinese spring roll wrappers (6-8 inches)
- Oil for deep-fat frying

DIRECTIONS

1. Pour the brown sugar, cornstarch, and bouillon granules into a small saucepan and bring to a boil over medium heat. When the mixture is smooth, add water and vinegar. Add the green peppers, pimientos, soy sauce, garlic, and ginger to the mixture. Simmer the liquid once you've added it. Set aside after cooking and stirring for 2 minutes or until thickened.

2. Mix the flour, sugar, and salt in a small bowl. After pouring miso and stirring until smooth

3. , set away.Stir-fry shrimp and garlic in 1 tsp oil in a large pan or wok until shrimp becomes pink. Then, take and keep warm.

4. In the remaining oil, cook the cabbage, mushrooms, water chestnuts, and carrot for 2 to 3 minutes, until the carrot is crisp-tender but not mushy.

5. Pour in the cornstarch mixture once it has been stirred up. For 1 minute or before the sauce thickens, bring the mixture to a boil. Add the shrimp and green onions; leave aside to chill.

6. Place 1.4 cup of the shrimp mixture in the center of the egg roll wrapper with the corner facing you. Before using the leftover wrappers, dampen a paper towel with water. Fold the bottom corner over the filling. Wet the remainder of the wrapper's edges. Fold the corners of the filling toward the center. To seal the spring roll, coil it up tightly and press down on the tip. Repeat.

7. Heat oil to 371° in an electric skillet or deep fryer. A couple at a time, fry spring rolls for 3-5 minutes or until golden brown, flipping often. Drain on a few paper towels. With sauce, of course.

147. CRISPY TOFU SUSHI BURRITO RECIPE

Prep Time: 20 minutes
Cook Time: 15 minutes
Cooling: 1 hour

INGREDIENTS

- Sushi Rice
- 1 cup of sushi rice
- 3 tbsp rice vinegar
- 1 tbsp raw caster sugar
- ½ tsp sea salt
- Crispy Tofu
- 250 grams firm tofu cut into 4-inch long blocks of firm tofu, 1 inch wide
- 3 tbsp potato or corn starch
- ½ tsp sea salt
- ¼ tsp cayenne pepper
- Sushi Burrito
- 6 nori sheets
- ¼ cup of chipotle mayonnaise
- ½ avocado, peeled and sliced
- ½ cup of matchstick carrots
- ½ cup of vegan kimchi
- ½ cup of baby spinach
- 1 tbsp Japanese pickled ginger

INSTRUCTIONS

1. Rinse the sushi rice well, but not until the water is clear. It takes me at least five washes and a few rinses to get it clean.
2. Rinse and drain the rice, then put it to a medium pot that has a cover. Add 1 and 14 cups of cold water and bring to a boil. Bring the water to a boil over low to medium heat before lowering the heat, putting on the saucepan cover, and simmering the water until it's completely cooled. Take the rice from the heat and let it in the pot with the cover on for 15 minutes after the water has absorbed.
3. Mix vinegar, sugar and salt in a small bowl, and whisk until the salt and sugar have dissolved and the vinegar has a tart flavor.
4. Using a wooden spoon, incorporate the vinegar mixture into the rice once it has been placed to a bowl. Set the rice aside in a cool, dry place until it reaches room temperature, then cover it with a clean towel.
5. minutes in a kitchen towel will help remove as much moisture from the tofu as possible. You'll then be able to cut the tofu into two-inch slices.
6. Toss the tofu in a small dish of corn starch, salt, and cayenne pepper and toss to coat.
7. Simmer the sunflower oil in a large saucepan. Take a pan and fry each block of tofu in it for 2 minutes on every side. Tofu should be placed on an absorbent cloth after cooking.
8. Make the burrito by gluing two nori sheets together by soaking the short edge of one and squeezing it into a rough ride up. Nori length is what we're aiming for.
9. The sushi rice should be pressed into the nori until it is as even as possible, starting an inch or two from the edge. In order to make a nori sheet-sized square, use three inches of rice and press it down firmly. Chipotle mayonnaise, crispy tofu blocks, avocado slices, matchstick carrots, kimchi, baby spinach, and pickled ginger are all great additions to this dish.
10. You can start by rolling the nori toward you, starting at the edge closest to you. When you turn the nori over, all defects will be hidden. There's no need to worry about the nori buckling or tearing apart.. Seal the

roll by running a line of cold water along the nori's far edge. Make sure the roll is fully sealed by laying it seam-side-down for a minute. Serve the tortilla by slicing it in half.

148.   FRESH FRUIT SUSHI

INGREDIENTS

- 1 ½ cup of short-grain rice(300 g)
- 2 cup ofs water(480 mL)
- 3 tbsp sugar
- ¼ tsp salt
- 1 cup of coconut milk(240 mL)
- 1 ½ tsp vanilla
- A VARIETY OF FRUIT
- pineapple
- strawberry
- mango
- kiwi
- 1 pt blackberry(475 g)
- raspberry

PREPARATION

1. I Toss the rice with the other ingredients in a medium saucepan.On a low heat, cook the rice for about twenty minutes, or until the rice has absorbed all of the water, on a low heat.
2. Coconut milk and vanilla extract should be added. Moldability is a must. If it's too runny, cook it for a few more minutes.
3. Carve a wide swath of the fruit of your choosing.
4. Use a potato peeler to cut the mango into thin pieces.
5. On a counter top, place a wax paper rectangle on top of a wooden rolling pad.

Over the paper, create a 7x5-inch (17x12-cm) rectangle by spreading the rice out to a thickness of about 12 inch (1 centimeter).

6. 3 minutes of toasting 14 cup (25g) coconut shreds.
7. Carefully roll the rice with fruit bits on it. Try spreading the rice a bit thicker if it's sticking to the paper too much.
8. The mango slices or the toasted coconut can be used to coat the rolls.
9. Cut each roll into six equal pieces.
10. Roll the remaining rice into little balls (like nigiri).
11. A half-blackberry on top of kiki or strawberry slices makes it seem like fish eggs.
12. Make a dipping sauce by combining 14 cups of (25 g) raspberries with 1 cup of (60 ml) water.
13. Enjoy!

149.   FAT ROLLED SUSHI WITH VEGETABLES

Prep: 90 mins
Cook: 20 mins
Total: 110 mins

INGREDIENTS

- For Kanpyo
- 1 ounce dried kanpyo (calabash gourd)
- Water, for soaking
- 2/3 cup of dashi stock
- 3 tbsp soy sauce
- 2 tbsp granulated sugar
- 1 tbsp mirin
- For Tamagoyaki (Egg Omelette)
- 2 large eggs
- 2 tsp granulated sugar

- 1 tbsp Canola oil
- For Futomaki Rolls
- 4 sheets nori (dried seaweed)
- 6 cup of cooked sushi rice
- 1 small cucumber, quartered lengthwise

STEPS

1. It is time to make Kanpyo
2. Prepare the ingredients by gathering them all together.
3. Kanpyo should be cleaned, rinsed, and drained in a small basin (dried calabash gourd).
4. Soak for about an hour in freshwater to make it flexible.
5. The kanpyo has to be squeezed dry.
6. Cut the kanpyo into 8-inch pieces once it has been softened.
7. Soy sauce, sugar and mirin are combined in a medium saucepan with dashi stock.
8. Add kanpyo and simmer on low heat until the liquid is almost gone, then remove from the fire. Let it cool down for a while.
9. Tamagoyaki is ready to be made.
10. Gather the materials.
11. In a bowl, beat the eggs & sugar.
12. together.Heat canola oil in a small pan, being careful to cover the pan thoroughly with oil. Add a thin coating of the egg mixture on top.
13. Continue rolling or folding the omelet until it is thick and puffy.
14. Serve when it has cooled. Slice it into long pieces.
15. Futomaki Sushi Rolls may be made at home.
16. Gather the materials.
17. Wrap the bamboo mat in plastic wrap and set it aside to dry. (This facilitates the process of cleaning.) On a bamboo mat, spread a big layer of dried, roasted seaweed (nori).
18. On top of the dried seaweed sheet, evenly distribute 1/4 of the sushi rice.
19. Put rice in the middle of the kanpyo, omelet, and cucumber sticks and spread them out horizontally.
20. Roll the bamboo mat into a cylinder, pushing forward as you go, to make sushi.
21. Remove the sushi by pressing hard on the bamboo mat.
22. Make three additional futomaki rolls and set them aside.
23. Before slicing the futomaki, wipe a knife with a damp towel. Snip portions of sushi from the futomaki roll with your knife.

150. SPICY CUCUMBER & AVOCADO ROLLS

30 Minutes Total time
30 Minutes Prep time

INGREDIENTS

- 2½ cup of warm cooked microwaveable sticky rice
- 2 tbsp rice vinegar
- 2 tsp granulated sugar
- 2 tbspless-sodium soy sauce
- 1 tbsp fat free mayonnaise
- 1 tsp prepared wasabi
- 4 sheets sushi nori
- 1 DOLE® Avocado, peeled, pitted and thinly sliced
- 1 cup of DOLE® Colorful Coleslaw
- ⅓ cup of finely chopped English cucumber

DIRECTIONS

1. Rice, vinegar, and sugar should be mixed together in a medium-sized bowl before being served. In a separate medium bowl, combine the soy sauce, mayonnaise, and wasabi.
2. Use plastic wrap to cover a bamboo sushi mat and arrange it horizontally on a counter top. Brush the top and bottom edges of 1 nori sheet with water after placing it lengthwise and shiny side down on the mat. Over nori, spread 2/3 cup of the rice mixture lengthwise and 1/4 of the avocado, coleslaw, cucumber, and soy sauce mixture down the middle of an 8 x 5-inch rectangle. Use a mat to firmly coil the nori and rice mixture around the filling, starting at the long end. Make three additional rolls using the leftover nori, rice mixture, and fillings.
3. Slice each roll into 34-inch-thick sections crosswise.

151. TRADITIONAL GEFILTE FISH

Time > 60 Minutes

INGREDIENTS:

- 2 lb. carp fillets
- ½ cup of breadcrumbs
- 3 onions
- 2 carrots
- 2 cloves garlic
- 3 celery stalks
- 2 eggs, beaten
- salt
- pepper

DIRECTIONS:

1. Grind the fish with 112 onions. Salt, pepper, and bread crumbs should be added to the mixture.
2. Make balls out of the fish mixture by rolling it into balls of equal size.
3. Bring a saucepan halfway full of water to a boil. In a mixing dish, combine the vegetables and fish balls.
1   hours on low heat, covered.

152. BANANA SUSHI ROLLS

Prep time 3 mins
Cook time 1 min
Total time 4 mins

INGREDIENTS

- 1 large (8-inch) whole-wheat tortilla (can sub a gluten-free tortilla, if needed)
- 3 tbsp peanut butter, divided (can sub sunflower seed butter, soy butter, pea butter, or a nut butter of choice)
- 1 banana, peeled
- 1 strawberry, sliced
- ½ kiwi, sliced
- 1 tbsp unsweetened shredded coconut

INSTRUCTIONS

1. Spread half of the peanut butter on a tortilla and roll it up.
2. To make a banana roll, place the banana on one end of the tortilla, then wrap it up.
3. Slice the roll into equal pieces and top each piece with a strawberry and a kiwi slice.
4. Microwave for 31 seconds on high or until melted the remaining peanut butter.
5. Apply peanut butter and coconut flakes to a roll of sushi made from bananas.

153.   GODZILLA ROLL (FRIED SHRIMP TEMPURA ROLL)

INGREDIENTS

- Sushi Rice (2 cup of, uncooked) click HERE
- Shrimp tempura (8 pieces) click HERE
- Imitation crab sticks-8
- Cucumber or avocado (cut into fine sticks)-1
- Cream cheese- 5 oz
- Toasted Nori seaweed-4
- For Serving:
- Spicy Mayo
- Soy sauce
- Yum yum sauce

INSTRUCTIONS

1. Using a big pan, heat about 1 cup of oil to 350 F / 175 C. Then, deep-fry sushi rolls.
2. Make sure to cover the bamboo sushi rolling mat with plastic wrap. Spread out a nori sheet on the mat, with the glossy side down, in the center.
3. Keep a bowl of water available for emergencies. To keep the rice from sticking to your hands, squirt some water on your hands and grab a bunch. Apply a small coating of sauce on the nori sheet. Carefully turn the nori over.
4. Make sure the seaweed is long enough to hold the shrimp tempuras, cucumber sticks, crab sticks, and 2 tablespoons of cream cheese. Keep the filling inside the bamboo mat as you roll it forward. Place on a tray after being removed from the mat. Recreate this process with the rest of the nori sheets.

5. Using the shrimp tempura batter as a substitute is an option. Deep-fry each roll for about two to three minutes, rotating it halfway through the frying process, until it's golden brown on all sides. removing and putting on a plate coated with paper towels
6. Use a very sharp knife to cut a Godzilla roll into five to six pieces.
7. Spicy mayo or yum yum sauce can be drizzled on top.

154.   CATERPILLAR ROLL

INGREDIENTS:

- 2 fully made sushi rolls
- 1 avocado, peeled, cored
- 1 tsp of lemon juice

DIRECTIONS:

1. The avocado should be sliced horizontally into thin slices (short way across.) A sushi roll should have enough slices overlapping each other to completely cover the top. (A quarter of an avocado should be enough to cover one piece of bread.)
2. The avocado should be patted into the ceramic wrap, which should be over the roll (DO NOT ROLL the whole rollover.)
3. Slice the roll into eight equal pieces after removing the bamboo mat and ceramic wrap. Remove the wrap and sprinkle the sauces of your choice over the wrap.

155.   PALEO CAULIFLOWER RICE SUSHI ROLLS

Prep Time 10 minutes
Cook Time 30 minutes
Total Time 40 minutes

INGREDIENTS

- Cauliflower rice
- 1 head Cauliflower
- 1 tbsp Olive oil
- Sea salt (as need)
- Sushi filling
- ounces Tuna (sashimi grade)
- 2 tbspAvocado mayonnaise
- 2 tsp Sriracha
- Sea salt (as need)
- 1 small Cucumber
- 1/2 medium Avocado
- 2 sheets Nori
- Pickled ginger
- Wasabi
- Coconut amines

INSTRUCTIONS

2   The oven should be preheated to 426°F.
3   Cauliflower should be cut into pieces small enough to go into your food processor. Pulse the cauliflower for two seconds at a time until it resembles rice.
4   Spray a baking sheet with olive oil and spread the mixture out evenly. Toss with the olive oil and then spread it out to make an equal layer if desired.
5   Stir the bread every few minutes to ensure even cooking in the oven for around 30 minutes.
6   Sushi making instructions
7   Make a paste out of mayonnaise, sriracha, and salt to taste, then add the tuna.

8   Make long strips of cucumber by slicing the cucumber thinly.
9   Using a mandolin, thinly slice the avocado.
10 Get some nori and cover it with the "rice," leaving a 1-inch space at one end.
11 The end closest to you is where you'll put your toppings.
12 Start rolling the sushi away from you using the mat or cloth.
13 Serve with wasabi, coconut amines, and pickled ginger once it's been rolled up.

156.   CHAIKIN TOFU IN GINGER BROTH

PREPARATION 20MIN
COOKING 20MIN

INGREDIENTS

- 400 block good-quality firm tofu
- 2 dried wakame seaweed
- 200 minced chicken breast
- 1 tipsy sauce
- 1 tbspsake
- 1egg white
- 50 carrot, finely chopped
- 3spring onions, finely chopped
- 2 supinely grated ginger
- 1 tbsp cornflour
- 1 tsp baking powder
- salt and ground white pepper
- For the ginger broth
- 750 ml dashi stock
- 3 tbsp soy sauce
- 2 tbspsake
- 2 tbsp mirin
- 4shallots, thinly sliced
- The mixture of 1 tbsp cornflour and 1 tbsp iced water

INSTRUCTIONS

1 Squeeze out as much water as possible from the tofu by wrapping it in muslin fabric. Roughly chop the ingredients and place them in a separate bowl.

2 Dried wakame can be soaked for 5–10 minutes in a dish of cold water. slice it into little pieces after draining and squeezing off the water

3 In a large bowl, combine the chicken, soy sauce, sake, and the egg white, and stir thoroughly with your hands. Incorporate the tofu with the carrots and onions, as well as the 1 tbsp. grated ginger and the wakame. Before everything is incorporated, continue to mix thoroughly.

4 Place a quarter of the tofu mixture in a small rice bowl and cover with cling film. The tofu should be tightly wrapped in cling film like a little package. Make three additional packages by securing the top with a rubber band and repeating the process. Steam the packages for around 20 minutes at a low temperature in a steamer.

5 Make the broth while the packages are steaming. Simmer the dashi stock for 3–4 minutes with the sake, mirin, soy sauce, and salt. After 2 minutes of boiling, add the shallots and season to taste with salt and white pepper. Cook, stirring constantly, for about 20 seconds or until the broth has thickened and turned glossy after adding the cornflour mixture.

6 Remove the tofu packages from the cling film and serve each one in a separate dish. Serve with the leftover grated ginger and the broth on the side.

157. CREAMY CRAB SUSHI ROLL

Prep Time 10 mins

INGREDIENTS

- 2 legs of imitation crab OR 1/2 cup of crab meat shredded or diced
- 1 tbsp softened cream cheese
- 1 tbsp mayo
- 1/4 of a cucumber cut into long thin strips
- 1 tsp sriracha optional
- 1 cup of cooked sushi rice cooled
- 1 nori wrap if using a full size sheet cut 3/4ths of the wrapper and set aside the other 1/4 of it to make a standard-sized roll.
- french fried onions
- sesame seeds
- spicy mayo
- eel or unagi sauce
- 2 tbsp dark soy sauce
- 3 tsp oyster sauce
- Pinch of sugar

INSTRUCTIONS

1. Use a rolling pin to flatten and uniformly press the sushi rice to match the nori wrap's size and shape. Then cover the top of the rice with plastic wrap.

2. The seaweed should be placed rough side up.

3. A tiny bowl is all that is needed for chopping or shredding the fake crab meat or actual crab meat.

4. Mix crab with cream cheese and mayonnaise until it is covered and creamy.

5. Crab salad and cucumber slices should be placed in the centre of the nori wrap.

6. If you're using sriracha, drizzle it down the centre of the roll.

7. To construct the sushi roll, you need to pull the ends together and compress them into a cylinder, pressing together with your hands and then using a sushi mat or cloth to press and form the sushi roll.

8. Slicing the rice using a water or rice vinegar-coated serrated knife is done slowly and delicately, re-dipping the knife if the rice becomes stuck on the serrated blade.

9. Enjoy with sauces and other toppings if preferred.

158. CHICKEN SUSHI RECIPE

Prep Time: 20 minutes
Cook Time: 50 minutes
Total Time: 1 hour 10 minutes

INGREDIENTS

- 1 medium carrot (shredded)
- 2 medium chicken breasts (cooked and shredded)
- 2 large eggs (scrambled and optional)
- 3 cups of cooked brown rice (sticky is best -see link above)
- 4 large nori (sheets)
- tsp. toasted sesame seeds (optional for garnish)

INSTRUCTIONS

1 Sticky rice should be ready to eat now.

2 Lay your Nori out on a level and firm work surface.

3 It's important to leave at least a quarter-inch of rice-free space around the perimeters of your rice.

4 Sprinkle the rice liberally with sesame seeds if you're using them.

5 Your other ingredients (chicken, eggs, and some vegetables) should be placed up in a single row at the front of your Nori strips. Only a fourth of the space on your Nori should be used for it.

6 Your sushi should be rolled tightly, but not so tightly that you rip the Nori sheet. Once you've made one roll, you'll get a sense of how it works.

7 Make sure that the nori's open edge is sealed by putting your finger in water and dragging it across it. Using this method will ensure that the roll doesn't unravel.

8 A sharp knife is all that is needed to slice and serve if you're serving others. For those who plan on eating sushi on the go, it becomes a lot more convenient to not slice it. It's best eaten in the style of a burrito.

9 It's important to maintain the rice layer thin and add only a modest amount of additional ingredients to get the best results. A large number of components will put Nori under too much strain.

NOTES

Please keep in mind that the nutrition information provided here is a rough estimate. Exact data is not feasible here.

159. DELICIOUS UME SHISO MAKI ROLLS RECIPE

Serves: 24

INGREDIENTS

- To make the sushi rice:
- 240 g of boiled brown rice
- 20 g rice vinegar
- 20 g of agave concentrate (agave syrup)
- Fine gray salt
- For the sushi:
- 3 slices of lightly toasted nori seaweed
- Green shiso leaves
- pieces of frozen sea urchins

INSTRUCTIONS

1 Rice should be smeared on the nori seaweed sheets.
2 Glue three sheets of shiso to each nori and rice sheet.
3 Approach 15 unfrozen Hedgehog yolks per Shiso leaf.
4 Compress after rolling.
5 With this, you'll be able to enjoy:
6 sesame seed oil that is certified organic
7 Tamari
8 Slice the buns into 2cm broad slices. '
9 With a dropper, season each piece with oil and tamari.

160. SWEET FRUIT SUSHI (DESSERT SUSHI)

Prep Time: 30 minutes
Total Time: 30 minutes

INGREDIENTS

- ½ cup of raspberries
- ½ cup of blackberries
- 1 cup of strawberries
- 3 cup of coconut sticky rice cooked
- Optional
- shredded coconut to top
- kiwi or your favorite fruit

INSTRUCTIONS

1. Set up the steamed rice
2. My fruit sushi is usually made with a delicious coconut rice. To continue the process, you must first prepare and cool the ice cream. Even when it's heated, the rice might still be somewhat mushy, making it difficult to roll into sushi.
3. Make the fruit ready to eat.
4. You'll want to cut lengthy 'baton' strips of any fruit you're using while preparing sushi rolls. Set aside the raspberry halves for later.
5. Strawberry, kiwi, and mango are the ideal fruits to use for the sushi balls, which require very thin slices of fruit (you may use a mandolin or a sharp knife).
6. To make a rectangle 'nigiri,' cut your fruit into pieces large enough to sit on top of the rice; raspberries can be left whole once again.
7. The dessert should be molded into a shape. Sushi
8. Use a bamboo sushi mat and cover it with cling film (plastic wrap) when making sushi rolls. If you don't have any parchment paper, a sheet of aluminum foil will suffice (with or without cling film).
9. The mat/parchment paper should be rolled into a 'nearly square,' so one side has to be narrower so it's more of a rectangle.' Use around 1 cup of rice each roll.
10. The fruit batons should be about 1.5" (cm) away from the rice. You don't want to

overfill the sushi since it will be tough to wrap it.

11. Start rolling the sushi forward, creating a log form, using the sushi mat or just your hands. Form a full roll by softly pressing the two rice edges together.

12. Wrap the log in cling film or parchment paper, tying the ends together like a candy wrapper, and secure it with double-sided tape. Bring to room temperature before serving.

13. To cut the roll, use a sharp knife dipped in water to create rapid, firm slices about 1-2" apart after removing it from the parchment paper/plastic wrap.

14. To begin, finely slice your fruit for the Sushi Balls. Strawberries, kiwi, and mango work well with these balls since they can be cut extremely thinly.

15. Slice the fruit as thinly as possible with a mandolin or a razor-sharp knife. Then, on top of a sheet of cling film or plastic wrap, arrange them in a circle with a tiny overlap (6-8" wide).

16. Drop 1-1 1/2 tbsp of the sweet rice in the center of the fruit circle for a simple rice center. A raspberry or blackberry in the heart of the rice will give it the appearance of an unexpected berry center.

17. Squeeze and twist the plastic wrap to hold it in place around the perimeter of the wall, then remove the plastic wrap. After a few minutes, you might be able to pry it out of the mold. I, on the other hand, prefer to chill it for an hour in the refrigerator.

18. The simplest form to make is 'Nigiri,' which is rectangular in shape. The only thing you'll need to do is divide the rice into 2-4tbsp portions (depending on your preference). Shape them into a rectangle

log and then decorate with your preferred fruits.

19. Honey (non-vegan) or another sticky syrup (maple syrup isn't sticky enough) can be used to help the fruit adhere to the top. Alternatively, a small amount of berry jam might do.

20. (Optional) Decoration and dips are the final steps in the process.

21. Your sweet sushi is now ready for consumption after completing the preceding two processes. To make them stand out even more, there are a number of other decoration options available (listed above).

22. Some of my favorite ways to serve sushi are with a variety of toppings sprinkled on top, including fresh mint leaves.

23. Prepare and sprinkle the 'dip'/'drizzle' you intend to use at the same time. For an acidic flavor, try melting some chocolate, watering down a jam, or using one of the berry sauces.

24. Also, you may serve it with a scoop of your favorite frozen treat or some coconut-whipped-cream on the side.

161.   DESSERT SUSHI

Prep Time 20 mins
Refrigerate 3 hrs
Total Time 20 mins

INGREDIENTS

- Chocolate Layer
- 2 pkg chocolate crackers(300grams)
- tbsp coconut oil
- 2/3 cup of hot coffee
- 3/4 cup of powdered sugar
- 3 tbsp cocoa powder

- 1/2 tsp Chocolate Liqueur
- Coconut Filling
- 3 cup of unsweetened desiccated coconut
- tbsp coconut oil
- -10 tbsp Agave Nectar/Honey
- 1/2 tsp Vanilla extract
- Fruit Filling
- raspberries
- strawberries
- mango
- kiwifruit

INSTRUCTIONS

1 Layers of dark chocolate
2 Crumble the crackers first in a food processor or blender.
3 Place crumbs from a chocolate biscuit in a bowl.
4 Whisk powdered sugar and coconut oil into a cup of hot coffee. If used, stir in the cocoa powder and liqueur once the coconut oil has melted.
5 Incorporate the cookie crumbs with roughly half of the heated mixture Stirring using a spatula is a good option. Pour in the remaining heated liquid. Frigerate for at least one hour before serving.
6 Filling made from coconuts
7 For around 5-10 seconds, reprocess the desiccated coconut and oil mixture in the food processor before adding the Agave Nectar and vanilla essence.
8 Assembly
9 Form a 6-inch log from 1 cup of chocolate dough. Make use of a piece of plastic wrap to protect your work surface.To make a chocolate rectangle, roll out the dough using a silicone rolling pin. With a ruler, measure and cut it to 8 (20cm) by 7 inches (21cm) (17 cm).
10 Allowing for approximately an inch of empty space on each bottom and top end, spread the coconut filling evenly over the middle. Stack the fruit in the middle of the plate. Fold the chocolate layer over the fruit filling, pressing gently but firmly with your fingers, and tuck it in with the plastic wrap up. Continue rolling for one more turn once you've tucked the fruit layer in, and your role should be complete.
11 It's still mushy, so don't even think of slicing it just yet. Refrigerate for six hours after wrapping in plastic wrap.
12 Slice it with a serrated knife after unwrapping it. Don't rush the process. Layer between parchment-lined sheets in the fridge for up to 3 days.
13 Repeat the process with the leftover dough.

162.   PISTACHIO CHOCOLATE BANANA SUSHI

PREP TIME 15 mins
TOTAL TIME 15 mins

INGREDIENTS

- 1 banana
- 50-gram dark chocolate
- pistachio nuts a handful

INSTRUCTIONS

1. The chocolate should be melted.
2. Slice the pistachios.
3. You'll need to remove the skin off the banana.

4. Melt the chocolate and spread it over the banana.
5. Pistachios sliced and sprinkled over the cocoa banana.
6. Slice the remaining pistachios and banana into sushi and top with them.

NOTES

Try eating dessert sushi with chopsticks for a more authentic Japanese experience.

163.   CALIFORNIA ROLL

Prep Time 5 minutes
Cook Time 15 minutes
Total Time 20 minutes

INGREDIENTS

- 1 medium-sized avocado peeled and sliced into 1/4-inch thick pieces
- sheets sushi nori
- 1/4 cup of sesame seeds
- 1 small cucumber peeled, seeded
- 4 pieces crabsticks
- 3 cup of cooked sushi rice
- 4 tbsp rice vinegar
- 2 tbsp granulated sugar
- 1 tsp salt

INSTRUCTIONS

1. Add sugar and salt to rice vinegar in a small bowl, then mix thoroughly.
2. After about 10 seconds in a microwave, mix again to ensure that all of the ingredients are dissolved.
3. Mix thoroughly the vinegar, sugar, and salt combination with the sushi rice. Remove from consideration.
4. It's time to halve the sushi nori (nori).

5. Lay a sushi nori on a level surface with the glossy side down.
6. Spread some sushi rice on top of the sushi nori, then top with a few pieces of sushi (make sure to distribute the rice evenly)
7. Top sushi rice with sesame seeds.
8. The mat (or bamboo mat) should be covered with plastic (such as cling wrap)
9. On a level surface, layout the sushi nori and rice on top of the mat. The rice should be on the bottom of the piece.
10. To serve, place the crabstick, cucumber, and avocado on a large plate in the middle of the plate.
11. Roll it into a tight cylinder by grasping the mat's edge and rolling it into a tight cylinder with your fingers. Remove from consideration.
12. Continue the process until all of the rice has been consumed. '
13. Using a sharp knife, split the sushi cylinder in half along its long axis.
14. Slice each half into three equal pieces crosswise.
15. Serve with soy sauce and wasabi on a serving platter. It's time to get together and have fun!

164.   COCONUT FRUSHI RECIPE

INGREDIENTS

- 1/4 c water
- 2 c uncooked sushi or other short-grain rice
- 1/4 c sugar
- 1/4 coconut milk
- dash salt

- cooking spray
- tangerine or orange sections
- about 20 raspberries
- 1 6oz carton vanilla yogurt

HOW TO MAKE

1 A medium saucepan should have water and rice boiling over medium heat. Set a timer for 15 minutes and simmer until the liquid has been absorbed. Leave covered for 15 minutes once you've removed the pan from the heat.

2 To prepare the rice, place it in a big bowl and cover with water. Stir in the brown sugar, coconut milk, and salt until everything is well-combined, then serve immediately. Wait for 20 minutes before removing the lid.

3 Spray some cooking spray on your hands to protect them. Form each of the 20 equal amounts of rice mixture into a sphere. Then, using your palms, gently flatten each rice ball into an oval shape before placing it on a wax paper-lined baking sheet. Add 1 tangerine segment to the center of each of the ten ovals and gently press to attach. 2 raspberries should be placed on top of the remaining ten ovals. Before serving, refrigerate the dish completely covered in plastic wrap. Use yogurt as a dipping sauce.

4 Two tablespoons of yogurt and four fresh pieces.

5 Adding a dab of honey will help the fruit adhere to the rice if it doesn't attach on its own.

6 This dish may be made with any type of fresh fruit.

7 This is a recipe adapted from Cooking Light.

165. SUSHI-STYLE BEEF ROLL-UPS

Prep 25 Min
Total 5 Hr 15 Min

INGREDIENTS

- 2 cup of warm cooked medium-grain white rice (cooked as directed on package)
- 2 tbsp seasoned rice vinegar
- 3 (3-oz.) pkg. cream cheese, softened
- 3 tsp whipped horseraBowl
- 2 (7 or 8-inch) flour tortillas
- 1 (2.5-oz.) pkg. thinly sliced corned beef
- 1 (7 to 8-inch) cucumber
- cup roasted red bell pepper chunks

STEPS

1. Vinegar and cooked rice should be properly mixed in a medium bowl. Refrigerate for at least 31 minutes, or until the mixture has cooled to room temperature.

2. Stir together the cream cheese and horseradish in a small bowl until well-combined. The oven should be preheated at 351 degrees Celsius. The cream cheese mixture should be spread evenly over each tortilla, reaching the edges. Place corned beef slices on top of cream cheese, overlapping as necessary and leaving 1 inch of each tortilla's top and bottom borders exposed.

3. Place a third of a cup of the cooled rice mixture in the center of each tortilla and roll tightly into a 2-inch wide by 1/2-inch thick strip before serving.

4. Transversely slice a cucumber in half. Set aside three portions of the table for future usage. Remove the seeds from a quarter of a cucumber and slice it into three long

strips. Every rice strip should have a single strip pressed into the middle of it. Slice thinly roasted peppers. To create a lengthy crimson stripe, place next to the cucumber.

5. Stack another 1/3 cup of rice mixture on top of the cucumbers and roasted peppers on each tortilla. Form rice into firm rolls, coating cucumber and roasted pepper thoroughly with damp palms.

6. Every tortilla should be rolled tightly around rice starting from the bottom border. Wrap each roll with a piece of plastic wrap and fasten it. Refrigerate for at least four hours, or until completely cooled. To serve, cut each roll into eight 3/4-inch-thick slices; trim the uneven ends.

166.   CALIFORNIA ROLLS
Prep Time 60 minutes
Cook Time 20 minutes

INGREDIENTS

- Prepared sushi rice - 540 gm.
- Cooked crab meat- 230 gm.
- Japanese mayonnaise- 05 tbsp.
- English cucumber- 1/2
- Avocados- 02 nos.
- Lemon for Avocado - 1/2
- Nori sheets - 08
- White sesame seeds- ¼ th cup of
- Black sesame seeds- ¼ th cup of
- For Preparing the California Roll:
- Bamboo mat, covered with plastic wrap
- Tezu (vinegared hand-dipping water): 1/4 cup of water + 2 tsp. rice vinegar
- For Toppings: (Optional)
- Ikura (Salmon Roe)
- Tobiko (Flying fish Roe)
- For Accompaniments:

- Wasabi Sauce: 60 ml (1/4 cup of)
- Pickled Ginger: 60 gm (1/4 cup of)
- Chopsticks: 15 pairs

INSTRUCTIONS

1. Pre-preparation: To prepare the crab meat, combine the crab meat with Japanese mayonnaise. Remove the seeds from the cucumber. Cut the nori sheet into the equal length of long, thin strips.

2. Slice the avocado into ¼" thick slices and pour the lemon juice over it to keep it from turning brown (enzymatic browning). To utilize nori, cut off ⅓ of the nori and use a nori sheet.

3. Set up a Tezu-coated bamboo mat on a piece of plastic wrap (vinegared hand-dipping water).

4. You'll need a bamboo mat and a nori sheet for this step. Spread 1 cup of rice evenly on a nori sheet by wetting your fingertips with tezu. Rice can be topped with sesame seeds.

5. Rice should be face-up on the nori sheet. The bottom of the bamboo mat should be lined with a nori sheet.

6. Place the cucumber, crab meat, and avocado on the nori sheet at the bottom. Keeping the contents firmly in place with your fingers, grab the mat's lower edge and roll it into a tight cylinder.

7. Gently roll the bamboo mat forward, lifting the edge of the mat slightly while maintaining a soft grip on the mat. A sharp knife is needed to cut each roll in half and then cut each half into three equal halves.

8. In order to keep the knife from clinging to the rolls as it slices, wipe it off with a moist towel after each cut. OPTIONAL Ikura (Salmon Roe) and Tobiko can be added to

the sliced California rolls before serving them on their side (Flying fish Roe)

9. On a sushi plate, place everything. Chopsticks, Wasabi sauce, and pickled ginger are all good additions.

167.   COOK TIMECREAM CHEESE AND CRAB SUSHI ROLLS

INGREDIENTS

- 1 cup of white rice
- tsp minced ginger
- tbsp rice vinegar
- 1 tsp salt
- 1 cucumber
- imitation crabmeat, leg style
- cream cheese
- nori sushi sheet

DIRECTIONS

1. Add the rice and ginger to 2 cups of boiling water. Place a lid on the pot and let it cook for 20 minutes, or until the rice is done cooking.
2. Rice vinegar and salt should be mixed into the rice.
3. Prepare your seaweed sheets by laying them out on the floor.
4. Put water on your hands and distribute the rice evenly between the two seaweed sheets, then press the rice down into a flat surface. Leave approximately a half-inch of space at the top of the sheets unfilled with rice. This will make it easier to seal the sushi roll.

5. Crab, cucumber, and cream cheese should be arranged in a straight line about an inch from the bottom of the dish (left to right).
6. Be cautious not to tear the seaweed sheets by gently but forcefully squeezing the sushi as tightly as possible (from bottom to top).
7. Cut the sushi into individual pieces by wetting a very sharp knife and using it to slice the rolls.

168.   SPICY CRAB ROLL RECIPE

Prep Time: 15 minutes
Cook Time: 45 minutes
Total Time: 1 hour

INGREDIENTS

- For Sushi Rice
- 2 cup of sushi rice short-grain sushi rice
- 3 cup of water
- 1 ½ tbspsushi vinegar (or mix 1 tbsp rice vinegar, 1/2 tbsp sugar, and 1/2 tsp salt)
- Spicy Mayo
- 3 tsp mayonnaise
- 1 ½ tsp sriracha sauce
- For the Spicy Kani Roll
- 2 oz Kani crab meat
- 2 sheets nori seaweed
- 1 tbsp sesame seeds

INSTRUCTIONS

1. Make Rice for Sushi
2. Add the rice to the rice cooker once it has been rinsed. In this case, add water and follow the recipe's directions.
3. Once the food has cooled, put it to a big bowl. Pour sushi vinegar into the mixture

while it's still lukewarm (or the mixture of rice vinegar, sugar and salt).

4. Make a Spicy Sriracha Mayonnaise Recipe

5. Stir together mayonnaise, Sriracha, and salt. Depending on your own preference, you may increase or decrease the quantity of Sriracha sauce.

6. Crab Salad with Spicy Sauce

7. Use your hands or two forks to pulverize the imitation crab flesh into small pieces.

8. Then, add Sriracha mayonnaise and thoroughly combine.

9. Make the Spicy Crab Roll now.

10. Using kitchen scissors, cut the nori sheet in half.

11. You'll want to make sure that the nori sheet is placed on the bamboo mat with the shiny side down.

12. Sushi rice (about 3/4 cup) should be spread evenly over nori. Gently knead the rice with your fingertips. The rice will not adhere to your hands if you dip your hands in Tezu water.

13. Top the rice with sesame seeds.

14. Make sure the rice side is facing down when you flip the sheet.

15. Serve with some hot Kani crab salad in the center.

16. Lift the bamboo mat's edge up and over the filling with your thumbs below the mat.

17. Press the rice and filling together with the bamboo mat as you roll it away from you. You'll get there if you keep going till the finish.

18. Cut the roll into eight pieces after transferring it to a cutting board.

19. Add a little more spicy mayo sauce on the top of the roll if you'd like.

NOTES

The simplest way to produce Tezu water is to combine 1/4 cup water with 2 teaspoons of rice vinegar.

What's wrong with my sushi roll? If you used the wrong rice or if you didn't crush the rolls properly, you may have ended up with this problem. The bamboo mat has to be tucked in and rolled securely.

169.   CALIFORNIA CRAB ROLLS

INGREDIENTS

- 500g sushi rice
- tbsp sushi vinegar
- ripe medium avocado, halved and stoned
- juice of ½ lemon
- 4 sheets toasted sushi nori
- meat from 2 small dressed crabs (or 240g tinned white crab meat, drained)
- 2 tbsp sesame seeds
- 4 tbsp sushi ginger, to serve
- a squeeze of wasabi, to serve
- 2 tbsp soy sauce, to serve

STEP BY STEP

1. Soak the rice in 850ml of water for 30 minutes in a medium pot. Add water and bring to a boil, then cover and simmer for an hour or more. For 10 minutes, lower the temperature to a simmer and stir often. Before adding the sushi vinegar, spread the rice out on a baking sheet and allow it to cool.

2. Slice the avocado into long, thin strips and add the lemon juice. You may use a nori sheet to make this dish, but you can also use

a nonstick baking sheet to make it. Spread nori on top of the rice, then line up a quarter of the avocado strips and a quarter of the crabmeat along the long bottom border. Using the paper to assist, roll the sushi into a cylinder; hold onto the contents with your fingers while you do so.

3. Cut the roll into 2cm-thick slices and top with sesame seeds before slicing with a moist knife. Use a new piece of baking paper each time you add a new ingredient. Pickled ginger, wasabi, and soy sauce are all great accompaniments.

4. Make sure your soy sauce is gluten-free if you want this to be a gluten-free dish.

170. CALIFORNIA - CREAM CHEESE SUSHI ROLL

Prep Time: 45 minutes
Cook Time: 15 minutes
Total Time: 1 hour

INGREDIENTS

- 2 cup of uncooked short-grain white rice
- 1 cup of water
- ¼ cup of rice vinegar
- 1 tbsp white sugar
- sheets nori dry seaweed
- ½ tbsp sesame seeds
- 1 whole cucumber cut into thin spears
- 1 whole carrots cut into thin spears
- 2 whole avocados - pitted peeled, and sliced the long way
- ½ cup of imitation crabmeat finely chopped
- 1 block cream cheese cut into long strips about ¼ inch thick

INSTRUCTIONS

1. After many changes of water, strain the rice thoroughly, and put it in a covered pan or rice cooker with 1 cup of water.
2. Bring to a boil, then turn down to low and keep warm.
3. Allow 16 minutes for the rice to cook before the top begins to dry out.
4. minutes after turning off the heat, allow the pasta to soak up the remaining water.
5. Before the sugar dissolves, combine the rice vinegar and sugar in a small basin. Stir the mixture into the cooked rice only until it is fully incorporated.
6. Set aside the rice to cool.
7. To roll the sushi, use a Ziploc bag or plastic wrap to cover a bamboo rolling mat.
8. Nori should be placed on the plastic wrap or Ziploc bag with its glossy side down.
9. Gently pat a thin, uniform layer of prepared rice over the nori, leaving about an inch of the bottom border of the sheet uncoated.
10. Gently push around 12 tsp of sesame seeds into the rice to coat it.
11. For an outer nori look, simply leave it as is, or flip it carefully over so that the seaweed-facing side is up.
12. Stack 2 or 3 long cucumber spears, 2 or 3 carrots spears and a few slices of avocado in a line across the nori sheet about 14 from the exposed side of the nori sheet with 1 tbsp of imitation crab in the middle.
13. Roll the sushi into the cylinder approximately 1 12 inches in diameter by picking up around the edges of the bamboo rolling sheet and folding the bottom edge up, encasing the contents.
14. Squeeze the sushi securely into the mat once it's been rolled.

15. Use a very sharp knife soaked in water to cut each roll into 1 inch pieces.

171. SUSHI ROLL

Prep: 45 mins
Total: 45 mins

INGREDIENTS

- ⅔ cup of uncooked short-grain white rice
- 3 tbsp rice vinegar
- 3 tbsp white sugar
- 1 ½ tsp salt
- sheets nori seaweed sheets
- ½ cucumber, peeled, cut into small strips
- 2 tbsp pickled ginger
- o 2 avocado
- ½ pound imitation crabmeat, flaked

DIRECTIONS

a. 1/3 cup water boiled in a medium saucepan Mix in the rice. 20 minutes covered on low heatRice vinegar, sugar, and salt should be combined in a small bowl for the final product. Add the mixture to the rice and stir it in.

2. The oven should be preheated at 300 degrees Fahrenheit (150 degrees C). Nori may be roasted in a preheated oven for up to two minutes on a medium baking sheet.

3. It's a sushi mat made out of bamboo and nori. Wet fingers Hand-press a small layer of rice onto the nori sheet. Line up 1/4 of the cucumbers, ginger, avocado, and imitation crabmeat on the rice. When you've lifted the end of the mat, carefully roll it over the ingredients and press lightly.

Make a full roll by rolling it forward. Repeat with the remaining ingredients.

4. Using a moist, sharp knife, slice each roll into four to six pieces.

172. SALMON CUCUMBER NIGIRI

Prep Time: 15 minutes

INGREDIENTS

- 6 oz salmon sashimi-grade
- 1 tsp roasted sesame seeds
- 1 Tbsp ponzu sauce
- ½ cucumber
- 1½ cup of cook sushi rice
- 2 Tbsp sushi vinegar or 2 Tbsp rice vinegar + 1 tsp sugar + ¼ tsp salt
- 1 Tbsp nori bits crush and crumble nori/seaweed

INSTRUCTIONS

1. Mix sesame seeds, ponzu, and chopped salmon together. It's ready to go.

2. Cucumbers should be peeled lengthwise and sliced into long, broad strips.

3. Preserve the moisture in the cucumber slices by wrapping or covering the container. It is not self-adhesive if they are dry, thus additional binding strength is needed (i.e. toothpick)

4. Set aside a container and combine the sushi rice with the sake vinegar (or any vinegar of your choice) (see notes).

5. To make sushi rice balls, take about 2 tablespoons of sushi rice and mold them into oblong or oval shapes.

6. Keep going until you've used up all of the sushi rice.

7. Wrap a cucumber slice around each rice ball, making careful to leave an opening at the top to accommodate the salmon filling. If 1 slice of cucumber isn't broad enough, place another slice on top of it.
8. Fill each ball with a spoonful of salmon once the cucumber slices are wrapped around it.
9. Serve on serving dishes with crushed nori pieces as a garnish.
10. Sushi made with cucumbers can also be served with this.

173. CUCUMBER SUSHI

INGREDIENTS

- 2 Lebanese cucumbers
- 1/2 red capsicum
- 1/2 avocado
- 1/2 cup of sushi rice cooked
- 1 tbs soy sauce *to serve

METHOD

1. Slice the avocado and capsicum into small pieces.
2. The rice should be cooked according to the directions on the package. Let it cool down.
3. After each cucumber has been sliced in half, remove the centers using an apple corer. Depending on how well the rice sticks to the pan, you may have to dry out the cavity first. To accomplish this, swab the cavity dry with a paper towel-wrapped chopstick.
4. Rice should be stuffed into the cavity, then a knife is used to push it aside so that other vegetables can be added.
5. Add a few slices of avocado and capsicum to the cavity before it is completely filled.
6. Serving suggestion: Slice and drizzle with soy sauce on the side.

7. All the notes are here.

NOTES

Cucumber sushi may be stuffed with anything you choose, from carrots and tuna to pickled ginger and more ponzu sauce.

174. DECONSTRUCTED SUSHI BOWL WITH SWEET SESAME DRESSING

INGREDIENTS

- 1½ cup of (278 g) uncooked brown rice, soaked overnight, drained*
- 2¼ cup of (540 mL) water*
- 1½ cup of (225 g) frozen shelled edamame beans
- ½ cup of (85 g) wakame seaweed salad
- 2 cup of (70 g) shredded red cabbage
- 3 mango, chopped
- 3 avocado, chopped
- 1 stalk green onion, chopped
- ¼ cucumber, chopped
- ½ small red onion, minced
- The dressing
- Tbsp (30 mL) sodium-reduced soy sauce
- tsp (10 mL) sesame oil
- tsp (10 mL) agave syrup
- 1 lime, juiced
- 1 tsp (3 g) garlic powder
- 1 tsp (2 g) onion powder
- Optional garnishes
- fried onions
- toasted sesame seeds

DIRECTIONS

1. Bring the water & brown rice to a boil in a medium saucepan over high heat, then reduce the heat and partly cover the pot with a lid,simmering until the rice is done, about 20 minutes. Allow it cool for five minutes after removing from the heat and covering with a lid.
2. Beans were boiled for 3 minutes, then drained. They were cooked according to the instructions on the package.
3. You may just put all of the ingredients into a container, seal the top and shake briskly until the dressing is thoroughly mixed.If you want, you may just whisk the ingredients together in a bowl.
4. Put rice in first, then add any prepped fruits or vegetables of your choice on top, then add the garnish and pour the dressing. Enjoy!

NOTES

Cooking time and water should be increased if soaking is not possible.

175.   FRIED CALIFORNIA SUSHI ROLL

Prep Time 15 mins
Cook Time 5 mins

INGREDIENTS

- 1-2 cup of cooked sushi rice – cooled
- 1-2 sheets seaweed nori wraps
- 3 sticks imitation crab meat
- 1/2 avocado
- 1/2 cucumber
- 2 ounces cream cheese – roughly
- 2 egg
- 2 tsp sriracha
- 1 tsp soy sauce
- 1 cup of panko bread crumbs
- oil for frying corn, canola, peanut or any preferred frying oil
- 1 tbsp eel or oyster sauce – can be found in the Asian food aisle.
- French fried onions – optional
- 1 tbsp spicy mayo

INSTRUCTIONS

1. Slice all of your fillings into long, thin strips before preparing them for the dish.
2. To begin rolling, cover your sushi mat with plastic wrap or parchment paper before you begin rolling.
3. Add sushi rice that has been prepared.
4. Then, using a rolling pin, flatten the rice until it's approximately 1/2 inch thick and large enough to cover with nori wrap before covering it with that.
5. Remove the top layer of plastic wrap or parchment paper.
6. If the nori wrapper's shiny side is facing up and the rough side is facing down, it's ready to eat.
7. A little spicy mayo and eel or oyster sauce are all that's needed to finish the dish.
8. Fold over one end of each plastic wrap so that the roll may be joined.
9. Press the roll into a long cylinder with the sushi mat, a towel, or your hands, then fill the ends with rice to seal the roll.
10. Whisk together the egg, sriracha, and soy sauce in a rectangular baking dish large enough to hold the sushi roll.
11. Panko bread crumbs are used to coat the outside of the roll.
12. Add roughly 1-2 inches of oil to a pan and bring the temperature to 350 to 360 degrees Fahrenheit.

13. Place the sushi roll on a pan and cook for 2-3 minutes on each side, or until the outsides are golden brown, draining the excess oil.
14. If desired, top with fried onions, eel or oyster sauce, and spicy mayo.
15. A sharp or serrated knife, drizzled with rice vinegar or water between each slice, can help you slice the roll without it becoming sticky and ruining the whole roll.

176. BACON-WRAPPED CREAM CHEESE CALIFORNIA ROLL

Prep Time: 10 minutes
Cook Time: 20 minutes
Total Time: 30 minutes

INGREDIENTS

- Bacon Thick Cut
- oz Crab Meat canned shredded or lumps in water
- 4 tbsp Kewpie Mayo
- 1/2 tsp Monkfruit Erythritol Blend
- 1/4 tsp Rice Vinegar
- 1/2 Whole Avocado
- 1/2 Whole Persian or Japanese Cucumber
- 1/4 oz Cream Cheese
- 1/8 tsp Sesame Seed optional
- Toothpicks
- 2 Sq Ft Aluminum Foil

INSTRUCTIONS

1. Cooking time: 400F. Cover the baking sheet in the oven with aluminum foil or a silicone baking mat.
2. The pieces of bacon should be around 5 inches long (you should end up with 10 slices). Wrap a cylinder-shaped item with a diameter of roughly 3-4" in 3-4" wide sheets of aluminum foil (or you can use your fingers). Wrap the bacon around the foil and secure it with a toothpick at the end. Make sure the bacon is arranged vertically on the oven tray before placing it in the oven. Repeat for each of the 10 bacon rolls. Turn oven on and bake for 16-19 more minutes until crispy.
3. Cucumber slices should be sliced in half and placed aside. For each role, you'll need a piece.
4. The avocado should be peeled and chopped into 1" x 1/2" pieces and stored in an airtight container. For each role, you'll need a piece. If you'd want to see how we do it, here it is.
5. It is best to slice the cream cheese into one-ounce chunks (using the marker on the cream cheese wrapper). In order to get 8 pieces for 1 ounce of cream cheese, cut it into eighths and leave it aside. Every roll will require a piece.
6. Drain canned crab meat by squeezing the flesh with a spoon to remove the water. A lack of moisture will alter its final texture. Crab flesh, Kewpie Mayo, Monkfruit Erythritol Blend, and Rice Vinegar are mixed together in a mixing dish. Set aside until the mixture has reached a consistency similar to potato salad
7. Remove the toothpicks once the bacon is cooled enough to handle. Undo the bacon rolls with 2 fingers and add a cucumber, cream cheese, avocado, and a tsp of crab mixture in the center of the bacon. Place the bacon back on the plate. Form a roll out of the bacon and place it on a serving dish.

8. Enjoy with optional Sesame Seeds if desired!

NOTE –

Soy sauce is unnecessary because the bacon already has enough salt.

177.   CHICKEN SUSHI

INGREDIENTS

- ½ cup of sushi rice
- ½ tsp salt
- 3 Tbsp sushi vinegar
- 4 nori sheets
- 2 bamboo sushi mat
- Roast chicken, shredded
- 3 avocado, halved, stoned, peeled and chopped
- 1 small carrot, cut into thin strips
- soy sauce to serve
- pickled ginger to serve
- wasabi to serve
- Heinz Seriously Good Japanese Style Mayo

METHOD

1. In a sieve, rinse the rice well under cold water. Bring 2 1/2 cups cold water and 1/2 teaspoon salt to a boil in a pot. When you put the mixture on high heat, it will come to a rapid boil quickly. With the cover on, cook for 12 minutes. Remove from the heat for 10 minutes and cool completely with the lid on before serving. Pour the sushi vinegar into a bowl and mix thoroughly. Then transfer the mixture to a cooling tray.
2. Nori should be placed on a sushi mat with the glossy side facing down and horizontally aligned. Rice should be distributed over the nori with damp fingertips, leaving a 2cm strip free of rice on one side of the sheet.
3. Sliced avocado and carrots are arranged on top of a bed of rice containing shredded chicken mixed with Heinz Seriously Good Japanese Style Mayo.
4. In order to help you roll the sushi away from you, use the bamboo mat as a guide.Refrigerate for 30 minutes after wrapping with cling film. Continually add in the other ingredients as needed.
5. Soy sauce, pickled ginger, and wasabi sauce go well with sashimi-style slices.

178.   SPICY TUNA ROLL

PREP TIME: 30 mins
TOTAL TIME: 30 mins

INGREDIENTS

- ½ cup of sushi rice (cooked and seasoned) (every roll requires ¾ cup of (135 g) sushi rice. 1 rice cooker cup of (180 ml /150 g) makes 330 g (12 oz, 1 ¾ cup of) of cooked rice.)
- oz sashimi-grade tuna
- 2 tsp sriracha sauce
- ½ tsp roasted sesame oil
- green onions/scallions (cut into thin rounds)
- sheet nori (seaweed) (every roll requires half sheet; cut in half crosswise)
- 3 tbsp toasted white sesame seeds
- spicy mayo
- For Vinegar Water for Dipping Fingers (Tezu)
- ¼ cup of water (4 Tbsp)

- 2 tsp rice vinegar

INSTRUCTIONS

1. Make a list of everything you'll need to make the dish. The time required to prepare the sushi rice is not included in the cooking time. Please refer to the sushi rice recipe for a detailed instruction to making sushi rice. Always keep a moist towel over the sushi rice to keep it from drying out. Apply a layer of plastic wrap on your bamboo sushi mat.

2. Combine 14 cup (4 Tbsp) of water and 2 tsp rice vinegar in a small basin to make vinegar water for dipping fingers (Tezu). Rice will not adhere to your fingers if you dip them in water.

3. Make 14-inch (0.5 cm) cubes of tuna (or you can mince the tuna).

4. Mix the tuna with the Sriracha sauce, sesame oil, and green onion in a medium bowl (save some for topping).

5. Place a half-sheet of nori on the bamboo mat, shiny side down. Spread 34 cups of the rice out evenly on the nori sheet using Tezu-wet fingertips. Rice can be topped with sesame seeds.

6. Make sure the rice-facing side is down on the nori sheet before flipping it over. Line the nori sheet's bottom border with the bamboo mat's bottom end. Place half of the tuna mixture on the nori sheet's bottom end.

7. Using your fingers to hold the contents in place, grab the bamboo mat's lower edge and roll it up into a tight cylinder. Roll the bamboo mat forward while maintaining a moderate pressure on the surface of the mat.

8. Cut each half of the roll into three equal pieces using a very sharp knife.. Every few cuts, wipe the knife off with a moist towel. Use Tezu or plastic wrap to keep the rice from sticking to your fingers when cutting sushi rolls.

9. Top each piece of sushi with a dollop of spicy mayo and the last of the green onions.

10. TO KEEP ACCESSIBLE

11. On the same day, it's ideal to have sushi rolls. Refrigeration causes rice to become hard and dry. In order to store sushi rolls in the refrigerator, I recommend covering them with plastic and a thick kitchen towel so that the rice remains fresh and safe, but does not get very cold. '

179. VEGAN BLACK RICE SUSHI ROLLS

INGREDIENTS

- SUSHI
- ⅓ cup of organic tempeh (55 g), cut into thin strips
- ⅓ cup of soy sauce (80 mL)
- 2 medium carrot, grated
- ¼ head purple cabbage, grated
- 2 sheets toasted nori
- black rice
- ½ cup of avocado (75 g), thinly sliced lengthwise
- ⅓ cup of English cucumber (50 g), seeded, cut into thin strips
- ⅓ cup of cashews (45 g), coarsely chopped
- water, for sealing
- SESAME MISO SAUCE

- 3 tbsp olive oil
- ¼ cup of lime juice (60 mL)
- 1 tbsp maple syrup
- 2 tsp white miso paste
- 2 tsp black sesame seeds
- 1 tsp fresh ginger, grated, optional
- SPECIAL EQUIPMENT
- bamboo sushi mat, optional

INSTRUCTIONS

1. Soy sauce is poured over the tempeh in a medium dish. Set aside for at least 25 minutes to marinate. Meanwhile, prepare the other components for the dish.

2. A medium nonstick frying pan should be heated to a high temperature. Add the tempeh strips that have been marinated. When the outsides are golden brown and somewhat burnt, remove them from the pan. Set aside to cool once you've removed it from the pan.

3. Toss the carrots and cabbage together in a medium-sized bowl.

4. Downn on the bamboo mat or clean work surface You should leave approximately a 14 inch (1 14 cm) of space at the top of the nori for the rice to rest on.Rice and a few avocado slices should be placed on top of nori sheets. A few cukes, some carrot-cabbage mix, a few tempeh cubes, and around 1 tbsp. of chopped cashews complete the dish.

5. Close the sushi roll by sprinkling some water on the nori's open edge. Carefully tuck the ingredients within the nori sheet by rolling the filled end of the sheet over onto itself with both hands. Make sure to keep rolling until the rice is completely covered by the nori sheet. Re-fill the remaining nori sheets and repeat the process.

6. Each roll should be sliced into six to eight pieces, depending on personal choice. If you moisten your knife before slicing, you'll be able to slice more easily through the nori. However, be careful!

7. To make the sesame miso sauce, combine the olive oil, lime juice, maple syrup, miso, sesame seeds, and any more ginger you'd like to include in the mix. In a large mixing basin, whisk together all of the ingredients until smooth and creamy.

8. Toss the sushi rolls in the sauce and serve.

9. Enjoy!

180.　BLACK RICE SUSHI

Prep Time: 45 mins
Cook Time: 50 mins
Total Time: 1 hour 35

INGREDIENTS

- 2 cups of black rice
- 3 ½ cup of water
- 1 cucumber
- 1 avocado
- 1 cup of shredded carrots
- ¾ lb cooked shrimp, thinly sliced
- ⅓ cup of rice vinegar + 1 tbsp for coating avocado
- 10 stevia drops
- 1 tbsp salt
- sheets nori
- coconut aminos for dipping (optional)
- wasabi (optional)

INSTRUCTIONS

1. Rice should be cooked according to the package's directions. As a result, make sure

you follow the manufacturer's directions about the rice-to-water ratio while shopping. Cook the rice for 45 minutes after bringing it to a boil and then lowering the heat to a simmer.Please refrain from peeping! In order to get the food to cook correctly, you must keep the pot steaming hot at all times. Remove the lid at the 35-minute mark to examine if all of the water has been drained. Then mix it, put the cover back on, and remove it off the stovetop for 5 minutes. Stir and let it rest for 6 minutes if there is any water remaining in the pot before the water is absorbed.

2. Large mixing basin: Add the cooked rice to the bowl. Let it cool down to room temperature before serving. Using a heat-safe spatula or a wooden rice spoon, gently fluff or stir the rice if you're in a rush. It may take a few 5-minute intervals in the freezer (shaking between) until it's cold.

3. Prepare your vegetables while the rice cools.

4. Using a spoon, carefully scrape the seeds out of the cucumber after cutting it in half lengthwise. Next, cut the cucumber into 1/4-inch broad strips. There should be a small amount of green peel on each strip of the pizza crust.

5. After you've removed the pit and halve the avocado, slice the flesh into thin ribbons inside its skin (without cutting through the skin). I use a paring knife and hold the avocado half in one hand while slicing it. Once you've removed the skin, use a spoon to remove the meat. Rice vinegar can be used to prevent avocado from oxidizing and becoming brown (yuck!) since you won't be using it right away.

6. As the Japanese do, you'll want to set up a sushi bar. I prefer to put out all of the contents (in this example, cucumber, avocado, carrots, and shrimp) on a large cutting board before assembling the sushi. Stack nori sheets on a clean counter or table, cover your sushi roller in plastic wrap (or not, just additional clean-up), and then take a small basin of warm water and a kitchen towel (for your fingers*). Your work area is now complete!

7. Mix the rice vinegar, stevia, and salt in a small bowl until the salt is dissolved. Make sure that you mix thoroughly so that all of your rice is coated. To prevent the rice from sticking together like typical sticky white rice, crush it with the back of the spoon as you stir.

8. Once you've added the bowl of rice to your setup, you're ready to go! Literally! Let's get to work making sushi!

9. Use your sushi roller to roll a sheet of nori with its glossy side down and the vertical lines facing up.

10. You may use a spoon or your fingers to distribute 2/3 cup of rice onto the nori. Cover the nori save for the top 2 inches. Use this place to help close up the roll! ' Warm water and a kitchen towel can be used to keep your fingers from sticking while you distribute the rice around.

11. Starting approximately an inch from the bottom of the nori sheet, start placing your fillings in a horizontal row across the sheet. If you're just getting started with sushi rolling, keep it simple. If you overfill your dish, you'll wind up with a massive mess.That should be avoided. To ensure that each mouthful contains a little something from each ingredient, be sure to

spread the ingredients out evenly throughout the sheet.

12. It's now or never! Do not feel disheartened if it takes some time to achieve your goals. Lift the nori's bottom edge and wrap it over the fillings using the sushi roller as a guide. Squeeze the roll toward your body with a light hand. The roller comes in helpful in this situation. The fillings will pour out if you push too hard, but you need to hold the roll together so it doesn't split apart when you remove it from the roller. Squeeze and tuck the roll in order to keep it tight while you continue rolling. Nearing the end! Use warm water to run a finger down the top of the sheet just before rinsing it off. This will help you remember it better. A few squirts of water might be enough. Using the roller, gently press and form the sushi roll into a lovely cylinder shape from the top to the bottom.

13. A cutting board should be used for this task. Cut each roll as you create them, or wait till the end and cut all of them at once. At the end, I like to cut them all.

14. Using a very sharp knife, dip it in your warm water, and then cut the rolls. When cutting the roll, you won't have to worry about the knife becoming stuck. As required, rewet the knife and slice the roll into eight equal pieces.

15. It's done! * As you labor, your hands will become somewhat dirty. Just dip them in the basin of water and dry them off with a dish towel anytime they get a bit out of hand. It couldn't be easier now!

181.   BLUEBERRY FRUIT "SUSHI"

INGREDIENTS

- 3/4 cup of short-grain rice
- 1/4 cup of water
- 2 tbsp sugar
- Pinch salt
- 1/2 cup of coconut milk
- 1/2 tsp vanilla extract
- 1/2 cup of blueberries
- 1/2 avocado
- 1 small p every, apple or plum cut into small cubes
- Dipping Sauce Ingredients
- 1 cup of frozen blueberries
- 1/3 cup of vanilla yogurt
- 1 tbsp honey

INSTRUCTIONS

1   Pour water, sugar, and salt into a medium saucepan and bring to a boil. Add rice and heat to a boil.

2   After 16 minutes of cooking, the rice should be soft but still chewy.

3   Add the vanilla and coconut milk and mix well. This should be a thick mixture. Let it become a little lukewarm.

4   Wet your hands and pat half of the rice into a 7 × 5-inch rectangle on a piece of parchment paper.

5   On one side, place half of a rectangle's blueberries. Add a quarter of the avocado and apple pieces to the salad.

6   Wrap the fruit in the parchment to make a long, tightly rolled log.

7   Unwrap the parchment; cut the rice roll into 1-inch pieces to form "sushi rolls" out of the parchment.

8   The leftover rice and fruit combination may be used in the same manner.

9   Instructions for making a dipping sauce

10   Blend the blueberries, yogurt, and honey in a blender until they're smooth and creamy. Before smoothing, puree the ingredients.

182.   BOSTON ROLL

Prep Time: 10 minutes
Cook Time: 50 minutes
Total Time: 1 hour

INGREDIENTS

- 1 cup of sushi rice short-grain sushi rice
- 1 cup of water
- 1 ½ tbspsushi vinegar (optional) or mixing 1 tbsp rice vinegar, 1/2 tbsp sugar, and 1/2 tsp salt
- 3-6 tbsp tobiko (or masago)
- oz shrimp
- 1/2 cucumber cut into ½-inch strips
- 2 sheets nori seaweed sheet
- 2 avocado ripe but still firm
- Optional for Serving:
- soy sauce
- wasabi paste

INSTRUCTIONS

1.   To begin the process of cooking rice, rinse it and put it to a rice cooker with water. Once the food has cooled, transfer it to a large mixing bowl. Make sure it's still a little warm before adding the sushi vinegar

2.   Shrimp may be poached with only a sprinkle of salt. Turn off the heat and add shrimp. Allow the shrimp to rest for around 3-5 minutes before slicing into them. To halt the cooking process, transfer the shrimp to a dish of cold water. Remove the tails and peel the shrimp.

3.   Layout a bamboo mat with a sheet of plastic wrap on top of it to produce Boston Sushi Rolls

4.   .

5.   Using a knife, cut the roll into eight pieces.

6.   Stack one-third to one-half the nori on the bottom side of your mat.

7.   Pour 3/4 cup of cooked rice into a bowl and squirt some water on it. The rice should be spread out evenly to the borders of the pan. Rice that's been cooked with too much pressure will turn out mushy.

8.   Switching positions, place the rice and nori on top of each other, with rice on the bottom.

9.   Place shrimp, avocado, and cucumber on nori. If you overfill a roll, it won't seal properly.

10. With your thumbs below the bamboo mat's edge, lift it over the filling.

11. Tighten the bamboo mat by rolling it away from you. You'll get there if you keep going.

12. Remove the bamboo mat before using tobiko.

13. Cover the sushi mat with the plastic wrap. Wrap the tobiko around the sushi roll.

14. Discard the plastic wrap but save the bamboo mat. Using a knife, cut the roll into eight pieces. Remove the plastic wrap from all of the food. It's time to eat!

NOTES

Pour 1/4 cup of water and 2 tablespoons of rice vinegar into a bowl and stir to combine.

Avoid putting sushi rice in the refrigerator to chill down as this will alter the flavor and texture.

What's wrong with my sushi roll? Using the incorrect rice or not squeezing the rolls tightly enough might be to blame. While rolling, you must tuck in and pull the bamboo mat.

NUTRITION

There are 51kcal in this serving of food, with 6 grams of carbohydrates, 2 grams of protein, and 2 grams of fat. There is also 1 grams of fiber, 1 gram of sugar, and 1 milligram of vitamin A, C, and iron.

183. HEALTHY AVOCADO SUSHI WITH BROWN RICE
READY IN: 1hr 15mins

INGREDIENTS

- 1 cup of short-grain brown rice
- 1 -2 tbsp brown rice vinegar (or apple cider vinegar)
- nori sushi sheets
- 1 avocado
- 1/4 red pepper
- 1/2 cup of alfalfa sprout

DIRECTIONS

1   Add 2.1 cups of water and a pinch of sea salt to the rinsed and drained rice. Cook for 45 minutes once it reaches a boil.
2   After that, the rice must be allowed to cool. Add enough vinegar to make the rice stick to itself.
3   Place a nori sheet on the rolling mat. These grooves are used to indicate where you should cut your sushi, and should be aligned with the direction you're looking in.
4   Cover the nori sheet with rice, leaving a little gap at the rear for the roll to be sealed.

5   Perpendicular to the direction you're facing, place a few veggies at the near edge of the sheet. Overlap the row of veggies with the sheet and roll it up. Press down on the roll while returning the pressure to you. Don't crush the roll, but make sure it's tight.
6   Continue rolling after removing the rolling mat from the front edge. To finish, seal the roll with a strip of rice-free paper at one of the ends.
7   A few minutes before slicing, let your sushi roll to sit on the counter to allow the rice to soften the nori. Tamari (or soy sauce), pickled ginger, and wasabi are frequent accompaniments offered for dipping with Asian cuisine.

184. CALIFORNIA ROLLS WITH BROWN RICE
PREP TIME15 Min
TOTAL TIME 60 Min

INGREDIENTS

- 1 ½ cup of (375 mL) UNCLE BEN'S® Wholegrain Brown Rice
- 1 Tbsp (15 mL) rice wine vinegar
- 1 Tbsp (15 mL) granulated sugar
- ¾ tsp (4 mL) salt
- nori sheets
- ½ English cucumber, cut into matchsticks
- 1 avocado, thinly sliced
- 8-piece leg-style imitation crab
- soy sauce, wasabi and pickled ginger

DIRECTIONS

1. In a saucepan, heat the UNCLE BEN'S® Wholegrain Brown Rice with no butter or salt. In a small bowl, combine vinegar,

sugar, and salt. 45 to 60 seconds or until sugar is dissolved in the sugar can be microwaved. Incorporate the vinegar mixture into the rice with your hands.

2. Use parchment paper to lay down a single sheet. Place the crab on the parchment with the nori trimmed to fit its length. Leave a 1-inch (2.5 cm) strip of nori exposed at the top and spread roughly half a cup (125 mL) of rice over it.

3. The bottom of the nori should be filled with cucumbers, avocados, and crab flesh. Wrap the nori around the filling and tightly roll it into a log using the parchment paper. Assemble by sprinkling water on the nori and cutting into four pieces. Repeat with the remaining ingredients. Soy sauce, wasabi, and pickled ginger are all condiments that can be served alongside the meal.

185. CHICKEN AND AVOCADO BROWN RICE SUSHI ROLLS

INGREDIENTS

- 1 cup of short-grain brown rice
- 1 tbsp gluten-free unseasoned rice vinegar
- 1 boneless skinless chicken breast
- pinch every salt and pepper
- 1/2 tsp vegetable oil
- 1/4 cup of light mayonnaise
- 2 tsp gluten-free Tamari
- 2 tsp sesame oil
- 1 tsp liquid honey
- 1/2 tsp Asian chili sauce (such as sriracha)
- 3 sheets roasted nori
- 1-piece English cucumber halved, seeded and cut in strips
- half avocado peeled, pitted and sliced

METHOD

1. Add vinegar to the rice when it's still hot and ready to eat, if desired. Let it cool down before handling.

2. Salt and pepper the chicken while it's cooking, if you want. Cook the chicken for 10 to 12 minutes, tossing it once, in a small nonstick pan with vegetable oil heated to medium. Slice into thin lengthwise pieces after allowing it cool fully. Remove from consideration.

3. Mayonnaise, tamari, sesame oil, honey and chili sauce are all mixed together in a small bowl; leave away.

4. On a bamboo sushi rolling mat, place 1 nori sheet shiny side down and long side nearest to you. Gently sprinkle approximately half a cup of rice evenly over the nori with wet fingertips, leaving a 1-inch (2.5 cm) border around each side.

5. Line up one-quarter of the sauce approximately 2 inches (5 cm) from the nearest long edge and drizzle it in a thin, even stream. Add one-fourth of the cucumber, chicken, and avocado on the plate.

6. Using a mat to raise, roll up tightly, encasing the filling, starting at the nearest long edge. To dry, lay flat with the seam side down. Make three additional rolls by repeating the process with the remainder of the ingredients. Evenly cut the ends of the meat using a sharp chef's knife. Using a moist towel to clean the knife between cuts, slice each roll into eight equal pieces.

7. Sushi rolls are a wonderful way to use up any leftover rice or chicken in your fridge, according to the chefs at Test Kitchen. Use 2 cups of cooked rice and 2 cups of sliced cooked chicken from your leftovers to make this dish. Reheat the rice and add the vinegar after the first two paragraphs have been removed. Continue following the recipe.

186. SOBA NOODLE SUSHI ROLLS

PREP TIME 10 mins
COOK TIME 10 mins
TOTAL TIME 20 mins

INGREDIENTS

- 2 ounces soba noodles
- 3 leaves Swiss chard
- 3 sheets nori
- 1/4 bell peppers red
- 1 avocado
- 1 carrot large
- 1 leaves cabbage (Savoy)
- 2 tbsp plum chutney or plum butter
- 2 tbsp Bragg's liquid aminos (or tamari)
- 1 tbsp maple syrup
- 1 tbsp apple cider vinegar
- 1 tbsp mint leaves (fresh)
- 1/2 tsp chili-ginger paste

INSTRUCTIONS

1. For 8 minutes, cook the soba noodles in a pot of boiling, salted water. Cut the stem from the chard leaves once they have been folded in half. The chard leaves should be added to the water just before draining the noodles, about 15 seconds before they begin to wilt.

2. In a colander or colander with cold water, rinse the chard leaves and noodles, then drain them thoroughly. When it's time to dry the leaves, wrap them in a towel and place them in the sink to drain thoroughly.

3. When cutting the red pepper, be sure to do it in a thin, long strip. Carrots should be scrubbed and then peeled into long, thin strips using a peeler. Cabbage should be sliced very thinly.

4. Using a knife or spoon, halve the avocado and remove the pit.

5. Mince the mint finely. When ready to serve, add mint and whisk together the sauce components (plum butter through apple cider vinegar).

6. Keep a small basin of water nearby for rinsing hands and tools between tasks.

7. To begin, lay out a single nori sheet vertically on a sushi mat or other strong cloth. Leave about two inches of nori at the top of each chard leaf. In the center, spread a thin layer of soba noodles (one third of what you cooked). Put about a third of the remaining vegetables on top and arrange them so that they run lengthwise along the plate.

8. Using a cloth or a mat as a rolling surface, begin to roll the sushi away from you (using the mat or towel to help you get it started)Toss in the vegetables one cup at a time. Hold the roll in one hand while dipping the other in water, then wet the exposed edge with your fingertips after you've reached the top. Take care to seal the sushi when you've finished rolling it. To dry, lay flat with the seam side down.

9. Then cut the rolls into six equal pieces. Seam-side down, use a very sharp knife to

cut them after at least five minutes of resting (or they can come apart).

187.   BUFFALO CHICKEN SUSHI

Prep Time: 15 minutes
Cook Time: 20 minutes
Total Time: 35 minutes

INGREDIENTS

- 1 cup of short-grain rice rice, sushi rice
- 2 cups of water
- 1/4 cup of rice vinegar
- 1 tbsp sugar
- 1/2 tsp salt
- sheets nori
- 1 cup of chicken cooked shredded
- 1/4 cup of hot sauce
- 2 celery ribs
- 2 carrots peeled
- 1/2 cup of blue cheese crumbled
- 1/2 cup of tortilla chips cheese, crumbled, optional

DIRECTIONS

1. Cook rice for around 18-22 minutes after bringing water and rice to a boil, then decrease heat and cover to simmer.
2. meantime, cook the vinegar, sugar, and salt over medium heat until the sugar and salt have dissolved, then put aside and cool.
3. Rice should be mixed completely with the vinegar mixture before it is served.
4. Nori should be placed on a sushi mat with the glossy side down and rice should be placed on the other side, covering about three quarters of it. Stack 1 inch from the edge of a tortilla with a row of buffalo

chicken, celery, carrots, blue cheese, and tortilla chips. Do it again three times.
5. Using a bread knife, cut the rolls into six equal pieces!

188.   CALIFORNIA ROLL

Prep Time: 20 minutes
Total Time: 20 minutes

INGREDIENTS

- 1 batch prepared sushi rice
- 1 avocado (sliced into 16 wedges)
- 200 grams crab meat (or imitation crab)
- 1 small cucumber (julienned)
- 3 sheets unseasoned nori
- 1 tbsp toasted sesame seeds

STEPS

1. Sushi rice is ready to be made.
2. In order to protect the rice from adhering to your bamboo mat, you must use plastic wrap to cover your makisu (bamboo mat). Preparing a small dish of water for dipping your fingers in can help prevent the rice from sticking to them.
3. You should be able to get two 3.75-inch × 8-inch pieces of nori after carefully folding it in half. You may toast nori by gently waving it over an open flame, or just use a pair of scissors if it's stable and won't split.
4. Lay a single sheet of nori at the bottom of the mat, if desired. Add a tiny bit of rice to the bowl of water and moisten your fingers.
5. Gently spread the rice out to the corners of the nori with your fingertips, making sure your fingers are wet to avoid the rice from sticking. Rice that's been cooked with too much pressure will turn out mushy.

6   Rice and nori are flipped over so that rice is on top and nori is on bottom. Sprinkle with sesame seeds.

7   A few slices of cucumber and avocado should be placed on the nori's bottom edge. Spread some crabmeat on top of the roll to finish it off. If you overfill your roll, it won't be able to seal correctly.

8   Using your thumbs and fingers, you can raise a bamboo mat with rice over the filling and then roll the sushi.

9   Turn rice and nori over so that the contents are on one side.

10 Working from home

11 Remove the nori and discard the rice after rolling it over the mixture one more time.

12 At this stage, you'll probably need to peel the mat back away from the rice if you want to avoid accidentally rolling the mat into the rice.

189.   SALMON CALIFORNIA ROLLS

Total Time 1 hr 10 min
Prep 40 min
Cook 15 min

INGREDIENTS

- Rice, white, dry 1 cup of(s), (sushi), 200g
- Caster sugar 1 tsp
- Vinegar ¼ cup of(s), (rice vinegar), 60ml
- Dried nori seaweed 3 sheet(s), (toasted)
- Sesame seeds 1½ tbs, toasted
- Lebanese cucumber 1 medium, cut into batons
- Snow peas 50 g, shredded
- Skinless salmon 200 g, (sushi grade) cut into long 1cm thick batons
- Wasabi paste 10 g, (2 tsp)
- Ginger, pickled 90 g, (1/3 cup of)
- Reduced salt soy sauce 1 tbs
- Table salt, non-iodised ¼ tsp

INSTRUCTIONS

1   In order to get the water virtually clear, repeat the washing process multiple times. In a saucepan, combine rice with 112 cups (375 ml) water. Set a high heat source to the mixture and bring to a rapid boil. Reduce the temperature under the cover. The water should be absorbed after 15 minutes or so. Cook for 15 minutes, then remove from the heat and let stand covered until done.

2   Meanwhile, in a separate basin, mix the sugar, salt, and half of the vinegar.

3   In a wide, shallow bowl, spread out the rice evenly. Use a spatula to incorporate the vinegar mixture into the dough.

4   Stir together 14 cup (60 ml) water and the remaining vinegar in a small dish.

5   A nori sheet should be laid out on a bamboo sushi mat, then rolled. Spread one-third of the rice on the nori sheet after dipping your hands in the vinegar mixture. A third of the sesame seeds should be sprinkled on top. Turn the rice side of the sheet over. Place one-third of the cucumbers, snow peas, and salmon 5cm from the edge closest to you on the rice. Spread a little amount of wasabi on top of the fish.

6   Hold the filling in place as you roll the mat to encompass it. Make two more rolls using the leftover nori sheets, rice, sesame seeds, and filling. To make four pieces, cut the rolls in half. Soy sauce, pickled ginger, and

wasabi are all excellent accompaniments to sushi.

NOTES

Extra cucumber ribbons are a good idea for serving.

Sushi mats made of bamboo may be found in supermarkets' Asian sections.

190. CALIFORNIA ROLL SUSHI CAKE

INGREDIENTS

- 2 cups of cooked brown rice
- 2 tbspmayonnaise
- 1/2 tbsp soy sauce
- 1/2 tbsp rice vinegar
- 1/2 cup of cooked crab meat
- 1 avocado, thinly sliced
- 1 Persian cucumber, thinly sliced
- cherry tomatoes, halved
- 1 tbsp microgreens

DIRECTIONS

1. Before serving, mix brown rice, mayonnaise, soy sauce, and rice vinegar in a medium bowl.
2. Begin by layering the crab first in a jar or straight-sided dish. Assemble the dish by layering rice, cucumbers, avocados, and the rest of the crab. Each layer should be flattened and compressed before going on to the next, so that when it is taken from the mold, it preserves its shape.
3. Carefully invert your mold onto a plate when it has been filled to the brim.
4. Microgreens and cherry tomatoes adorn the bottom of the plate.

191. CALIFORNIA ROLL BOWL

INGREDIENTS

- cups of Cooked Rice, kept warm
- 1/4 cup of Seasoned Rice Vinegar
- 1 English Cucumber, Chopped
- 1 Avocado, peeled, pitted and chopped
- 1 Packages (8 oz. every) Crab Delights® Flake or Chunk, chopped
- Toasted Sesame Seeds

DIRECTIONS

1. Soy Sauce, Wasabi and Pickled Ginger are optional additions to this dish
2. Rice should be mixed with vinegar and served in four separate bowls. Sprinkle sesame seeds on top of the cucumber, avocado, and Crab Delights®. Toss with Sriracha mayonnaise and serve.
3. (Optional) Sprinkle with nori flake and garnish with pickled ginger, wasabi, and soy sauce for added flavor.

192. CALIFORNIA ROLL
PREP TIME: 1 hr.
TOTAL TIME: 1 hr.

INGREDIENTS

- cup of sushi rice (cooked and seasoned) (Since every California Roll requires ¾ cup of sushi rice, you need to cook 3 ½ rice cooker cup ofs, which will yield 1155 g. Make sure to cover the prepared sushi rice with a damp cloth at all times to prevent it from drying.
- sheets nori

- tbsp toasted white sesame seeds
- For Fillings
- oz cooked crab meat
- tbsp Japanese mayonnaise
- ½ English cucumber
- 2 avocados
- ½ lemon (for avocado)
- For Vinegar Water for Dipping Fingers
- ¼ cup of water
- 2 tsp rice vinegar
- For Toppings (Optional)
- ikura (salmon roe)
- yuzu-flavored tobiko (flying fish roe)

INSTRUCTIONS

1. Tabletop temperature rice is ideal for slicing into sushi. Every every Californian To create 8 sushi rolls, you'll need 6 cup of sushi rice (135 g) each roll, or 1080 g of sushi rice.
2. You may prevent your fingers from adhering to the bamboo sushi mat by covering it with plastic wrap and preparing vinegar water (Tezu).
3. Fillings to be Made
4. To prepare the crab meat, combine the crab meat with Japanese mayonnaise.
5. Using a spoon, separate the cucumber's seeds from the skin. The nori sheet should be the length of your thin long strips.
6. Slice avocados into 14-inch (0.5-centimeter) thick slices (See How To Cut Avocado). Lemon juice, drizzled over the avocado, prevents browning.
7. Cut off one third of a nori sheet and use the other two thirds.
8. To make sushi by rolling it
9. The glossy side of the nori sheet should face down on the bamboo sushi mat. You can wet your fingers with Tezu and put 34 cup (135 g) of the rice equally on the nori sheet after wetting them.
10. Take some sesame seeds or tobiko and sprinkling the rice.
11. Rice should be face-up on the nori sheet. The bottom of the bamboo mat should be lined with a nori sheet. Place the cucumber, crab meat, and avocado on the nori sheet at the bottom.
12. Keeping the contents firmly in place with your fingers, grab the mat's lower edge and roll it into a tight cylinder.
13. Gently roll the bamboo mat forward, lifting the edge of the mat slightly while maintaining a soft grip on the mat. To keep the finished rolls from drying out, use a moist towel to cover them at all times. If you haven't finished your rolls, don't stop creating them!
14. It's possible to produce Ikura Sushi with the remaining third of a nori sheet. In the middle of the nori sheet, cut a huge slit. Make sushi rice balls and wrap them in nori sheets. Top with ikura.
15. A sharp knife is needed to cut each roll in half and then cut each half into three equal halves. Using a moist towel, wipe off the blade of the knife after each use.

TO KEEP ACCESSIBLE

On the same day, it's ideal to have sushi rolls. Refrigeration causes rice to become hard and dry. When it comes time to store sushi rolls in the refrigerator, If you want to keep the rice cold and safe, but not frozen, I suggest wrapping it in plastic and then wrapping it in a thick dish towel.

193. INSIDE-OUT CALIFORNIA ROLL

Total: 15 min
Active: 15 min

INGREDIENTS

- 1 sheet nori
- 1 cup of sushi rice that has been cooked and seasoned
- Tobiko, for garnish
- Black and blond sesame seeds, for garnish
- Black and blond sesame seeds, for garnish
- 2 cooked snow crab legs, shelled and meat reserved
- 2 cooked snow crab legs, shelled and meat reserved
- 1 avocado, diced
- 1 cucumber, peeled and julienned
- Pickled ginger, for serving
- Wasabi, for serving

DIRECTIONS

1. Special tools: The sushi mat
2. Sushi rice should be thinly coated with rice seasoning before the nori is laid out on top, making sure to cover the whole sushi mat. Toss some sesame seeds and tobiko into the mix. You may do this by turning the nori sheet over and putting sushi rice on top of it. When you're done placing the snow crab flesh on a nori sheet, spread some avocado and cucumber slices horizontally over it in a 1-inch-by-1-inch grid. Using the mat, tightly roll-up. Serve with pickled ginger and wasabi on the side.

194. CANNED TUNA SUSHI

INGREDIENTS

- 2 tbsp sugar
- 2 tsp mirin
- 1 1/2 cup ofs cooked sushi rice
- 1 small tin tuna in brine, drained
- tbsp sweet chili sauce
- 1/2 small onion, finely diced
- 5 sheets toasted nori (seaweed)
- 1 tsp wasabi, optional

DIRECTIONS

1. Add sugar and mirin to the sushi rice after it has been cooked. Let it cool down.
2. Tuna, chili sauce, and chopped onions are mixed together in a bowl.
3. A sushi mat should be used to place a nori sheet with the rough side facing up. Press firmly but leave a 5cm space on the side closest to you while spreading the rice over nori.
4. Closest to the edge, place the tuna. To begin, place the sushi on a mat and begin rolling it up into a roll. Use water to help seal the nori roll by moistening the 5cm space at the end. Before you need it, chill.
5. Slice the rolls into 1 1/2cm pieces just before serving.
6. Alternatively, you may offer the sushi with wasabi on the side and allow your guests select how much they want to eat.

195. CAPRESE SANDWICH

Total: 11 min
Prep: 10 min
Cook: 1 min

INGREDIENTS

- Kosher salt
- 2 heirloom tomatoes, sliced
- 1 large baguette, split
- 3 balls fresh mozzarella, thickly sliced
- Fresh basil leaves
- Basil Oil, recipe follows
- Basil Oil:
- 2 bunches fresh basil, stems removed
- 1 cup of extra-virgin olive oil
- Kosher salt and freshly ground black pepper
- Juice of 1 lemon

DIRECTIONS

1. The mozzarella and basil go on top of the salted tomatoes, which are then layered on the bottom slice of bread. Basil Oil can be drizzled on top. The final slice of bread should be topped with the rest of the toppings. Slice into sections.

2. Mix in 45 seconds to a minute of boiling water for the basil to infuse. Stop additional cooking by placing it in a cold water bath. Add to a blender once it has been drained and dried. Blend in the olive oil until smooth. Strain into a basin using cheesecloth. Salt and pepper can be added as needed. Before serving, add the lemon juice.

196. SUSHI-ROLL RICE SALAD

Active Time 40 min
Total Time 1 1/2 hr

INGREDIENTS

- 1 1/2 cup of short-grain sushi rice
- 1 3/4 cup of + 1 1/2 tbspwater
- 1/4 cup of seasoned rice vinegar
- 1 tbsp sugar
- 1 tsp salt
- 1 medium carrot
- 1 1/4 tsp wasabi paste (Japanese horseraBowl paste)
- 1 1/2 tbsp vegetable oil
- 1/2 large seedless cucumber (usually plastic-wrapped), peeled, halved lengthwise, cored, and chopped (1 cup of)
- 3 scallions, thinly sliced diagonally
- 3 tbspdrained sliced Japanese pickled ginger, coarsely chopped
- 1 tbsp sesame seeds, toasted
- 1 firm-ripe California avocado
- fresh shiso leaves (optional)
- 1 (6-inch) square toasted nori (dried laver), cut into very thin strips with scissors

STEPS

1 Drain the rice after 30 minutes of rinsing in a colander with numerous changes of cold water until the water is virtually clear.

2 Bring 3 cups of water and 1 3/4 cups of rice to a boil in a heavy pot, then cover and simmer for 2 minutes. Remove the rice from the stove and let it stand for 10 minutes with the lid on (do not lift lid).

3 Prior to adding the rice to the sugar, the sugar should be dissolved in water.Allow

the vinegar mixture to cool for two minutes while the rice is standing.

4 Using a spoon, stir the vinegar mixture into the rice and spread it out on a baking pan.

5 Shave long strips from the carrot with a vegetable peeler and cut them diagonally into 1/4-inch wide strips.

6 Toss rice, carrots, cucumbers, scallions, pickled ginger, and sesame seeds with the wasabi, remaining 1 1/2 tbsp water, and oil in a dish.

7 Remove the pit by slicing the avocado in half, and peel it before slicing it into 1/4-inch-thick slices. Every 4 plates, place 2 shiso leaves (if using). Sprinkle nori strips on top before adding avocado and rice mixture.

197. CATERPILLAR ROLL (WITH AN AVOCADO TOPPING)

Prep time: 20 minutes
Cook time: 50 minutes

INGREDIENTS

- For Sushi Rice
- 1 1/2 cup of sushi rice short-grain sushi rice
- 1 ½ cup of water
- 1 ½ tbsp optional sushi vinegar
- For Caterpillar Rolls
- oz unagi
- 1/2 cucumber
- 2 sheets nori
- 2 avocado ripe but still firm

INSTRUCTIONS

1. Rinse sushi rice in cold water before adding it to the rice cooker, and then cook it until the water is clear.

2. When you're ready to serve, transfer the rice to a large bowl and let it cool for a few minutes.

3. Stir in additional sushi vinegar when the mixture reaches a scalding temperature (or the substitute mixture).

4. Unagi: the art of preparing raw fish

5. The unagi should be baked for 10 to 12 minutes at 360 degrees Fahrenheit, or according to the box instructions.

6. When the unagi is done cooking, slice it into half-inch strips.

7. To make caterpillar rolls, follow these instructions:

8. To make cleanup a breeze, place the bamboo mat on a flat surface and cover it with plastic wrap.

9. After that, cut the nori sheets in half and lay one half on top of the other.

10. After immersing your hands in vinegar water to prevent the rice from sticking to them, spread 3/4 cup of cooked rice evenly over the nori.

11. Unagi strips and cucumbers should be placed on top of nori after the rice has been flipped over.

12. After placing your thumbs beneath the bamboo mat, begin pulling the edge of it up and over your filling.

13. Apply some pressure when rolling the bamboo mat away from you before the ends come together.

14. To make the avocado topping, follow these directions:

15. You may split an avocado in half and remove the pit and skin before slicing it thinly.

16. Spread the layer on the counter, then lift the Caterpillar Sushi Roll with a big knife and set it on top of the layer.

17. The avocado should now be wrapped in plastic wrap and covered with a sushi mat before being gently squeezed to form it around the roll.

18. When you've finished slicing your Caterpillar Sushi Roll, remove the mat but keep the plastic wrap, then remove the plastic wrap and eat your sushi.

198.   SALMON CARROT CUCUMBER SUSHI

rep Time 25 Minutes
Cook Time 25 Minutes

INGREDIENTS

- 1 x 95g can Safcol Salmon in Springwater, drained
- 1 Lebanese cucumbers, cut in thin batons
- 2 large carrots, cut in strips
- 1 cup of sushi rice, cooked following pack instructions
- 1 pack nori sheets for sushi
- 3 to 4 tbspsushi rice wine
- to serve
- 3 tbsp toasted sesame seeds
- Japanese soy for dipping
- wasabi
- Japanese style pickled ginger

INSTRUCTIONS

1. The product instructions for sushi rice should be followed. Add a dash of sushi vinegar to the mix. You may adjust the amount of vinegar to your preference.

Allow to cool before covering with cling film.

2. Using a double layer of baking parchment or a bamboo sushi mat, arrange a nori sheet shiny side down on the baking paper or paper. Then, leaving a few centimeters of nori sheet exposed at the end, cover the bottom half of the sheet with a thin coating of sushi rice.

3. Place slices of cucumber and carrot in the centre of the sushi rice and add a thin wasabi swab if desired. On top of the veggies, spread a thin layer of salmon flakes. Lift the end of the nori nearest to you and roll it into a tight log with the mat.

4. Arrange on a serving platter after being cut into eight equal pieces using a sharp knife. You may do that again and again until all the rice is gone.

5. Refrigerate the nori for about 30 minutes before serving to soften it somewhat. With a side of Japanese soy and wasabi and pickled ginger, this dish is best served cold.

199.   CALIFORNIA ROLL RECIPE

INGREDIENTS

- rice mixed with Japanese sushi vinegar
- Japanese cucumber, cut in strips - lengthwise
- Tobiko
- avocado, sliced
- nori
- Prepared raBowl, cut in strips - lengthwise
- Japanese mayonnaise

- crab stick, cut in strips – lengthwise shopping

HOW TO MAKE IT

1. Using a spoon, transfer the rice to a serving bowl (DO NOT use metal bowl)
2. Before adding the vinegar, wait for the rice to cool down a little.
3. Toss in some acidity. Do not pulverize the kernels of wheat.
4. Use a damp cloth to cover the device while it's not in use.
5. Clipwrap your bamboo mat to protect it.
6. Lay rice on the mat.
7. Top the rice with a nori sheet.
8. Place the nori, cucumber, raBowl, crabstick, avocado, and mayonnaise on top of the steamed vegetables.
9. Let's get this party started. Roll with a gentle squeeze.
10. Tobiko can be spread around the mat's edge once the roll has been made.
11. Let the tobiko 'stick' to the roll by gently rolling in your hands.
12. Slice the roll into equal halves.

200.   SPICY TUNA ROLL

INGREDIENTS

- 2 cup of sushi rice (460 g), cooked
- ¼ cup of seasoned rice vinegar (60 mL)
- half sheets sushi-grade nori
- TUNA FILLING
- can tuna, drained
- 1 ½ tbsp mayonnaise
- 1 ½ tsp sriracha
- 1 green onion, thinly sliced
- 1 tsp sesame oil

PREPARATION

Rice vinegar is a traditional way to season sushi rice, and it should be used as soon as the rice reaches room temperature.

Rough side up, place nori sheet on the rolling mat.

Mix the ingredients for the tuna filling in a small dish. Remove from consideration.

Then, wet your hands, grab a little amount of rice, and lay it on the nori. The rice should be spread out evenly throughout the nori without being smushed down.

Large spoonfuls of the tuna filling should be placed 1 inch (2.5 cm) apart in a horizontal row.

To construct a tight roll, grab both nori sheets and a mat and roll them over the filling until the additional space at the bottom hits the opposite side. To prevent the roll from keeping its form, squeeze it down as you go along the way.

A cutting board should be used to transfer the roll. After rubbing the knife on a wet paper towel, cut the roll into six equal pieces.

201.   SANDWICH SUSHI

Prep Time: 10 mins
Total Time: 10 mins

INGREDIENTS

- Sliced sandwich bread
- Ranch Dressing
- Sliced Turkey Lunch Meat
- Cucumber
- Carrot

- String Cheese

INSTRUCTIONS

1. Every piece of bread should be flattened with a rolling pin before you begin making your dish. Slice your carrot and cucumber with a vegetable peeler, then cut your string cheese into strips with a knife.
2. Using a knife, spread ranch dressing on the bread.
3. The turkey should be placed on top. Make careful to fold over the leftover bread once you've covered the entire piece.
4. Stack the turkey, cheese, and vegetables in a symmetrical configuration. Then do it again.
5. Make two rolls from each piece of bread by rolling up the bread, cutting both ends straight, and then slicing the bread in half.
6. And that's it! You can serve it with ranch or any other dipping sauce you choose!

202.   SUSHI ROLL RICE SALAD RECIPE

INGREDIENTS

- 1/2 cup of short-grain sushi rice
- 1 3/4 cup of + 1 1/2 tbspwater
- 1/4 cup of seasoned rice vinegar
- 1 tbsp sugar
- 1 tsp salt
- 1 medium carrot
- 1 1/4 tsp wasabi paste (Japanese horseraBowl paste)
- 1 1/2 tbsp vegetable oil
- 1/2 large seedless cucumber (usually plastic-wrapped), peeled, halved lengthwise, cored, and chopped (1 cup of)
- 1 scallions, thinly sliced diagonally
- 2 tbspdrained sliced Japanese pickled ginger, coarsely chopped
- 1 tbsp sesame seeds, toasted
- 1 firm-ripe California avocado
- fresh shiso leaves (optional) *
- 1 (6-inch) square toasted nori (dried laver), cut into very thin strips with scissors

HOW TO MAKE

1. Drain the rice after 30 minutes of rinsing in a colander with numerous changes of cold water until the water is virtually clear.
2. The rice should be cooked for 2 minutes after it is brought to a boil in 3 to 4 cups of water and 1 3/4 cups of rice. Turn off the heat and cover the pot with a lid for 10 minutes
3. to allow the rice to cool.
4. Prior to adding the rice to the sugar, the sugar should be dissolved in water. Allow the vinegar mixture to cool for two minutes while the rice is standing.
5. Using a spoon, stir the vinegar mixture into the rice and spread it out on a baking pan.
6. Shave long strips from the carrot with a vegetable peeler and cut them diagonally into 1/4-inch wide strips.
7. Toss rice, carrots, cucumbers, scallions, pickled ginger, and sesame seeds with the wasabi, remaining 1 1/2 tbsp water, and oil in a dish.
8. Before slicing the avocado into 1/4-inch thick slices, cut it in half, remove the pit, and peel it.
9. Enjoy.

CONCLUSION

Printed in Great Britain
by Amazon

32759372R00090